THE GLOSSARY OF
PROJECT
MANAGEMENT

Compiled & Edited By:
Dr.Padmaja Saha
Sachin Pasayat

Rhythm

Independent
Publication

THE GLOSSARY OF PROJECT MANAGEMENT

Compiled & Edited By:
Dr.Padmaja Saha
Sachin Pasayat

ISBN:9798861276955

9798861276955

Published by:
Rhythm Independent Publication,
Jinkethimmanahalli, Varanasi, Bengaluru, Karnataka, India - 560036

For all types of correspondence, send your mails to the provided address above.

The information presented herein has been collated from a diverse range of sources, comprehensive perspective on the subject matter.

Acceptance Criteria

In the context of Agile Process and Project Management disciplines, acceptance criteria refer to the specific conditions or requirements that a product or feature must meet in order to be considered satisfactory and accepted by stakeholders. These criteria are typically defined collaboratively by the project team, including product owners, developers, and stakeholders, during a planning or refinement session.

Acceptance criteria are written in a clear and concise manner, using language that is easily understood by all parties involved. They are typically expressed as statements or scenarios that describe the desired behavior or functionality of the product or feature. Acceptance criteria should be measurable and testable, allowing the project team to determine whether the desired outcome has been achieved. They may include details on performance, functionality, usability, security, compatibility, and other relevant aspects.

Acceptance Testing Criteria

Acceptance Testing Criteria refers to the set of conditions or requirements that must be met in order for a product or deliverable to be accepted by the stakeholders. In the context of Agile Process and Project Management disciplines, acceptance testing criteria play a crucial role in ensuring that the product meets the expectations and needs of the customer or end-user.

Unlike traditional software development methodologies, Agile places a strong emphasis on collaboration and continuous feedback. Acceptance testing criteria are defined collaboratively by the development team, product owner, and other stakeholders during the early stages of the project. These criteria are based on the project's goals, user stories, and acceptance criteria, which are used to define the specific requirements and desired outcomes for the product.

Acceptance Testing

Acceptance Testing is a crucial phase in Agile Process and Project Management disciplines. It is a formal method of evaluating the functionality, usability, and performance of a software application or system. This testing phase ensures that the developed product meets the requirements and expectations of the end users and stakeholders.

During the acceptance testing process, the product is tested in a real-world scenario to determine its compliance with the defined business requirements, user stories, and acceptance criteria. The focus is on validating that the system behaves as expected and produces the desired results. This phase is typically performed by the end users or the client, providing an opportunity for them to gain confidence in the product.

Action Item

The Agile Process is a project management approach that emphasizes flexibility and collaboration in order to deliver high-quality results in a timely manner. It is characterized by its iterative and incremental nature, allowing for continuous improvement and adaptation throughout the project lifecycle.

In Agile, projects are divided into small, manageable tasks called "user stories." These user stories are prioritized by the project stakeholders and are developed by cross-functional teams during short time periods known as "sprints." Each sprint typically lasts between one and four weeks, during which the team works collaboratively to deliver a potentially shippable product increment.

The Agile Process fosters frequent communication and close collaboration between the

1

development team and the stakeholders, enabling rapid feedback and continuous improvement. This close interaction helps ensure that the project remains aligned with the stakeholders' needs and expectations throughout its development.

Key principles of the Agile Process include:

1. Individuals and interactions over processes and tools: Agile values the importance of effective communication and collaboration among team members, rather than relying solely on formal processes and tools.

2. Working software over comprehensive documentation: Agile prioritizes delivering functional software that meets the stakeholders' requirements over extensive documentation, while still recognizing the importance of relevant documentation.

3. Customer collaboration over contract negotiation: The Agile Process encourages a collaborative relationship between the development team and the stakeholders, involving them throughout the project to ensure a shared understanding of goals and requirements.

4. Responding to change over following a plan: Agile embraces change as a natural part of the development process, allowing for flexibility and adaptation based on feedback and evolving requirements.

In summary, the Agile Process is a project management approach that promotes flexibility, collaboration, iterative development, and continuous improvement. By focusing on delivering incremental value and fostering effective communication, Agile helps teams deliver high-quality results that meet the stakeholders' needs.

Activity Duration

Activity Duration refers to the amount of time required to complete a specific activity or task within the Agile Process and Project Management disciplines. It is an essential aspect of project planning and scheduling, as it helps determine project timelines, resource allocation, and overall project success.

In the context of Agile Process, activity duration is often estimated using techniques such as Story Points or Ideal Days. These techniques are used to assign a relative measure of effort or complexity to each activity, allowing the team to estimate how long it will take to complete them. The Agile approach emphasizes flexibility and collaboration, which means that activity durations can be adjusted as the project progresses, based on new information and insights.

Activity Resource Requirements

Activity Resource Requirements refer to the identification and allocation of necessary resources for executing project activities in both Agile Process and Project Management disciplines.

These requirements play a crucial role in project planning and execution, ensuring that the appropriate resources are available to complete each activity effectively and efficiently. The resources may include various elements such as human resources, equipment, materials, software, and facilities.

In the Agile Process, activity resource requirements are determined during the sprint planning phase. The team identifies the activities that need to be completed within the sprint, and then determines the resources needed to execute those activities. This could involve allocating specific team members with the required skills and expertise, determining the availability of necessary tools and equipment, and ensuring access to relevant software and technology.

In Project Management disciplines, activity resource requirements are typically identified and listed in the project plan. The project manager collaborates with the stakeholders to determine the resources needed for each activity, taking into consideration factors such as budget, timeline, and project scope. The allocation of resources is then managed throughout the project lifecycle, ensuring that the necessary resources are available at the right time and in the right quantities.

Effective management of activity resource requirements is essential for project success. It ensures that the project team has the necessary resources to complete their tasks, minimizes delays and bottlenecks, and optimizes resource allocation for maximum productivity and efficiency.

Agile Coach

An Agile Coach is a professional who guides teams and organizations through the implementation and adoption of Agile principles and practices in their project management processes. The role of an Agile Coach is multifaceted and involves facilitating effective communication, fostering collaboration, and promoting continuous improvement within the team.

The main goal of an Agile Coach is to assist teams in embracing the Agile mindset and adhering to the values and principles outlined in the Agile Manifesto. This involves coaching team members on the various Agile frameworks, such as Scrum or Kanban, and helping them understand how to apply these methods in their day-to-day work.

Agile Coaches act as mentors, providing guidance and support to team members as they navigate the challenges and complexities of Agile project management. They help teams identify and overcome obstacles, such as bottlenecks or lack of alignment, by facilitating discussions and encouraging self-organization.

In addition to working with individual teams, Agile Coaches also collaborate with stakeholders and senior management to foster an Agile culture across the organization. They provide insights and feedback on the progress and effectiveness of Agile practices, and advocate for continuous learning and improvement.

Agile Contracts

Agile contracts are agreements between a customer and a supplier that define the terms and conditions of a project or deliverables in an Agile environment. They are tailored to support the iterative and collaborative nature of Agile project management.

Unlike traditional contracts that focus on detailed documentation and fixed requirements, Agile contracts promote flexibility and adaptability. They prioritize delivering value to the customer through continuous collaboration and feedback.

Agile contracts emphasize the following key principles:

1. Collaboration: Agile contracts encourage close collaboration and communication between the customer and the supplier throughout the project. Both parties work together to define project goals, prioritize requirements, and make decisions collectively.

2. Adaptability: Agile projects often involve changing requirements and evolving priorities. Agile contracts accommodate these changes by allowing for adjustments to the scope, timelines, and costs. They promote an iterative approach where the contract evolves as the project progresses.

3. Value-driven: Agile contracts prioritize delivering value to the customer. They focus on outcomes rather than rigid specifications. The contract may include metrics or performance indicators that measure the success of the project based on the customer's desired outcomes.

4. Transparency: Agile contracts promote transparency in project progress, costs, and decision-making. They may include provisions for regular reporting, frequent demonstrations of deliverables, and open communication channels.

Overall, Agile contracts foster a collaborative and adaptive environment where both the customer and the supplier share the responsibility of delivering value. They enable flexibility and promote a focus on customer satisfaction by embracing change and continuous improvement.

Agile Estimation Techniques

Agile Estimation Techniques refer to the methods used in Agile Process and Project

Management disciplines to estimate the size, effort, time, and cost for completing project tasks and delivering features. These techniques are designed to provide accurate and reliable estimates in an environment characterized by changing requirements, uncertainty, and complexity.

One commonly used Agile Estimation Technique is Planning Poker, in which team members collaborate to estimate the effort required to complete a specific task or user story. Each member privately selects a number from a predefined set of values, typically representing complexity or effort. The team then shares their estimates, discuss any discrepancies, and repeat the process until a consensus is reached. This technique encourages active participation and engagement from all team members, fostering a better understanding of the work involved and increasing the accuracy of the estimates.

Another technique used in Agile estimation is the Relative Sizing method. This approach involves comparing the size or effort of one task or user story to another, rather than providing absolute values. The team assigns a story point value to a reference story, known as the baseline, and then estimates the size of other stories relative to this baseline. This technique allows for quicker and more intuitive estimation, especially when working with large backlogs or a high number of tasks.

Agile Feature Driven Development (FDD)

Agile Feature Driven Development (FDD) is an iterative and incremental software development approach that belongs to the Agile Process and Project Management disciplines. It focuses on delivering high-quality software features in a timely manner while emphasizing collaboration, flexibility, and adaptability.

At its core, FDD revolves around a set of five iterative and repeatable processes. The first process, 'Develop an Overall Model,' involves creating a high-level object model that serves as the foundation for the project. The second process, 'Build a Feature List,' entails identifying and prioritizing all the features that need to be implemented. These feature lists are then divided into smaller, manageable chunks called 'feature sets' in the third process, 'Plan by Feature.' Each feature set is assigned to a specific team or individual for development. The fourth process, 'Design by Feature,' focuses on designing and developing the features assigned to respective teams. Finally, the fifth process, 'Build by Feature,' involves coding, testing, and integrating the features into a working system.

Agile Manifesto

The Agile Manifesto is a set of guiding principles that is followed in the Agile Process and Project Management disciplines. It provides a formal definition of the values and principles that underlie the Agile approach to managing projects and processes.

The Agile Manifesto emphasizes four key values:

1. Individuals and interactions over processes and tools: This value emphasizes the importance of putting the focus on the people involved in the project or process and promoting effective communication and collaboration. It recognizes that the success of a project or process depends on the individuals and their ability to work together effectively.

2. Working software over comprehensive documentation: This value emphasizes the importance of delivering a working product or solution over spending excessive time and effort on extensive documentation. It recognizes that the primary measure of progress is the delivery of working software or solutions that meet the needs of the customer or user.

3. Customer collaboration over contract negotiation: This value emphasizes the importance of actively involving the customer or user throughout the project or process. It recognizes that collaboration and continuous feedback from the customer or user leads to better results and customer satisfaction.

4. Responding to change over following a plan: This value emphasizes the importance of being flexible and adaptable in the face of changing requirements and circumstances. It recognizes

that the ability to respond quickly to change is crucial for project success in a dynamic and unpredictable environment.

By adhering to these values, the Agile Manifesto helps guide Agile practitioners in making decisions and taking actions that align with the principles of Agile Project Management and Process Management. It promotes a customer-centric and iterative approach to project and process management, where continuous improvement, collaboration, and adaptability are key.

Agile Portfolio Management

Agile portfolio management refers to the practice of strategically selecting and prioritizing a portfolio of projects within the context of Agile process and project management disciplines. It is a dynamic and iterative approach that aims to ensure alignment between the organization's overall strategic goals and the projects being executed.

In an Agile portfolio management framework, projects are organized into portfolios based on their strategic relevance, potential value, and resource requirements. The key objective is to optimize the allocation of resources and achieve the highest value delivery by continuously refining and reprioritizing the portfolio as new information emerges.

Agile Process

The Agile Process is a project management approach that emphasizes flexibility, collaboration, and continuous improvement. It is designed to help teams adapt to changing requirements and market conditions, enabling them to deliver value quickly and efficiently.

In Agile, projects are divided into small segments called sprints, each typically lasting one to four weeks. The development team collaborates closely with stakeholders, including the product owner and end users, to define and prioritize the work to be done in each sprint.

At the start of each sprint, the team creates a sprint backlog, which is a prioritized list of tasks or user stories that need to be completed. The team then works on these tasks using an iterative and incremental approach, focusing on delivering working software at the end of each sprint.

Throughout the sprint, the team holds regular meetings, such as daily stand-ups, to track progress, identify and resolve any issues, and make adjustments as needed. This frequent communication and feedback loop allows for quick decision-making and helps to ensure that the project remains aligned with the stakeholders' goals.

After each sprint, the team conducts a sprint review and retrospective to gather feedback, reflect on their performance, and identify areas for improvement. This continuous learning and adaptation enable the team to deliver value in a predictable and efficient manner.

Agile Product Backlog

The Agile product backlog is a dynamic and prioritized list of all user stories, features, and enhancements that are necessary to deliver a successful product. It serves as a single source of truth for the entire Agile team, including the product owner, Scrum master, developers, and testers.

The backlog is a living document that is constantly refined and adjusted throughout the project lifecycle. It represents the evolving requirements and stakeholders' needs, allowing the team to respond to changes in market conditions and customer feedback promptly.

Agile Release Planning

Agile release planning is a key activity in the Agile process and project management disciplines. It involves creating a high-level plan for delivering increments of value to customers throughout the project. The goal of agile release planning is to prioritize and schedule features, user stories, and other project requirements in a way that ensures the most important and valuable items are delivered early in the development process. Unlike traditional project management approaches, agile release planning is an iterative and adaptive process. It allows the team to continuously refine and adjust the plan as new information becomes available and priorities change. This flexibility is essential in Agile, as it allows the team to respond to changing customer needs and market dynamics. Agile release planning typically begins with the creation of a product backlog, which is a prioritized list of features and user stories. The team then collaborates to estimate the effort required to implement each item and assign them to specific iterations or sprints. During the planning process, the team considers various factors such as dependencies, resource availability, and risks. They also take into account feedback from stakeholders, customers, and end users to ensure the plan aligns with their expectations and needs. The output of agile release planning is a roadmap or schedule that outlines the planned releases and the features or user stories included in each release. This roadmap serves as a guide for the development team, stakeholders, and other project participants, helping them stay focused and aligned with project goals. In summary, agile release planning is a crucial activity in Agile project management. It enables the team to prioritize and schedule project requirements, ensuring the most valuable items are delivered early and allowing for flexibility and adaptability throughout the development process.

Agile Release Train (ART)

An Agile Release Train (ART) is a core construct in the Scaled Agile Framework (SAFe) that helps manage and coordinate the delivery of complex solutions across multiple agile teams. It combines Agile and Lean principles to provide a structured and synchronized approach to managing large-scale projects, ensuring alignment, collaboration, and quality.

Within the context of Agile process and project management disciplines, an ART involves multiple agile teams working together to deliver value to the customer in the form of a fully integrated solution. It represents a virtual organization that has all the necessary roles and responsibilities to plan, develop, test, and deploy software incrementally and iteratively. The ART concept promotes collaboration, transparency, and efficiency by providing a high level of visibility and coordination across teams.

Agile Scrum Master

An Agile Scrum Master is a key role in Agile project management that facilitates the use of the Scrum framework to effectively deliver high-quality software products. The Scrum Master serves as a servant leader of the Scrum team, helping them understand and embrace Agile values and principles.

The primary responsibility of an Agile Scrum Master is to ensure that the Scrum team functions smoothly and efficiently. This involves removing any impediments that may hinder the team's progress, such as excessive workloads, conflicts, or dependencies on other teams. The Scrum Master also acts as a facilitator in Scrum events, such as daily stand-up meetings, sprint planning sessions, sprint reviews, and retrospectives, ensuring that they are conducted effectively and that the team has opportunities for continuous improvement.

The Agile Scrum Master is responsible for coaching and guiding the team on Agile practices and ensuring adherence to the Scrum framework. They are also responsible for promoting self-organization and empowerment within the team, encouraging collaboration, and fostering a culture of trust and respect. The Scrum Master acts as a shield, protecting the team from external interruptions and distractions, allowing them to focus on delivering value to the customer through iterative and incremental development.

In summary, the Agile Scrum Master plays a critical role in enabling Agile project management by supporting and guiding the Scrum team throughout the development process. They facilitate effective collaboration, communication, and decision-making within the team and ensure that Agile principles and practices are followed, ultimately helping to deliver high-quality software products.

Agile Transformation Roadmap

An Agile Transformation Roadmap is a strategic plan for implementing and adopting Agile practices within an organization. It outlines the steps and activities required to transition from traditional project management methodologies to an Agile approach. The roadmap provides a clear path for change, highlighting the key initiatives and timelines necessary for a successful transformation.

The Agile Transformation Roadmap typically includes several key elements. Firstly, it defines the goals and objectives of the transformation, articulating the desired outcomes and benefits of adopting an Agile approach. These goals are aligned with the organization's overall strategic direction, ensuring that the transformation supports the broader business objectives.

Secondly, the roadmap outlines the specific steps and activities required to implement Agile practices. This includes establishing Agile teams, defining roles and responsibilities, and implementing Agile frameworks and processes. The roadmap may also include training and upskilling initiatives to ensure that team members have the necessary knowledge and skills to work effectively in an Agile environment.

Thirdly, the roadmap includes a timeline or schedule for the transformation, breaking down the implementation activities into manageable phases or iterations. This allows the organization to track progress and measure success against predefined milestones. The roadmap also identifies potential risks and challenges that may arise during the transformation, providing contingency plans and mitigation strategies.

In summary, an Agile Transformation Roadmap is a strategic plan for transitioning to Agile practices, outlining the goals, steps, and timeline required for a successful transformation. It provides a clear path for change, ensuring that the organization can adapt and thrive in today's dynamic business environment.

Agile

Agile is a project management methodology that emphasizes adaptability, collaboration, and continuous improvement. It is primarily used in software development but is also applicable to other disciplines.

In the Agile process, projects are divided into small increments called "sprints." Each sprint typically lasts for a few weeks and focuses on delivering a working product feature or increment. At the start of each sprint, the project team collaboratively determines which features to include in the sprint backlog.

Throughout the sprint, the team holds daily stand-up meetings to discuss progress, identify and resolve issues, and plan for the next day's work. The team may also conduct sprint reviews and retrospectives at the end of each sprint to evaluate the product increment and reflect on the team's performance, respectively.

Agile is characterized by its iterative and incremental nature. It encourages flexibility and responsiveness to changing requirements or circumstances. Instead of following a rigid plan, Agile projects embrace change and aim to deliver value early in the development process. Feedback loops and close collaboration among team members, stakeholders, and customers enable continuous improvement and ensure alignment with evolving needs and priorities.

Agile frameworks such as Scrum, Kanban, and Extreme Programming (XP) provide specific guidelines and practices to implement Agile principles effectively. These methodologies promote self-organizing teams, transparency, and frequent communication to foster productivity and customer satisfaction.

Agreement

An agreement, in the context of Agile Process and Project Management disciplines, refers to a mutual understanding or consensus reached between all stakeholders involved in a project or process. It serves as a formal acknowledgment of shared goals, objectives, commitments, and expectations, binding all parties involved to collaborate and work towards the successful completion of the project or process.

Agreements are essential in Agile methodologies as they establish a framework for effective communication, cooperation, and decision-making. They define the scope, timelines, and deliverables of the project, ensuring that everyone is aligned with the project's vision and objectives.

Agreements in Agile Process and Project Management typically cover various aspects, including but not limited to:

- Project Goals: Clear identification and agreement on the desired outcomes and objectives of the project.

- Roles and Responsibilities: Defining the responsibilities and roles of each team member and stakeholder involved.

- Communication: Establishing channels and frequency of communication between team members, project managers, and other stakeholders.

- Documentation: Agreement on the necessary documentation, artifacts, and reports required throughout the project.

- Change Management: Processes and protocols to handle changes, issues, and conflicts that may arise during the project.

- Risk Management: Identifying potential risks and agreeing on strategies to mitigate or address them.

In conclusion, agreements play a crucial role in Agile Process and Project Management by providing a structured framework for collaboration, defining expectations, and ensuring that all parties involved are working towards a common goal.

Backlog Grooming Session

Backlog grooming, also known as backlog refinement or backlog prioritization, is a critical step in the Agile process and project management disciplines. It involves regularly reviewing and refining the product backlog to ensure that it is up to date, well-organized, and ready for implementation.

In a backlog grooming session, the product owner, Scrum master, and development team come together to discuss and evaluate the items in the backlog. The main objective of this session is to clarify the user stories or requirements, break them down into smaller, actionable tasks, estimate their complexity or effort, and prioritize them based on their business value or customer impact.

The outcome of a backlog grooming session is a refined and prioritized product backlog, which serves as a roadmap for the development team. By discussing and understanding the items in the backlog, the team gains a better understanding of the project scope and the specific tasks or user stories that need to be completed in the upcoming sprints.

Backlog grooming sessions help reduce the risk of uncertainty or misunderstandings by clarifying the requirements and ensuring that they align with the project goals. It also helps optimize the team's productivity by breaking down complex user stories into smaller, more manageable tasks, allowing for better planning and estimation.

Overall, backlog grooming plays a crucial role in maintaining a healthy and effective Agile project management process. It promotes collaboration and transparency among the product owner, Scrum master, and development team, ensuring that everyone is on the same page and working towards a common goal.

Backlog Grooming

Backlog grooming is a crucial activity in Agile Process and Project Management disciplines. It involves continuously reviewing, refining, and prioritizing items in the product backlog to ensure a clear and well-defined set of user stories or requirements.

During backlog grooming, the project team, including the product owner, scrum master, and development team, collaboratively assesses and updates the backlog to maximize its value, clarity, and feasibility. The primary goal is to have a backlog that is ready for implementation in the upcoming sprints or iterations.

The process of backlog grooming includes several key activities. First, the team reviews the existing backlog items and user stories to ensure they are accurately defined, understood, and estimated. This might involve breaking down larger user stories into smaller, more manageable ones or merging similar stories together. The team also evaluates the priority of each item and adjusts it according to changing business needs.

Additionally, backlog grooming involves refining the user stories and requirements so that they are sufficiently detailed, unambiguous, and testable. This may require further discussions, clarification, and collaboration with stakeholders, subject matter experts, or users. The team also considers any dependencies, constraints, or risks associated with the backlog items.

In summary, backlog grooming is an ongoing process that facilitates effective backlog management. It ensures that the product backlog remains accurate, prioritized, and well-prepared for implementation. By continuously refining and updating the backlog, the project team can enhance collaboration, productivity, and the overall success of Agile projects.

Backlog Item

A backlog item, in the context of Agile process and project management disciplines, refers to a prioritized item or task that is yet to be completed or addressed in a project. It is a vital component of Agile methodologies such as Scrum, Kanban, or Lean, and serves as a central repository for all the work that needs to be done.

Backlog items are typically recorded and managed in a product or project backlog, which is a dynamic list that captures the requirements, features, enhancements, or defects identified for a particular project. These items are often described in the form of user stories, which are concise and measurable descriptions of a desired functionality or outcome. Each backlog item should be independent, negotiable, valuable, estimable, small, and testable.

The backlog item is prioritized based on its importance and value to the project stakeholders. The product owner or project manager, in consultation with the development team, assigns priority to each item, considering factors such as customer needs, business value, complexity, dependencies, and project timelines. The team then focuses on completing the highest priority items first during the iteration or sprint.

As backlog items are generally high-level requirements, they are frequently decomposed and refined into smaller, more detailed tasks during the planning phase. This breakdown helps in estimating effort, identifying dependencies, and defining the order of execution. By continuously reviewing and updating the backlog items, the project team can adapt and respond to changing priorities, refine scope, and ensure alignment with evolving customer needs.

Backlog Prioritization

Backlog prioritization is a critical aspect of Agile Process and Project Management disciplines. It refers to the process of ordering the backlog items based on their relative importance and value to the project. The backlog is a dynamic list of all the tasks, features, and requirements that need to be completed for the project.

Prioritizing the backlog is necessary to ensure that the most valuable and critical items are worked on first, while the less important ones are pushed further down the list. This allows the project team to focus on delivering the highest value to the stakeholders early in the project.

There are various techniques and approaches that can be used for backlog prioritization. One commonly used method is the MoSCoW method, which categorizes backlog items into four priority levels: Must have, Should have, Could have, and Won't have. This helps in identifying and focusing on the most important requirements first.

Another approach is the Weighted Shortest Job First (WSJF) prioritization technique, which assigns a value to each backlog item based on factors such as business value, time criticality, risk reduction, and dependencies. This allows for a more objective and data-driven approach to backlog prioritization.

Overall, backlog prioritization plays a crucial role in Agile Process and Project Management as it helps in maximizing value delivery, managing stakeholder expectations, and facilitating efficient resource allocation. By continuously reprioritizing the backlog based on changing project requirements and business needs, teams can ensure that they are always working on the most valuable and impactful tasks.

Backlog Refinement Meeting

A Backlog Refinement Meeting, also known as a Product Backlog Grooming or Sprint Planning Meeting, is an essential ceremony in the Agile process and Project Management disciplines. It is typically conducted by the Scrum Team, which includes the Product Owner, Scrum Master, and Development Team members.

The purpose of the Backlog Refinement Meeting is to refine and prioritize the items in the Product Backlog. The Product Backlog is a dynamic list of features, enhancements, and bug fixes that represents the requirements for the project. It serves as a single source of truth that guides the development team throughout the project lifecycle.

During the meeting, the Scrum Team reviews, discusses, and re-evaluates the items in the Product Backlog. They analyze the user stories, estimate effort, clarify requirements, and ensure that the backlog items are well-understood and ready for development. The team may also identify and define new user stories or split existing ones to enable more accurate estimation and planning.

The Product Owner takes the lead during the Backlog Refinement Meeting, providing guidance on prioritization and answering any questions from the team. The Scrum Master facilitates the meeting, ensuring that it stays focused and productive, while the Development Team members actively participate, sharing their knowledge and expertise.

Ultimately, the Backlog Refinement Meeting helps the Scrum Team to maintain a transparent and well-groomed Product Backlog. It enables a better understanding of the requirements, fosters collaboration within the team, and facilitates effective Sprint Planning. By continuously refining the backlog, the team ensures that they are delivering the highest value to the customer and meeting the project objectives.

Backlog Refinement

Backlog refinement is a critical practice in the Agile process and Project Management disciplines. It refers to the ongoing process of reviewing, prioritizing, and refining items in the product backlog.

During backlog refinement, the product owner, Scrum Master, and development team collaborate to determine the order, importance, and details of items in the backlog. This process ensures that the backlog remains relevant, up to date, and aligned with the goals and vision of the project.

The primary objective of backlog refinement is to ensure that the backlog contains well-defined, actionable, and valuable items that can be worked on in upcoming sprints. It involves breaking down large, complex user stories into smaller, more manageable tasks or sub-stories, estimating effort and complexity, and adding any missing details or acceptance criteria.

Backlog refinement sessions are typically held regularly, often during the sprint planning or retrospective meetings, to ensure that the backlog is continuously updated, refined, and prioritized. The frequency and duration of these sessions may vary based on the needs and complexity of the project.

By regularly refining the backlog, the team gains a clear understanding of the work that needs to be done and can plan and prioritize effectively. It also helps identify any dependencies, risks, or gaps, allowing for early mitigation and efficient allocation of resources.

In conclusion, backlog refinement is an essential practice in Agile project management, allowing teams to maintain a well-groomed backlog that reflects the current needs and priorities of the project.

Backlog

A backlog is a prioritized list of work items or requirements that need to be completed by a development team. It is a key component of Agile process and project management disciplines.

In Agile methodologies, such as Scrum, the backlog is commonly used to define and manage the scope of a project. It serves as a central repository for all the features, user stories, bugs, tasks, and other work items that the team needs to address. The backlog is dynamic and constantly evolves as new requirements arise or existing ones change.

The backlog is typically sorted in order of priority, with the most important and valuable items at the top. This allows the team to focus on delivering the highest value work first. Prioritization is often based on factors such as business value, customer needs, technical dependencies, or time constraints.

During sprint planning, a subset of items from the backlog is selected and committed to be completed in the upcoming sprint. The team then works on these selected items, in order of priority, until the sprint is finished. Any remaining items in the backlog are reevaluated and reprioritized for future sprints.

The backlog provides transparency and clarity to the team, stakeholders, and other project participants. It helps everyone understand what needs to be done, why, and when. By continuously refining and reprioritizing the backlog, the team can adapt to changes, reduce risk, and deliver value incrementally throughout the project.

Baseline Schedule

A baseline schedule in the context of Agile Process and Project Management disciplines refers to a predetermined plan that serves as a reference point for project execution and control. It is created during the project planning stage and provides a visual representation of the project's timeline, milestones, deliverables, and dependencies.

The baseline schedule is typically developed collaboratively by the project team, including the project manager, stakeholders, and subject matter experts. It takes into account various factors such as project objectives, available resources, and estimated effort required for each task or user story.

The baseline schedule helps in setting expectations, managing scope, and tracking progress throughout the project lifecycle. It provides a framework for measuring actual progress against planned progress, enabling project managers to identify delays, bottlenecks, or deviations from the original plan. By comparing the baseline schedule with the actual progress, project managers can analyze variances and take corrective actions to bring the project back on track.

The baseline schedule serves as a vital communication tool, ensuring that all team members are aligned and have a common understanding of the project's timeline and deliverables. It also helps in managing dependencies and resources effectively, enabling teams to prioritize tasks and allocate resources accordingly. Additionally, the baseline schedule provides a foundation for estimating and forecasting project completion dates, allowing stakeholders to plan accordingly.

In conclusion, the baseline schedule is an essential component of Agile Process and Project Management disciplines, providing a reference point for project execution, control, and communication. It allows project managers to measure progress, identify variances, and take timely corrective actions to ensure project success.

Baseline

The baseline in the context of Agile Process and Project Management disciplines refers to a reference point or starting point that is used to measure progress and performance throughout the project lifecycle. It serves as a foundation for establishing goals, determining scope, and tracking changes within the project.

In Agile processes, the baseline typically includes the initial set of requirements, specifications, and project plans that are agreed upon by the stakeholders and the project team. It provides a common understanding of the project's objectives and deliverables, acting as a blueprint for the development and execution of the project.

Behavior-Driven Development (BDD)

Behavior-Driven Development (BDD) is an agile software development approach that focuses on aligning the development team, stakeholders, and business representatives through the use of shared language and collaborative processes. BDD places a strong emphasis on creating and delivering software that meets the desired behavior and expectations of the end users.

In the context of Agile Process and Project Management disciplines, BDD is a methodology that helps bridge the gap between business requirements and technical solutions. It encourages communication and collaboration between different roles within the development team, including developers, testers, business analysts, and product owners. By fostering a shared understanding of the desired behavior, BDD helps to ensure that the development efforts are aligned with the business goals and objectives.

The core principles of BDD involve breaking down the software requirements into smaller, concrete examples that can be expressed in a common language understood by all stakeholders. These examples, often referred to as "scenarios," are written in a structured and human-readable format known as "Gherkin." Gherkin syntax allows for the specification of the system's expected behavior in a clear and concise manner.

During the development process, BDD encourages the implementation of the scenarios as automated tests, referred to as "executable specifications." These tests validate that the system behaves as expected and provide feedback to the development team by identifying any deviations from the desired behavior. By automating the tests, BDD enables continuous integration and delivery, ensuring that the software remains in a releasable state throughout the development cycle.

Benchmarking Analysis

Benchmarking Analysis is a practice used in the Agile Process and Project Management disciplines to compare the performance of a project or process against industry best practices or competitors' standards. It involves systematically measuring and evaluating various aspects of the project or process to identify areas for improvement or to determine if the current performance is meeting expectations.

During a benchmarking analysis, data is collected from multiple sources, such as internal project metrics, industry reports, and competitor information. The data is then analyzed and compared to establish benchmarks or benchmarks to assess the performance of the project or process. This analysis helps project managers and teams identify strengths, weaknesses, and areas where performance can be improved.

Benchmarking

Benchmarking is a formal process within the Agile Process and Project Management disciplines that involves comparing an organization's performance and practices against industry leaders or best-in-class companies in order to identify areas for improvement and enhance overall performance.

Agile project management is highly reliant on continuous improvement and learning from industry best practices. Benchmarking plays a crucial role in this process, as it helps Agile teams to determine where they stand in terms of performance and efficiency compared to other organizations. By evaluating the practices, strategies, and outcomes of industry leaders, Agile teams can uncover areas where they may be falling short or could enhance their performance.

Benefit Realization

Benefit realization, in the context of Agile process and project management disciplines, refers to the practice of identifying, tracking, and maximizing the value or benefits that are expected to be derived from a project or initiative. It is a proactive approach that ensures that the desired outcomes and benefits are achieved through continuous monitoring, evaluation, and adjustment of the project activities.

In the Agile framework, benefit realization is given significant importance, as it aligns with the core principles of delivering customer value and adapting to changing requirements. It involves the collaboration of the project team, stakeholders, and customer representatives to define clear and measurable benefits that the project aims to achieve.

The Agile project management team regularly reviews the benefits realization plan, which includes a set of key performance indicators (KPIs) and targets, to ensure that the project activities are on track to deliver the expected benefits. This allows for early identification of any deviations or risks that may impact the realization of benefits, enabling timely mitigation actions.

Throughout the project life cycle, Agile project teams continuously evaluate the progress and adjust their approach to maximize the value delivery. This iterative and adaptive approach is embedded in Agile methodologies, such as Scrum or Kanban, which promote regular reviews and feedback loops to enable continuous improvement and fine-tuning of the project activities.

Benefits Management

Benefits Management, in the context of Agile process and project management disciplines, refers to the systematic approach of identifying, planning, and realizing the benefits of a project or initiative. It involves assessing the value that the project brings to the organization and ensuring that the expected outcomes are achieved.

The primary goal of Benefits Management is to ensure that the project delivers the expected benefits to the stakeholders. This is done by clearly defining the desired outcomes, identifying the metrics to measure success, and continuously tracking the progress throughout the project lifecycle.

Within the Agile framework, Benefits Management is integrated into the project management process, as it aligns with the iterative and adaptive nature of Agile methodologies. It involves regular review and re-evaluation of the project objectives and benefits, allowing for adjustments and refinements as the project progresses.

Benefits Management begins with the identification of the stakeholders and their needs, followed by the establishment of clear goals and objectives. It then involves the development of a benefits realization plan, which outlines the specific actions and activities required to achieve the desired outcomes.

Throughout the project, Benefits Management focuses on monitoring and measuring the progress towards the anticipated benefits. This includes collecting relevant data, analyzing the results, and making informed decisions based on the findings.

By implementing an effective Benefits Management approach, Agile project teams can ensure that their efforts are aligned with the strategic objectives of the organization and deliver measurable value to the stakeholders. It enables project managers to make data-driven decisions and adapt the project direction as needed, ultimately increasing the chances of project success.

Benefits Realization

Benefits Realization, in the context of Agile Process and Project Management disciplines, refers to the practice of actively measuring the value and impact of the project outcomes, ensuring that the desired benefits, both tangible and intangible, are achieved.

When following an Agile approach, Benefits Realization becomes an integral part of the project management process. It involves defining clear objectives and measurable benefits at the outset of the project, aligning them with the organization's strategic goals. Throughout the project, regular checkpoints are established, allowing the project team to assess the progress made towards the desired benefits and make necessary adjustments as needed.

By continuously monitoring and evaluating the project's achievements against the defined benefits, Agile practitioners are able to identify any gaps or deviations from the intended outcomes early on. This enables them to take proactive measures and implement necessary changes to ensure the realization of those benefits. By doing so, Agile project management helps organizations maximize the value delivered by their projects.

Benefits Realization is a collaborative effort that involves stakeholders from various levels, ensuring their active participation throughout the project lifecycle. It helps establish a clear understanding of the expected outcomes and aligns the project execution closely with the organization's overall strategic direction.

In summary, Benefits Realization in Agile Process and Project Management focuses on actively measuring and ensuring the achievement of desired project benefits by aligning them with strategic goals, continuously monitoring progress, and making necessary adjustments to maximize value.

Best Practices

Agile Process: Agile Process refers to a software development approach that emphasizes flexibility, collaboration, and continuous improvement. It involves breaking a project into small, manageable tasks called user stories, which are then prioritized and completed in short iterations called sprints. The Agile Process encourages adaptive planning, early delivery, and rapid response to change. It promotes regular communication and collaboration among cross-functional team members, including developers, testers, and business stakeholders. Daily stand-up meetings are conducted to ensure transparency and address any roadblocks or impediments. The Agile Process aims to deliver value to the customer quickly and frequently through iterative development and feedback cycles.

Project Management: Project Management refers to the discipline of planning, organizing, and controlling resources to achieve specific project objectives while adhering to defined constraints such as time, cost, and scope. It involves initiating, planning, executing, monitoring, and closing project activities in a systematic and structured manner. Project Managers are responsible for defining project goals, creating project plans, allocating resources, and managing risks. They ensure effective communication, stakeholder engagement, and collaboration among team members. Project Management employs various methodologies, such as Agile, Waterfall, and Scrum, depending on the nature and complexity of the project. It requires strong leadership skills, effective decision-making, and the ability to adapt to change. The goal of Project Management is to deliver projects successfully, meeting client expectations and delivering value within the defined constraints.

Bottleneck

A bottleneck in the context of Agile Process and Project Management disciplines refers to a point in a system or process that causes a delay or impediment to the flow of work, impacting the overall efficiency and productivity of the project.

It is often characterized by a situation where tasks or activities are accumulating at a slower rate than they can be processed, leading to a build-up of work in progress (WIP). This can result in a decrease in throughput and an increase in lead time, causing delays in delivering value to the customer.

Budget Constraints

A budget constraint, in the context of Agile Process and Project Management disciplines, refers to the limitation or restriction on the amount of financial resources available for a project. It defines the financial boundaries within which the project team must operate in order to achieve its objectives.

Agile projects, characterized by their iterative and incremental approach, require careful management of resources, including budget. The budget constraint ensures that the project does not exceed the allocated funds and helps in maintaining financial discipline throughout the project lifecycle.

Budget Variance

Budget Variance refers to the deviation between the planned budget and the actual expenses incurred during the execution of an Agile project. It is a crucial metric in Agile Process and Project Management disciplines as it helps to assess the financial performance and control the project's expenditure.

In Agile, the budget is typically divided into iterations or sprints, with each iteration having a predetermined budget allocation. The budget variance is calculated by comparing the planned budget for a specific sprint or iteration with the actual expenditure incurred during that period.

A positive budget variance indicates that the actual expenses were lower than planned, implying that the project is performing well in terms of cost control. However, a negative budget variance suggests that the actual expenses exceeded the planned budget, which can be a cause for concern.

By monitoring the budget variance, Agile teams can identify any potential overspending or cost overruns early on and take appropriate corrective actions. This may involve reevaluating the project scope, adjusting resource allocation, or revisiting the budget planning process. It is essential for Agile teams to keep a close watch on the budget variance to ensure that the project remains financially viable and aligned with organizational goals.

Budget

A budget is a financial plan that outlines the estimated expenses and revenues for a specific project or period. It plays a crucial role in Agile Process and Project Management disciplines as it helps ensure that projects are executed within the available resources and constraints.

Agile Process and Project Management adopt iterative and incremental approaches to project execution, focusing on delivering value to customers in shorter timeframes. Budgeting in Agile aims to provide transparency and accountability in managing project finances while allowing flexibility to adapt to changing requirements and priorities.

Burn-Down Chart

The burn-down chart is a visual representation used in Agile Process and Project Management disciplines to track and communicate the progress of a project. It provides a clear and concise overview of the remaining work and the projected completion date.

The chart consists of two axes - the vertical axis represents the amount of work remaining, while the horizontal axis represents time. It shows the initial estimation of work and the ideal progress line, which is the projected amount of work that should be completed at each point in time. As the project progresses, the actual progress line is plotted based on the amount of work completed each day. By comparing the actual progress line with the ideal progress line, the burn-down chart helps identify any deviations and allows the team to take necessary actions to keep the project on track. If the actual progress line is above the ideal line, it indicates that the team is falling behind schedule. Conversely, if the actual line is below the ideal line, it means the team is working ahead of schedule. The burn-down chart also provides insights into the team's velocity, which refers to the rate at which work is being completed. By measuring the slope of the actual progress line, project managers can estimate the team's velocity and make informed decisions about the project timeline and resource allocation. Overall, the burn-down chart serves as a valuable tool for project managers and teams to monitor progress, identify potential issues, and make data-driven decisions to ensure successful project delivery within the Agile framework.

Burn-Up Chart

A burn-up chart is a visual representation used in Agile Process and Project Management disciplines to track progress and communicate the status of a project. It provides a clear visual depiction of how much work has been completed and how much work remains to be done, enabling the stakeholders to make informed decisions and identify potential bottlenecks or issues.

The burn-up chart consists of two axes: the horizontal axis represents time, while the vertical axis represents the amount of work completed. The chart includes two lines: the first line represents the original scope of the project, and the second line shows the actual progress made over time.

As the project progresses, the burn-up chart is updated regularly to reflect the completion of individual tasks or user stories. The actual progress line is updated by summing up the completed work, while the scope line remains fixed. By comparing these two lines, stakeholders can determine if the project is on track, ahead of schedule, or falling behind.

The burn-up chart also allows the team to forecast the completion of the project based on the current rate of progress. It helps identify any deviations from the original plan and prompts the team to take corrective actions if necessary. The chart is often used in conjunction with other Agile techniques, such as sprint planning, backlog grooming, and daily stand-up meetings.

In summary, a burn-up chart is a valuable tool in Agile project management, providing a visual representation of project progress and allowing the team and stakeholders to track and adjust their plans accordingly.

Business Analysis

A business analysis is a disciplined approach to identifying and solving business problems by studying and analyzing an organization's processes and systems. It involves understanding the current state of the business, identifying areas of improvement, and proposing solutions to meet the organization's goals and objectives.

In the context of Agile process and project management disciplines, business analysis plays a crucial role in ensuring that projects are delivered successfully. Agile methodologies focus on iterative and incremental development, with an emphasis on collaboration and adaptability. In an Agile environment, business analysis helps to bridge the gap between the business stakeholders and the development team, ensuring that requirements are well-understood and translated into working solutions.

During Agile project management, business analysts work closely with product owners, scrum masters, and developers to gather and prioritize requirements, create user stories, and clarify any ambiguities. They also facilitate communication between different teams and stakeholders, ensuring that everyone has a shared understanding of the project goals and requirements.

In addition to requirements gathering, business analysis in Agile also involves ongoing validation and verification of the developed solutions. Business analysts collaborate with stakeholders and conduct reviews and inspections to ensure that the delivered solution meets the defined requirements and provides value to the business.

Business Case

A business case is a formal document that outlines the justification for starting a new project or initiative. It provides a detailed analysis of the potential benefits, costs, risks, and constraints associated with the proposed project. The business case serves as a decision-making tool for stakeholders, allowing them to evaluate the feasibility and viability of the project before moving forward.

In the context of Agile Process and Project Management disciplines, a business case is particularly essential. As Agile methodologies emphasize iterative development and continuous delivery, a well-defined business case helps Agile teams prioritize work, align goals, and make informed decisions throughout the project lifecycle. By clearly articulating the intended outcomes, value proposition, and strategic alignment of the project, the business case ensures that Agile teams stay focused on delivering the highest value to the organization and customers.

Business Continuity Plan

A Business Continuity Plan (BCP) is a documented strategy that outlines how an organization will continue its operations after a disruptive event, be it a natural disaster, cybersecurity breach, or any other incident that threatens its ability to function. In the context of Agile Process and Project Management disciplines, a BCP ensures that essential business functions can be quickly resumed and sustained, minimizing the impact of the disruption on the overall project and its objectives.

The BCP establishes guidelines and procedures to facilitate a swift recovery and continuity of operations. It includes detailed instructions for handling critical processes, communication protocols, and the allocation of resources during the recovery phase. Within Agile frameworks, such as Scrum or Kanban, the BCP may also cover strategies to maintain productivity, adapt to changing circumstances, and ensure that project goals continue to be met despite the disruption.

Business Process Improvement (BPI)

Business Process Improvement (BPI) refers to the systematic approach used to identify, analyze, and implement enhancements to the existing processes within an organization. It involves the evaluation of current practices in order to optimize efficiency, effectiveness, and overall performance.

In the context of Agile Process and Project Management, BPI is an iterative and collaborative method that focuses on continuous improvement. It aligns with the core principles of Agile, such as adaptability, flexibility, and customer-centricity. BPI aims to streamline processes, eliminate waste, and increase value delivery to customers.

Cadence Planning

Cadence planning is a key practice in both Agile Process and Project Management disciplines. It refers to the process of establishing a predictable rhythm or schedule for work activities within a project. This rhythm helps create a sense of consistency and regularity, allowing teams to plan and execute their work effectively.

In an Agile context, cadence planning involves the establishment of regular time intervals, called iterations or sprints, during which work is planned, executed, and reviewed. These time intervals can range from a few days to a couple of weeks, depending on the needs and preferences of the team. Within each iteration, the team focuses on delivering a set of prioritized work items, which are typically represented as user stories or tasks on a team's backlog.

By adhering to a consistent cadence, Agile teams are able to improve predictability and adaptability in their work. Regular iterations enable teams to plan and estimate their work more effectively, as they gain clarity and insights into their velocity and capacity. Moreover, cadence planning empowers teams to maintain a sustainable pace of work, avoiding the pitfalls of over-commitment or under-commitment that can hinder productivity.

Similarly, in traditional project management, cadence planning plays a crucial role in ensuring the smooth execution and delivery of projects. Project managers establish a regular rhythm for activities such as project planning, progress tracking, team meetings, and stakeholder communication. This rhythm provides structure and accountability, enabling project teams to stay on track and deliver high-quality results within the defined timeframe.

In conclusion, cadence planning is a fundamental practice in both Agile Process and Project Management disciplines. It helps establish a predictable rhythm for work activities and enables teams to plan, execute, and deliver their work effectively. By adhering to a consistent cadence, teams can improve predictability, adaptability, and productivity, ultimately leading to successful project outcomes.

Capacity Planning

Capacity planning is a critical component of Agile Process and Project Management disciplines. It refers to the process of determining the resources required, such as manpower, infrastructure, and equipment, to meet the demands and goals of a project within a specific timeframe.

In Agile, capacity planning involves estimating the team's ability to deliver the required amount of work within each iteration or sprint. It takes into account various factors such as the team's velocity, individual team member's availability, and any external dependencies or constraints. By conducting capacity planning, project managers can effectively allocate resources and ensure that the team has the necessary capacity to complete the work.

Change Control Board (CCB)

A Change Control Board (CCB) is a group of individuals responsible for evaluating and approving or rejecting proposed changes to a project or product in the context of Agile Process and Project Management disciplines. The CCB serves as a governance body that helps ensure that changes to the project or product are properly assessed and controlled.

The primary role of the CCB is to evaluate the impact of proposed changes on the project's objectives, scope, timeline, resources, and budget. The CCB assesses the potential risks and benefits associated with each change request and makes decisions based on the overall impact to the project. This rigorous evaluation process helps minimize the chances of introducing unnecessary risks or disruptions to the project's progress.

The CCB reviews change requests submitted by stakeholders, team members, or the project manager. They consider the relevance and importance of each change before making a decision. The CCB may request additional information or analysis to aid in their evaluation process. They may also consult with subject matter experts or other relevant parties to gather insights and perspectives.

Once the CCB has evaluated a change request, they make a decision to either approve, reject, or defer the change. If approved, the change is implemented following predefined processes and procedures. If rejected, the change is not implemented, and the project proceeds as planned. If the CCB defers a change, it means further analysis or evaluation is needed before a decision can be made.

In summary, the Change Control Board plays a critical role in ensuring that changes to a project or product are carefully evaluated and controlled. Their decision-making process helps maintain the project's objectives, quality, and predictability. By providing governance and oversight, the CCB helps the Agile process and project management disciplines maintain focus and ensure successful outcomes.

Change Control Procedure

Change Control Procedure is a formal process followed in the Agile Process and Project Management disciplines to effectively manage and control changes to a project. It ensures that changes are properly evaluated, approved, and implemented in a systematic manner.

In Agile Process, change control is an important aspect as it allows teams to respond to changes and adapt to evolving requirements. The Change Control Procedure involves the following steps:

1. Identification: Any changes or potential changes are identified and documented. This may include changes to requirements, scope, schedule, or resources.

2. Impact Assessment: The impact of the proposed change is assessed, taking into account factors such as the project timeline, budget, and resources. This helps in understanding the potential risks and benefits of the change.

3. Evaluation and Approval: The change is evaluated by the relevant stakeholders, such as the project manager, product owner, and development team. The change is then approved or

rejected based on its alignment with project goals and priorities.

4. Implementation: If the change is approved, it is implemented following a structured approach. This may involve updating project documentation, revisiting user stories, modifying code, or adjusting the project plan.

5. Review and Documentation: After the change is implemented, a review is conducted to assess its effectiveness and impact on the project. The details of the change and its outcomes are documented for future reference.

The Change Control Procedure ensures that changes are carefully evaluated, managed, and controlled to minimize disruptions to the project while allowing for necessary adjustments. It promotes effective communication, collaboration, and decision-making within the Agile team.

Change Control

Change control refers to the systematic process of managing and implementing changes within an Agile process or project management discipline. It involves the identification, evaluation, and implementation of changes to ensure that they are properly planned, documented, and communicated to all stakeholders involved.

In the context of Agile, change control is crucial to maintain the project's flexibility and adaptability to changing requirements. It allows for the assessment of the impact of proposed changes on the project's scope, schedule, budget, and resources. By following a structured change control process, Agile teams can effectively manage change requests and ensure that they align with the project's goals and objectives.

Change Impact Analysis

Change Impact Analysis is a crucial activity in Agile Process and Project Management disciplines that aims to assess the potential effects of proposed changes on various aspects of a project or system. It helps the team in estimating the impact of these changes, identifying potential risks and dependencies, and making informed decisions about whether to implement the changes or not.

The purpose of Change Impact Analysis is to minimize surprises and disruptions that may arise from changes introduced during the agile development process. By analyzing the impact of proposed changes, the team can anticipate and evaluate the consequences on different project elements, such as requirements, design, implementation, testing, and deployment. This analysis helps in identifying the areas that may require modification, rework, or additional testing, allowing the team to plan and allocate resources accordingly in an agile manner.

Change Impact Assessment

Change Impact Assessment is a formal evaluation process that is conducted within the Agile Process and Project Management disciplines. It involves identifying, analyzing, and documenting the potential effects of a proposed change on various aspects of a project or organization.

This assessment is essential in Agile Process and Project Management as it helps stakeholders determine the magnitude and scope of the change and make informed decisions regarding its implementation. It provides a comprehensive understanding of the potential impacts on people, processes, technology, and resources, allowing for appropriate planning and mitigation strategies.

Change Log

Agile Process Change Log: A change log in the context of Agile Process refers to a record or document that captures all the changes made to the project throughout its lifecycle. It serves as a chronological record of modifications, updates, and revisions made to any aspect of the project, including requirements, design, code, tests, and documentation. The change log is a vital tool used by Agile teams to ensure transparency, traceability, and effective communication within the team and with stakeholders. It helps to keep everyone on the same page about the evolving nature of the project and facilitates decision-making based on accurate and up-to-date information. In Agile project management, change is expected and embraced, as it enables continuous improvement and adaptation to changing requirements and business needs. The change log captures the rationale behind each change, the person responsible for the change, and any relevant details or comments. It provides a historical record of the project's evolution, ensuring that all changes are properly documented and can be traced back to their origin. This helps in assessing the impact of each change and making informed decisions about whether to accept or reject a change request. The change log also serves as a reference for future projects, enabling teams to learn from past experiences and avoid repeating mistakes. It enhances accountability and transparency by providing visibility into the decision-making process and the reasoning behind each change. Overall, the change log is an essential tool in Agile process management, ensuring that all changes are properly documented, communicated, and understood by the team and stakeholders. It helps to maintain a clear and accurate record of the project's progress and facilitates effective collaboration within the team.

Change Management

Change Management in Agile Process and Project Management is the structured approach followed to manage and incorporate changes within the project, while ensuring minimal disruption and maximizing customer value. It involves developing strategies, processes, and techniques to seamlessly integrate changes into the project lifecycle, thereby enabling teams to adapt quickly and effectively to evolving requirements and circumstances.

In the Agile context, Change Management focuses on embracing change as a natural and inevitable part of the project. It involves continuously aligning team and stakeholder expectations, managing scope, and efficiently addressing change requests. The goal of Change Management in Agile is to maintain a balance between flexibility and stability, enabling teams to respond to customer needs and market dynamics while ensuring project goals and objectives are met.

Change Request Control

Change Request Control in the context of Agile Process and Project Management disciplines is a formalized process that manages and controls any changes to a project scope or requirements.

It involves a systematic and structured approach to assess, evaluate, approve, and implement changes in a controlled manner. The objective is to ensure that any changes made to the project are properly reviewed, analyzed, and integrated into the project without negatively impacting its quality, schedule, or budget.

Change Request Form

A Change Request Form is a formal document used in Agile Process and Project Management disciplines to capture and track requests for changes to a project's scope, deliverables, or requirements. It serves as a mechanism for managing and controlling changes within the project lifecycle.

The Change Request Form typically includes key information such as the reason for the change, the impact on the project, the proposed solution, and any supporting documentation or analysis. It also includes details related to the requestor, such as their name, contact information, and role within the project or organization.

By using a Change Request Form, project teams are able to effectively prioritize, evaluate, and manage change requests in a structured manner. It helps to ensure that changes are assessed for their feasibility, impact, and alignment with project objectives before being incorporated into the project plan.

As part of the Agile Process, Change Request Forms are often used in conjunction with other Agile techniques such as the Product Backlog or the Agile Kanban board. They enable project teams to maintain a clear and transparent record of all requested changes, allowing for better decision-making and stakeholder communication.

In summary, a Change Request Form is a formal document that plays a vital role in Agile Process and Project Management. It provides a structured approach to managing and controlling changes, helping to ensure that project objectives are met while minimizing disruptions and risks associated with uncontrolled change.

Change Request Log

A Change Request Log is a formal document used in the Agile Process and Project Management disciplines to track and manage changes that are requested during a project. It serves as a centralized record of all change requests, ensuring transparency and accountability throughout the project lifecycle.

The Change Request Log captures essential information related to each change request, including the requestor's name, description of the change, priority level, impact assessment, and the status of the request. This log acts as a communication tool for the project team and stakeholders, enabling them to understand the scope and impact of each change and make informed decisions regarding their implementation.

Change Request Tracking

Change Request Tracking is a fundamental process in the Agile process and project management disciplines. It involves managing and documenting any changes that impact the project scope, schedule, or budget. It enables teams to assess and evaluate the impact of requested changes, ensuring that they align with project objectives and can be effectively implemented.

Change Request Tracking allows for a systematic approach to handling change requests. It involves capturing and categorizing change requests, evaluating their impact, and making informed decisions about whether or not to implement them. This process helps prevent scope creep, ensures that changes align with project goals, and provides a clear audit trail of all requested changes throughout the project's lifecycle.

Change Request

An Agile Process is a project management approach that emphasizes flexibility, collaboration, and iterative development. It is based on the Agile Manifesto, which values individuals and interactions, working software, customer collaboration, and responding to change. Agile processes prioritize adaptability and continuous improvement, allowing project teams to respond to changing requirements and deliver value quickly.

An Agile Process typically involves breaking down the project into small, manageable chunks called sprints or iterations. Each sprint consists of a set of user stories or requirements that are prioritized and assigned to the team. During the sprint, the team collaborates closely, holding daily stand-up meetings to discuss progress and resolve any blockers. At the end of each sprint, the team reviews the work completed and adjusts the backlog and future priorities based on feedback and changing requirements.

In Agile Project Management, the emphasis is on empowering teams to make decisions and adapt to change. Project managers in Agile projects serve as facilitators and coaches, helping the team remove obstacles and ensure alignment with the project goals. Communication and collaboration are key in Agile projects, with frequent interactions between team members, stakeholders, and customers to ensure clarity and alignment.

Overall, Agile Process and Project Management are designed to enable organizations to deliver value faster, increase customer satisfaction, and adapt to changing market conditions. By prioritizing flexibility, collaboration, and iterative development, Agile provides a framework for managing projects in a dynamic and ever-evolving environment.

Charter

A charter is a document that outlines the purpose, objectives, scope, and deliverables of a project or initiative in Agile Process and Project Management disciplines. It serves as a formal agreement between the project team and the stakeholders, providing a clear understanding of the goals and expectations.

The charter defines the project's vision, mission, and objectives, highlighting the desired outcomes and benefits. It sets the direction for the project and serves as a reference point throughout its lifecycle. The document also includes a high-level description of the project's scope, identifying the major deliverables, milestones, and constraints.

Furthermore, the charter establishes the roles and responsibilities of the project team members, highlighting their involvement and accountability. It defines the governance structure and decision-making processes, ensuring a clear understanding of the project's organizational framework.

Additionally, the charter outlines the project's timeline, budget, and resource requirements. It helps in estimating and planning activities, ensuring that the necessary resources are allocated appropriately. The document also identifies the risks and dependencies associated with the project, enabling the team to proactively manage and mitigate them.

In conclusion, a charter is a key document in Agile Process and Project Management disciplines, providing a formal agreement that outlines the purpose, objectives, scope, and deliverables of a project. It sets the direction, establishes roles and responsibilities, defines the governance structure, and outlines the project's timeline, budget, and resource requirements.

Client

The Agile Process is a flexible and iterative approach to project management that emphasizes collaboration, frequent delivery of working software, and responsiveness to change. It aims to deliver value to stakeholders by continuously adapting to their evolving needs and requirements.

In Agile, projects are divided into short phases or iterations called sprints. At the beginning of each sprint, the team sets specific goals and selects a set of features or user stories to work on. The team then collaboratively plans, designs, develops, tests, and delivers the selected features within the sprint's timeframe.

Agile Process encourages daily communication and collaboration among team members through regular meetings such as daily stand-up meetings, sprint planning meetings, and sprint review meetings. This enables the team to quickly respond to changing requirements, identify and address potential issues, and prioritize tasks effectively.

As Agile focuses on delivering tangible results in short intervals, it allows project stakeholders to provide feedback and make adjustments throughout the project's duration. This iterative approach increases transparency, reduces risks, and enables the team to deliver high-quality software incrementally.

Overall, the Agile Process promotes a customer-centric mindset, emphasizing the importance of delivering a valuable product that meets customer needs. By embracing change, encouraging collaboration, and enabling continuous improvement, Agile helps teams to deliver projects on time, within budget, and to the customer's satisfaction.

Code Of Accounts

An Agile Code of Accounts is a structured and standardized system used in Agile Process and Project Management disciplines to categorize and track various elements and components within a project or organization. It serves as a comprehensive and organized framework for identifying, defining, and classifying items such as tasks, deliverables, resources, and milestones.

The Code of Accounts provides a common language and structure that enables effective communication, collaboration, and reporting among project team members, stakeholders, and other relevant parties. It helps ensure consistency and clarity in understanding and referencing project elements, facilitating transparency, efficiency, and accuracy in project management activities.

Collaborative Decision-Making

Collaborative Decision-Making is a process that is integral to the Agile Process and Project Management disciplines. It involves the active participation and input from all stakeholders, including team members, users, and customers, to collectively make decisions that impact the project's direction and outcomes.

In the Agile Process, collaborative decision-making is at the heart of effective teamwork and collaboration. It emphasizes open and transparent communication, where team members and stakeholders share their thoughts, ideas, and concerns to reach a consensus. This approach encourages the collective intelligence of the team, leveraging a diverse range of perspectives to drive innovative and successful outcomes.

Collaborative decision-making in Agile involves creating an environment of trust and respect, where everyone's ideas and opinions are valued. It promotes active listening and active participation, allowing individuals to express their views and provide input on important decisions that affect the project. This process creates a sense of ownership and engagement, as team members are personally invested in the decision-making process.

Through collaborative decision-making, Agile teams can rapidly respond to change and adapt their plans, as it allows for quick and efficient problem-solving. It supports the Agile principle of embracing change and iterative development, as decisions can be re-evaluated and adjusted based on new information or insights.

In summary, collaborative decision-making is a fundamental aspect of the Agile Process and Project Management disciplines. By involving all stakeholders in the decision-making process, it promotes teamwork, transparency, and adaptability, ultimately leading to successful project outcomes.

Collaborative Work Management

Collaborative Work Management (CWM) is a vital aspect of Agile Process and Project Management disciplines. It refers to the approach of organizing and coordinating various team members, tasks, and resources in a collaborative manner, with the goal of achieving project objectives efficiently and effectively.

In the Agile framework, CWM emphasizes the importance of collaboration and teamwork. It facilitates close collaboration between team members, stakeholders, and customers throughout the project lifecycle. The main aim is to foster effective communication, timely feedback, and the sharing of knowledge and expertise among all involved parties.

In Agile Project Management, CWM enables teams to work together seamlessly, promoting transparency and accountability. It allows team members to have a shared understanding of project goals, priorities, and requirements, leading to more accurate planning and improved decision-making.

CWM also supports the iterative and incremental nature of Agile processes. It provides the necessary tools and techniques for managing and tracking tasks, ensuring that work is distributed evenly, and progress is visible to all team members. This helps in identifying and resolving any issues or bottlenecks promptly, thus improving overall project efficiency and quality.

In summary, Collaborative Work Management in the context of Agile Process and Project Management disciplines involves fostering collaboration, facilitating effective communication, and providing the necessary tools and techniques for organizing and coordinating work in an Agile environment. It promotes teamwork, transparency, and accountability, ultimately leading to successful project delivery.

Communication Constraints

Communication constraints in the context of Agile Process and Project Management disciplines refer to the limitations or restrictions that impact effective communication within an Agile team or project. These constraints can hinder the flow of information, impede collaboration, and negatively impact overall project success.

In the Agile framework, effective communication plays a vital role in ensuring the success of the project. It enables team members to stay informed, align their efforts, and make timely decisions. However, various constraints can limit communication effectiveness, including:

1. Time Constraints: Agile projects often have tight deadlines, and team members may struggle to find adequate time for communication. This constraint can lead to rushed conversations, incomplete updates, and a lack of thorough understanding among team members.

2. Geographical Constraints: Agile teams are often distributed across different locations, which can create challenges in communication. Physical distance, time zone differences, and language barriers can hinder the flow of information and make it harder for team members to collaborate effectively.

3. Cultural Constraints: Cultural differences within an Agile team can impact communication effectiveness. Varying communication styles, norms, and expectations can lead to misunderstandings and misinterpretations, thereby affecting collaboration and productivity.

4. Technological Constraints: Inadequate or unreliable communication tools and technologies can hinder effective communication within Agile teams. Technical issues, connectivity problems, and limitations of virtual collaboration tools can impact the quality and timeliness of communication.

To overcome communication constraints, Agile teams should adopt strategies such as establishing clear communication channels, scheduling regular meetings, leveraging collaborative software tools, and promoting a culture of open and transparent communication. By addressing these constraints, Agile teams can enhance communication effectiveness and improve project outcomes.

Communication Management Plan

A Communication Management Plan in the context of Agile Process and Project Management disciplines is a formal document that outlines the communication approach for a project. It describes how information will be exchanged, who will be responsible for communication, and what channels and mediums will be used to distribute information.

The Communication Management Plan is an essential component of project management as it ensures that there is clear and effective communication throughout the project lifecycle. Agile projects, which are characterized by their iterative and collaborative nature, rely heavily on communication to facilitate regular feedback and collaboration between team members.

Communication Plan

A communication plan in the context of Agile Process and Project Management disciplines refers to a structured approach outlining how project stakeholders will communicate with each other throughout the project. It serves as a roadmap for effective and timely communication, ensuring that key information is shared, decisions are made collaboratively, and project progress is monitored.

The communication plan typically identifies the different types of information that need to be communicated, the frequency and channels of communication, and the responsible parties involved. It aims to promote transparency, enable efficient coordination, and foster a shared understanding among team members and stakeholders.

With Agile methodologies, such as Scrum, the communication plan is often tailored to the specific needs of the iterative and incremental development process. It emphasizes frequent and informal communication among team members, including daily stand-up meetings, sprint planning sessions, and regular retrospectives. The plan may also incorporate tools and techniques for virtual collaboration, such as online project management software or chat platforms.

Project managers play a crucial role in executing the communication plan and ensuring that all stakeholders have access to relevant information. They facilitate communication channels, manage conflicts, and identify potential risks or barriers to effective communication. Moreover, the communication plan is a dynamic document that evolves throughout the project based on feedback and lessons learned, enabling continuous improvement in communication practices.

Configuration Identification

Configuration Identification is a crucial aspect of both Agile Process and Project Management disciplines. It involves the systematic identification, labeling, and categorization of the components that make up a system or project.

In the context of Agile Process, Configuration Identification refers to the process of identifying and documenting the software configuration items (SCIs) that are part of the Agile project. SCIs can include code files, databases, documentation, test scripts, or any other item that contributes to the development and delivery of the software. The identification of these items is necessary for effective version control and change management within Agile projects. Configuration Identification ensures that every component of the system is properly tracked and documented, thereby enabling development teams to understand the current state of the project and make informed decisions about changes and updates.

In Project Management disciplines, Configuration Identification is equally important. It involves identifying and documenting the various components and deliverables of a project, including hardware, software, documentation, and other assets. This process allows project managers to establish a baseline configuration against which any changes can be measured and evaluated. Configuration Identification ensures that the project team has a clear understanding of the scope, requirements, and dependencies of the project, which is crucial for successful planning and execution.

Configuration Management

Configuration Management is a process in Agile Project Management that focuses on controlling and coordinating the projects' changes and maintaining the project's integrity. It involves identifying, documenting, and controlling the functional and physical characteristics of a product or system throughout its lifecycle.

In an Agile context, Configuration Management refers to the practices and techniques used to manage software development and delivery. It aims to ensure that all team members are working with the correct and up-to-date versions of the project's artifacts, such as source code, documentation, and dependencies. Configuration Management also helps in maintaining consistency and traceability between different versions and releases of the project.

Configuration Verification And Audit

Configuration Verification and Audit is a vital process in the Agile Process and Project Management disciplines. It refers to the systematic evaluation and validation of the configuration items, such as software, hardware, and documentation, that are part of a project or product. The aim is to ensure that these components are in line with the defined standards, requirements, and specifications.

During Configuration Verification and Audit, the project team follows a structured approach to review and assess the configuration items. This involves examining their completeness, correctness, and consistency. The team verifies that the items meet the established criteria, including technical, functional, and performance requirements. Additionally, the team also checks for compliance with industry best practices, regulations, and quality standards.

The process typically includes various activities, such as reviewing the documentation, inspecting the code, testing the functionality, and conducting interviews with stakeholders. It may also involve conducting physical inspections, where applicable. The team documents the findings, identifies any discrepancies or non-compliance, and defines corrective actions or improvement measures.

Configuration Verification and Audit are essential to ensure the integrity and quality of the configuration items throughout the project lifecycle. It helps in identifying and rectifying any inconsistencies or issues early on, reducing the risk of errors or failures later in the development or production phases. The process provides stakeholders with confidence that the project or product is built and delivered according to the defined requirements and specifications.

Conflict Resolution

Conflict Resolution in the context of Agile Process and Project Management disciplines refers to the process of identifying and addressing conflicts, disagreements, or issues that arise within a team or between team members during the course of a project.

Agile processes are characterized by their iterative and collaborative nature, with frequent interaction and communication among team members. As a result, conflicts may arise due to differences in opinions, priorities, or approaches to work. These conflicts can hinder progress, impact team morale, and ultimately affect the success of the project.

The purpose of conflict resolution in Agile is to facilitate open and transparent communication, encourage active listening, and find mutually agreeable solutions that address the underlying issues. This involves creating a safe and respectful environment where team members can express their concerns and perspectives.

Conflict resolution techniques in Agile include: - Facilitating discussions and meetings to encourage open dialogue and understanding - Identifying and addressing the root causes of conflicts rather than just the symptoms - Encouraging compromise and collaboration to find win-win solutions - Mediating between team members to facilitate effective communication and resolution - Promoting empathy and understanding among team members to build stronger relationships - Implementing retrospective meetings to reflect on conflicts and identify opportunities for improvement

By effectively managing and resolving conflicts in Agile, teams can foster a positive and productive work environment, enhance collaboration, and ultimately deliver high-quality results.

Conflict Of Interest

A conflict of interest refers to a situation in Agile Process and Project Management disciplines where an individual or entity has competing interests that may influence their decision-making or actions in a way that could undermine the fair execution of a project or the overall success of the Agile process. It occurs when personal, professional, or financial interests of the individual or entity conflict with the best interests of the project or the organization.

In Agile Process, conflicts of interest can arise in various scenarios. For instance, a project manager may have a close personal relationship with a team member, leading to favoritism and bias in assigning tasks or evaluating performance. Similarly, if a stakeholder in the project has financial investments in a vendor or supplier, their decisions regarding procurement or resource allocation may not be solely based on the project's best interests.

Conflicts of interest can have detrimental effects on the quality, transparency, and fairness of the Agile process and project management. They can compromise trust, create an unfair advantage for certain individuals or entities, and impede the objective evaluation of project goals and requirements. Consequently, conflicts of interest should be identified, addressed, and managed proactively to ensure the integrity of the Agile process and the successful delivery of the project.

Constraint

A constraint in the context of Agile Process and Project Management disciplines refers to any limitation or restriction that affects the planning, execution, and delivery of a project within the Agile framework. Constraints can arise from various factors such as time, budget, resources, scope, and quality.

Constraints play a crucial role in Agile project management as they help define boundaries and set realistic expectations for the project. By identifying and understanding these constraints, project teams can effectively prioritize and make informed decisions to ensure successful project completion.

Contingency Plan

A contingency plan in the context of Agile Process and Project Management disciplines is a predefined set of actions and procedures that are put in place to address potential risks and uncertainties that may arise during the course of a project.

Agile methodologies are iterative and dynamic, focusing on adaptability and flexibility. As such, it is crucial to have a contingency plan in place to handle unexpected events or obstacles that could potentially impact the project's success. The purpose of a contingency plan is to minimize the impact of these risks and ensure that the project can continue moving forward smoothly.

Contingency Planning

A contingency plan in the context of Agile Process and Project Management disciplines refers to a predetermined course of action to be taken in response to an unforeseen event or risk that may impact the successful delivery of a project.

Contingency planning is an essential aspect of Agile project management as it helps project teams identify and plan for potential risks, minimize their impact, and ensure that the project remains on track. It involves proactively identifying potential risks, determining the likelihood and impact of these risks, and developing strategies to address them.

Contingency Reserve

A contingency reserve, in the context of Agile Process and Project Management disciplines, refers to a specific amount of time and resources that are set aside to address unforeseen risks and uncertainties that may arise during the course of a project.

Agile methodologies, such as Scrum, recognize that project requirements and circumstances can change rapidly and unpredictably. As a result, it is essential to have a contingency reserve in place to effectively manage these changes and mitigate any potential negative impacts on the project's timeline, budget, and overall success.

Continuous Delivery Pipeline

The Continuous Delivery Pipeline is a fundamental concept within Agile Process and Project Management disciplines. It refers to the automated process of delivering software updates and enhancements to end-users on a continuous basis, ensuring a smooth and efficient workflow throughout the development and deployment phases.

In an Agile environment, the Continuous Delivery Pipeline plays a crucial role in enabling teams to achieve their goals by minimizing the friction and bottlenecks that can often occur during software delivery. It encompasses a set of practices and tools that facilitate the seamless flow of code changes from development to production environments.

The pipeline typically consists of several stages, each of which performs specific tasks and tests to ensure the quality and reliability of the software product. These stages include code compilation, unit testing, integration testing, artifact creation, deployment to various environments, and finally, release to end-users.

By automating these processes, Agile teams can accelerate the delivery of valuable features to customers while maintaining a high level of quality and stability. The use of automation tools, such as continuous integration servers and deployment scripts, eliminates manual and error-prone tasks, allowing teams to focus on delivering business value.

Furthermore, the Continuous Delivery Pipeline promotes collaboration and visibility among team members, as it requires extensive coordination and communication throughout the entire software delivery process. This helps to foster a culture of shared responsibility and accountability, ensuring that any issues or defects are addressed promptly and efficiently.

Control Charts

A control chart, in the context of Agile Process and Project Management disciplines, is a graphical representation that allows teams to monitor and control the performance of a process or project over time. It provides a way to identify common and special causes of variation, assess the stability and predictability of the process, and make data-driven decisions to improve the quality and efficiency of the work.

Control charts are based on the idea of statistical process control, where data is collected and analyzed to understand the natural variability in a process. By plotting the data points on the control chart, teams can visualize trends, patterns, and outliers, helping them to identify when the process is performing within acceptable limits (in control) or when it is deviating from the expected performance (out of control).

The control chart typically consists of a central line that represents the mean or target value of the process, as well as upper and lower control limits that define the acceptable range of variation. The data points are plotted over time, and if they fall within the control limits, the process is considered to be in a state of statistical control. If any data points fall outside the control limits or show non-random patterns, it indicates the presence of special causes of variation that need to be investigated and addressed.

By using control charts, Agile teams can proactively monitor their processes, identify potential issues early on, and take appropriate actions to prevent defects, reduce waste, and optimize productivity. This iterative approach to quality management helps teams to continuously improve their performance, deliver value to customers, and achieve project success.

Control Limits

Control Limits, in the context of Agile Process and Project Management disciplines, refer to predefined thresholds or boundaries that are used to determine whether a process or project is under control or not. They are statistical measures that help teams identify significant variations or deviations from the expected performance or quality levels.

Control Limits are typically set based on historical data, industry standards, or desired performance levels. They define the range within which a process or project can operate without causing significant concerns. These limits are used to identify both common cause variations (within the control limits) and special cause variations (beyond the control limits).

When a process or project performance falls within the control limits, it suggests that the variations or deviations observed are part of the normal and expected behavior. This indicates that the process or project is stable and predictable, ensuring consistency in terms of quality and performance levels.

On the other hand, when the performance exceeds the control limits, it indicates the presence of special cause variations. These variations may be attributed to factors that are not part of the usual performance patterns. In such cases, further investigation and analysis are required to identify the root causes and take corrective actions to bring the process or project back under control.

Control Limits provide a valuable tool for Agile teams in assessing and managing the performance of processes and projects. They enable teams to detect when a process or project is deviating from its expected behavior, allowing timely interventions to prevent or mitigate any negative impacts on quality, timeline, or budget.

Cost Control

Cost control in the context of Agile Process and Project Management disciplines refers to the practice of managing and monitoring project costs to ensure they stay within the allocated budget. It involves actively tracking and controlling expenses throughout the project lifecycle to minimize financial risks and optimize resource allocation.

In Agile, cost control is a fundamental aspect of project management as it helps to ensure that the project remains financially viable and delivers value to the stakeholders. It involves continuously monitoring and evaluating the project's financial performance to identify any deviations from the planned budget and taking appropriate actions to address them.

Cost Estimating

Cost estimating is the process of predicting the cost of a project, task, or feature within the Agile Process and Project Management disciplines. It involves determining the resources, materials, and efforts required to complete the project or task and assigning associated monetary values to them.

In Agile, cost estimating typically takes place during the initial stages of the project or when new tasks or features are being added. It is crucial to have accurate cost estimates to make informed decisions regarding project feasibility, budget allocation, and resource planning. These estimates help stakeholders understand the financial implications of the project and make informed decisions accordingly.

Cost estimating in Agile primarily relies on collaborative efforts, including discussions with team members, subject matter experts, and stakeholders. It involves breaking down the project or task into smaller, manageable components and assigning cost estimates to each component. Agile practitioners use techniques like story points, ideal hours, or t-shirt sizing to estimate the effort and cost associated with each component.

One notable aspect of cost estimating in Agile is that it is an ongoing and iterative process. As the project progresses and more information becomes available, cost estimates are refined and updated. Agile teams continuously review and revise their estimates to ensure they remain accurate and reflect the evolving project scope and requirements.

Cost Estimation

Cost estimation is a crucial aspect of Agile Process and Project Management disciplines. It refers to the process of determining the budgetary requirements for a project, taking into consideration both the tangible and intangible resources that will be needed.

In an Agile process, cost estimation is typically performed at the beginning of a project and is an ongoing activity throughout its duration. It involves breaking down the project into smaller, manageable tasks or user stories, and estimating the effort and resources required to complete each of these tasks.

This estimation is done by considering various factors such as the complexity of the task, the skills and expertise of the team members involved, the time required, and any potential risks or dependencies. The aim is to derive an accurate and realistic cost estimate that can guide project planning and decision-making.

Agile cost estimation techniques often rely on historical data, such as previous projects or similar tasks, as well as the expertise and knowledge of the project team. It is important to regularly review and update the cost estimates as the project progresses and more information becomes available.

Effective cost estimation in Agile Project Management ensures that the project stays within budget and helps in managing risk and resource allocation efficiently. It allows stakeholders to make informed decisions and prioritize tasks based on their economic feasibility. Moreover, it provides a basis for tracking actual costs against estimates, facilitating better financial management and reporting.

Overall, cost estimation plays a critical role in Agile Process and Project Management by assisting in project planning, budgeting, and decision-making, ultimately contributing to the successful delivery of the project.

Cost Management

Cost Management refers to the process of planning, estimating, budgeting, tracking, and controlling the costs of a project or process. In the context of Agile Process and Project Management disciplines, Cost Management plays a crucial role in ensuring the efficient use of resources and achieving the project's financial objectives.

Agile methodologies, such as Scrum or Kanban, focus on iterative and incremental development, where requirements and solutions evolve through collaboration between self-organizing and cross-functional teams. Cost Management in Agile requires a flexible and adaptive approach to budgeting and tracking expenses.

Cost Overrun

Cost overrun is a term used in Agile Process and Project Management disciplines to refer to a situation where a project exceeds its planned budget. It occurs when the actual cost of completing the project is higher than what was originally estimated or budgeted.

In an Agile process, cost overrun can happen due to various reasons. One of the main reasons is scope creep, which refers to the continuous addition of new features or requirements during the project, without proper evaluation of their impact on cost and resources. This can lead to an increase in the overall project cost and cause a budget shortfall.

Another reason for cost overrun in Agile project management is poor estimation. Agile projects require frequent iteration and adaptation, which can make it challenging to accurately estimate the cost of each iteration. If the initial estimates are too optimistic or if there are unforeseen circumstances that increase the cost, the project may exceed its budget.

Cost overrun in Agile projects can have detrimental effects on the overall success of the project. It can lead to delays in project delivery, reduced quality, and even project cancellation if the budget shortfall is significant. Therefore, it is crucial for Agile project managers to continuously monitor the project's cost and take proactive measures to prevent or mitigate cost overrun.

Cost Performance Baseline (CPB)

A Cost Performance Baseline (CPB) in the context of Agile Process and Project Management disciplines refers to a documented reference point that outlines the planned costs of a project over a specific time period. It serves as an important tool for monitoring and controlling the project's financial performance.

The CPB is typically established during the project planning phase and is based on the estimated costs of all the planned project activities, resources, and deliverables. It provides a comprehensive overview of the project's financial aspects, including budgeted costs, planned expenditures, and cash flow projections.

Cost Performance Index (CPI)

The Cost Performance Index (CPI) is a metric used in the context of Agile Process and Project Management disciplines to measure the efficiency of cost performance in a project. It is a ratio that compares the actual cost of work performed with the value of work completed, providing insights into the project's cost effectiveness.

The formula to calculate CPI is:

$CPI = EV / AC$

Where EV (Earned Value) represents the budgeted cost of work performed, and AC (Actual Cost) represents the actual cost of work performed. A CPI greater than 1 indicates that the project is performing better than expected in terms of cost, while a CPI less than 1 indicates cost overruns.

CPI offers valuable information to project managers and stakeholders, allowing them to assess and manage the project's cost performance. By monitoring the CPI throughout the project, any cost variances can be identified early on, enabling proactive measures to be taken to control costs and ensure budget compliance.

Cost-Benefit Analysis

A cost-benefit analysis is a systematic evaluation of the potential costs and benefits associated with a project or process, conducted in the context of Agile Process and Project Management disciplines. It serves as a decision-making tool that helps Agile teams and organizations assess the value and feasibility of undertaking a particular project or initiative.

During the Agile project planning phase, a cost-benefit analysis is performed to objectively analyze the financial and non-financial impacts of a proposed project. It involves identifying and quantifying the costs and benefits, and then comparing them to determine whether the project is worth pursuing.

Critical Chain Project Management (CCPM)

Critical Chain Project Management (CCPM) is a project management approach that is often used in the context of Agile Process and Project Management disciplines. It is based on the theory that the performance of a project is limited by a small number of critical tasks, known as the critical chain. In CCPM, the project plan is developed by identifying these critical tasks and then managing them in a way that maximizes efficiency and minimizes delays.

One of the key principles of CCPM is the concept of the "buffer." Buffers are time intervals that are strategically placed throughout the project schedule to account for uncertainties and potential delays. There are two types of buffers in CCPM: project buffers and feeding buffers.

The project buffer is placed at the end of the project schedule and acts as a safety net to protect project completion. It ensures that even if delays occur in non-critical tasks, the project will still be completed on time. Feeding buffers, on the other hand, are placed before critical tasks to protect them from delays in preceding tasks.

An important aspect of CCPM is the focus on resource utilization. In traditional project management approaches, resources are often overallocated, leading to inefficiencies and delays. In CCPM, resources are allocated based on the critical path, ensuring that they are utilized effectively and efficiently.

Critical Chain

Critical Chain is a project management technique that is often used in the context of Agile Process and Project Management disciplines. It focuses on optimizing the scheduling and resource allocation of tasks to complete a project on time and within budget.

The technique involves identifying the critical path, which is the sequence of tasks that determines the shortest possible duration to complete the project. In Agile Process and Project Management, the critical path is often depicted using a visualization tool such as a Gantt chart or a network diagram.

Once the critical path is identified, the next step is to identify resource dependencies and constraints. This includes identifying resource availability, considering any limitations or dependencies between tasks, and accounting for any potential risks or uncertainties.

Based on these factors, the critical chain is determined. The critical chain is the longest sequence of tasks within the critical path that takes into account resource dependencies and constraints. It considers not only the task duration but also any buffer time required to account for variability in task completion time.

The critical chain approach aims to optimize resource allocation by prioritizing tasks based on resource availability and dependencies. It involves carefully managing resources to avoid bottlenecks and ensure smooth project flow.

31

In Agile Process and Project Management, the critical chain technique can enhance project planning, improve resource utilization, and increase the likelihood of project success within the defined time and budget constraints.

Critical Path Analysis (CPA)

Critical Path Analysis (CPA) is a project management tool used in Agile Process and Project Management disciplines. It is used to identify the sequence of tasks that must be completed on time in order to ensure the successful completion of a project.

The critical path is the longest sequence of dependent tasks that must be completed in order to complete the project on time. It is determined by calculating the earliest and latest possible start and finish times for each task, taking into account dependencies between tasks and any constraints on the project timeline.

Critical Path Drag

The critical path drag is a concept in Agile Process and Project Management disciplines that refers to the total amount of time that a task or activity on the critical path of a project is delaying the project's overall completion date. It is a measure of the impact that a delay in a critical path task has on the project timeline.

The critical path is the longest sequence of dependent tasks that determines the project's minimum completion time. Any delay in a task on the critical path will directly affect the project's end date. The critical path drag quantifies the time impact of this delay and helps project managers prioritize tasks that need immediate attention to avoid further delays.

Critical Path Float

The critical path float, in the context of Agile Process and Project Management disciplines, refers to the amount of time that a task can be delayed without affecting the overall project timeline. It is a measure of flexibility within the project schedule and helps project managers identify tasks that have no potential for delay.

In Agile, where projects are divided into smaller iterations called sprints, the critical path float is crucial for managing priorities and maximizing efficiency. It allows teams to focus on completing essential tasks without being held up by non-critical activities.

Critical Path Method (CPM) Analysis

The Critical Path Method (CPM) Analysis is a project management tool employed in the Agile Process to identify the most critical tasks and determine the minimum project duration. It provides a visual representation of the project tasks and their dependencies, allowing project managers to allocate resources effectively and manage project timelines efficiently.

In the context of Agile Process and Project Management disciplines, CPM Analysis involves the following steps: 1. Identification of Tasks: The first step in CPM Analysis is to identify all the tasks required to complete the project. These tasks are listed in sequential order based on their dependencies and requirements. 2. Determination of Dependencies: Each task has dependencies on one or more preceding tasks. By identifying these dependencies, project managers can establish the sequence in which the tasks need to be completed. 3. Calculation of Duration: Assigning the duration estimate for each task allows project managers to calculate the overall project duration. This is done by considering the estimated time required to complete each task and the dependencies between tasks. 4. Identification of Critical Path: The critical path consists of tasks that must be completed in the shortest possible time for the entire project to be completed within the desired timeline. By identifying the critical path, project managers can focus their resources and attention on these critical tasks to ensure timely completion of the project. Thus, the Critical Path Method (CPM) Analysis in Agile Process and Project Management proves to be a valuable tool for visualizing project tasks, identifying dependencies, determining project duration, and focusing on critical tasks to manage project timelines effectively.

Critical Path Method (CPM)

The Critical Path Method (CPM) is a project management technique commonly used in Agile process and project management disciplines. It is a tool that helps project managers effectively plan and prioritize tasks to ensure the successful completion of a project within a given timeframe. In the Agile context, CPM involves breaking down a project into smaller, more manageable tasks, known as activities. Each activity is then assigned a duration, which represents the estimated time required to complete it. Additionally, relationships between activities are established to determine dependencies and create a logical sequence of work. By analyzing these activities and their dependencies, project managers can identify the critical path, which is the sequence of activities that determine the minimum amount of time required for project completion. Activities on the critical path have no flexibility and must be completed on time to prevent project delays. CPM provides project managers with a visual representation of the project timeline, allowing them to identify activities that can be sped up or delayed without impacting the overall project schedule. By understanding the critical path and its associated activities, project managers can make informed decisions on resource allocation, task prioritization, and risk mitigation. In summary, the Critical Path Method is a valuable tool for project managers in Agile process and project management disciplines. It helps them identify and prioritize tasks, determine dependencies, and optimize project timelines to ensure successful project completion within the given timeframe.

Critical Path

A critical path is a sequence of tasks or activities that must be completed in order to successfully complete a project. It represents the longest path through a project's schedule network diagram, as well as the shortest possible amount of time in which the project can be completed. In an Agile process, the critical path is often used to identify tasks that have dependencies and are critical to the overall project timeline.

In Agile project management, the critical path is a dynamic concept that evolves and changes as the project progresses. Unlike traditional project management methods, Agile projects are characterized by their iterative and incremental nature, with frequent delivery of working software or products. As a result, the critical path may shift or different tasks may become critical at different stages of the project.

Customer Collaboration

The term "Customer Collaboration" in the context of Agile Process and Project Management refers to the active involvement and continuous collaboration between the project team and the customer throughout the software development process. It is one of the core principles of Agile methodologies, such as Scrum, that emphasize the importance of satisfying the customer through early and continuous delivery of valuable software.

Customer collaboration involves the regular engagement of the customer in all stages of the project, including requirements gathering, prioritization, and feedback. The customer becomes an integral part of the project team, working closely with the development team to ensure that the end product meets their needs and expectations.

Customer Relationship Management (CRM)

Customer Relationship Management (CRM) is a strategy and approach in Agile Process and Project Management disciplines that focuses on building and maintaining strong relationships with customers. It involves managing interactions and communications with customers throughout their lifecycle, from initial contact to post-sale support. CRM aims to enhance customer satisfaction and loyalty by understanding and addressing their needs and expectations.

In the Agile Process and Project Management disciplines, CRM is implemented through various techniques and tools that facilitate effective customer engagement. This includes capturing and analyzing customer data to gain insights into their preferences and behaviors. Agile teams use this information to tailor their products or services to better meet customer requirements.

Customer Requirements

Customer requirements, in the context of Agile Process and Project Management disciplines, refer to the specific needs, expectations, and specifications that customers have for a product or service. These requirements are used to guide the development process and are crucial for ensuring that the final product meets the customer's needs and provides value.

Agile Process and Project Management disciplines approach customer requirements with a focus on continuous collaboration and feedback. The Agile methodology emphasizes close interaction with the customer throughout the development process, enabling quick and iterative delivery of valuable features. By continuously engaging with the customer, the project team can gather and refine requirements to ensure that the final product aligns with the customer's vision.

Customer requirements are typically captured in user stories or user scenarios, which are concise descriptions of specific features or functionalities from the end-user's perspective. These user stories serve as a communication tool between the development team and the customer, enabling shared understanding and validation of requirements.

Additionally, Agile Process and Project Management disciplines prioritize delivering working software over comprehensive documentation. This means that customer requirements are often captured in a lightweight manner, with an emphasis on conversations and face-to-face interactions rather than lengthy written specifications. This approach allows for greater adaptability and flexibility, as requirements can evolve and be refined as the development progresses.

Customer Satisfaction

Customer satisfaction in the context of Agile Process and Project Management disciplines refers to the degree to which the customer's expectations and requirements are met throughout the project lifecycle.

Agile methodologies prioritize customer collaboration and continuous delivery, aiming to deliver value to the customer early and frequently. Therefore, customer satisfaction is a central measure of project success in Agile environments.

Customer

An Agile Process is a flexible and iterative approach to project management, commonly used in software development. It emphasizes collaboration, adaptability, and continuous improvement through cross-functional teams and frequent feedback cycles.

Agile Process is guided by the Agile Manifesto, which values individuals and interactions, working software, customer collaboration, and responding to change. It focuses on delivering working software in small increments, with the aim of providing value to the customer early and frequently.

Daily Standup

The Daily Standup, also known as the Daily Scrum, is a time-boxed event (usually of 15 minutes) held by the Agile team on a regular basis, typically once a day. It is a key element of the Agile process and a widely used practice in project management disciplines.

During the Daily Standup, the Agile team gathers together, including the Product Owner, Scrum Master, and Development Team members. The purpose of this meeting is to provide a structured opportunity for team members to synchronize their activities and communicate progress and challenges.

Each team member should answer the following three questions during the Daily Standup:

1. What have I done since the last Daily Standup? This question allows team members to update the rest of the team on the progress they have made towards their Sprint goals, tasks completed, and any potential impediments encountered.

2. What am I planning to do until the next Daily Standup? This question helps team members inform the team about their upcoming tasks, commitments, and plans. It fosters transparency and enables other team members to understand the work in progress.

3. Are there any impediments or blockers that are preventing me from making progress? This question highlights any obstacles team members may be facing and provides an opportunity for the Scrum Master or other team members to offer assistance and remove these impediments.

The Daily Standup is crucial for facilitating collaboration, coordination, and communication within the Agile team. It promotes continuous improvement, enables early identification and resolution of issues, and ensures alignment towards achieving the Sprint goals and overall project success.

Dashboard Reporting

A dashboard reporting, within the context of Agile Process and Project Management disciplines, refers to a visual representation that provides key performance indicators (KPIs) and metrics for monitoring, analyzing, and communicating the progress and status of projects. It serves as a centralized tool for project stakeholders to quickly and easily access relevant information, enabling informed decision-making and effective project management.

A dashboard reporting typically consists of various charts, graphs, and data visualizations, presenting real-time data in a concise and user-friendly manner. It captures and displays critical project information, such as task completion status, resource utilization, timeline adherence, and overall project health. By condensing complex data into digestible visuals, the dashboard allows stakeholders to gain a comprehensive understanding of project performance at a glance.

Dashboard

A dashboard in the context of Agile Process and Project Management disciplines is a visual representation of key project data and metrics, typically displayed on a single screen or webpage. It provides a summary of the project's current status, progress, and performance, allowing project managers and stakeholders to quickly assess the overall health of the project.

The dashboard presents information in real-time, presenting up-to-date data based on the project's latest development activities. It serves as a central hub where project teams can access critical information, enabling effective decision-making and facilitating communication and collaboration among team members.

The key characteristics of an Agile dashboard include:

- Key project metrics: The dashboard highlights the most important project metrics, such as sprint progress, task completion rates, and project velocity. It provides an overview of the project's performance, allowing project managers to identify potential bottlenecks or areas for improvement.

- Visual representation: The dashboard uses charts, graphs, and other visual elements to present data in a clear and concise format. This visual representation helps project teams quickly analyze and interpret information, making it easier to identify trends and patterns.

- Real-time updates: The dashboard updates information in real-time, ensuring that project teams can access the most current data. This real-time visibility allows for proactive decision-making, enabling teams to address issues and make adjustments as necessary.

In summary, an Agile dashboard is a powerful tool for project managers and stakeholders to monitor and assess the project's progress and performance. It provides a centralized location for accessing critical project data, enabling effective decision-making and fostering collaboration among team members.

Data Analysis Techniques

Data Analysis techniques refer to the specific methods or procedures used to collect, organize, interpret, and present data in order to gain insights, make informed decisions, and support the successful execution of projects within the Agile Process and Project Management disciplines.

These techniques involve the application of statistical, mathematical, and analytical tools to analyze both quantitative and qualitative data. They can be used throughout the entire project lifecycle, starting from the initial planning and requirements gathering phase, through the execution and monitoring stages, and ultimately in evaluating the project's success and lessons learned.

Data Gathering Techniques

Data gathering techniques refer to the methods used to collect information and data that is relevant to an Agile process or project management discipline. These techniques are crucial in order to gather accurate and reliable data that can be used for decision-making and problem-solving.

In Agile processes, data gathering techniques are used throughout the project lifecycle to gather information about the project scope, requirements, user needs, and any potential risks or challenges. These techniques can include interviews, surveys, observations, and workshops. During the initial stages of the project, interviews can be conducted with stakeholders to understand their expectations and gather information about the project goals and objectives. Surveys can be used to collect data from a larger group of people and gather insights about user preferences or feedback.

Observations can be a valuable data gathering technique in Agile projects, as they allow project managers to observe how users interact with a product or system and identify any usability or functionality issues. Workshops are also commonly used in Agile processes to gather data through collaborative sessions with stakeholders, such as brainstorming sessions or design thinking workshops.

Using these data gathering techniques, project managers and Agile teams can identify the needs and requirements of the users, gain insights into the project scope, and gather relevant data to make informed decisions. It is essential to select the appropriate data gathering techniques based on the project requirements and objectives, ensuring that the collected data is accurate, reliable, and useful in driving the success of the Agile process or project.

Decision Tree Analysis

A decision tree analysis is a tool used in Agile Process and Project Management disciplines to systematically evaluate and select the best course of action or decision to be made. It involves breaking down complex problems or decisions into smaller, more manageable components, and analyzing the potential outcomes and alternatives at each step.

The decision tree analysis follows a hierarchical structure, resembling a tree, with branches representing different choices or options and nodes representing different decisions or events. The analysis begins with a root node, which represents the main decision or problem to be addressed. From there, the tree branches out into different paths, each representing a potential alternative or option. The branches continue to split until reaching the end nodes, which represent the final outcomes or conclusions.

Each branch and node in the decision tree analysis is assigned values or probabilities that measure the likelihood and impact of different outcomes. These values are determined based on available data and expert knowledge. By evaluating the probabilities and values associated with each possible outcome, decision makers can assess the potential risks, benefits, and trade-offs of different options.

In Agile Process and Project Management, decision tree analysis helps teams make informed decisions by considering multiple scenarios and their potential impacts. It provides a visual representation of the decision-making process, allowing stakeholders to understand the rationale behind the chosen course of action. Decision tree analysis also promotes transparency and collaboration, as it enables teams to collectively evaluate and reach a consensus on the best decision.

Defect

A defect, in the context of Agile Process and Project Management disciplines, refers to an imperfection or flaw in a software product or system that deviates from its specified requirements or expected behavior. It can also be seen as a variance between the actual and desired state of a feature or functionality. Defects can arise from errors or mistakes made during the development, testing, or implementation phases of a project.

In Agile methodologies, defects are typically identified through various quality assurance practices such as continuous integration, automated testing, and user acceptance testing. They are captured and tracked in defect management tools or systems, allowing the development team to prioritize and resolve them efficiently.

Effective defect management is crucial in Agile project management to ensure the delivery of high-quality software products. Defects can hinder the progress of the project, impact user satisfaction, and cause delays or additional costs if not addressed promptly. Agile teams often adopt a proactive approach to defect management by implementing strategies like early defect prevention, regular inspections, and continuous improvement of development processes.

The Agile approach encourages collaboration among team members, including developers, testers, product owners, and stakeholders, to identify, report, and resolve defects. Defects are typically categorized based on their severity and impact on the system's functionality. High-priority defects that severely affect critical features or cause system failures are given immediate attention, while lower-priority defects may be deferred to a later iteration or release.

Definition Of Ready (DoR)

The Definition of Ready (DoR) is a term used in Agile Process and Project Management disciplines to define the criteria that a user story must meet before it can be considered for inclusion in a sprint or iteration. It ensures that the story is well-defined, feasible, and ready for development.

In order for a user story to be considered "ready," it should meet the following criteria:

- The user story should be written in a clear and concise manner, using a standard format that includes a description of the feature or functionality, the intended user or customer, and any acceptance criteria or test scenarios.

- The user story should have a clear business value or benefit, and should align with the overall project goals and objectives.

- The user story should be small enough to be completed within a single sprint or iteration, and should not have any external dependencies that could delay its implementation.

- The user story should have been reviewed and validated by the product owner and other relevant stakeholders, ensuring that it accurately represents their needs and expectations.

- The user story should have a clear estimate of its complexity or effort required for implementation, based on prior experience or knowledge.

By ensuring that user stories meet these criteria before they are included in a sprint or iteration, the Definition of Ready helps to reduce ambiguity and improve the efficiency of the development process. It enables the development team to focus on delivering value and meeting the needs of the customer, while also facilitating effective planning and prioritization.

Deliverable

A deliverable refers to any tangible or intangible output or outcome that is produced as a result of completing a specific task or activity within the Agile process or Project Management disciplines. It typically represents a milestone, a completed phase, or a final product that can be measured, tested, or evaluated against predefined criteria or requirements.

Deliverables act as a measurable indication of progress and serve as a means of communication between the project team and stakeholders. They are essential for ensuring transparency and providing clarity on what is expected to be achieved within a given timeframe. By clearly defining and documenting deliverables, project managers can effectively manage expectations and track progress towards project goals.

Delphi Technique

The Delphi Technique is a structured communication method used in Agile Process and Project Management disciplines to gather and assimilate input from a group of experts in a particular field. It aims to achieve a consensus or convergence of ideas by eliminating bias and promoting anonymity among participants.

In the context of Agile Process and Project Management, the Delphi Technique is typically used in situations where there is a need for expert opinions or predictions but there is no possibility of face-to-face interaction. It allows geographically dispersed experts to contribute their insights and knowledge without being influenced by external factors or group dynamics.

Dependencies

A dependency in the context of Agile Process and Project Management disciplines refers to a relationship between two tasks or activities where one task is dependent on the completion or availability of another task in order to start or be completed. Dependencies help in determining the sequence and timing of activities within a project, ensuring that tasks can be executed in a logical and efficient manner.

Agile methodologies, such as Scrum, Kanban, or Lean, emphasize the importance of identifying and managing dependencies to optimize project delivery and minimize risks. Dependencies can be classified into two types: external and internal dependencies.

External dependencies are related to factors outside the control of the project team, such as dependencies on external stakeholders, vendors, or third-party systems. These dependencies often require effective communication and coordination between different parties to ensure smooth execution of the project.

Internal dependencies, on the other hand, are dependencies within the project team itself. These can include dependencies between tasks, user stories, or features. Identifying and managing internal dependencies is critical to avoid delays or bottlenecks in project execution.

By understanding and managing dependencies, Agile teams can effectively plan, organize, and execute project activities. Dependency management techniques, such as dependency mapping, dependency tracking, and dependency resolution, are used to identify and address dependencies throughout the project lifecycle. This helps teams deliver value incrementally and iteratively, while adapting to changing requirements and priorities.

Dependency Constraints

Dependency Constraints, in the context of Agile Process and Project Management disciplines, refer to the limitations or restrictions imposed by the relationships and dependencies between tasks, features, or deliverables within a project. These constraints determine the sequence or order in which activities need to be completed or the conditions under which certain tasks can be started or finished.

In an Agile environment, where iterative and incremental development is practiced, dependency constraints play a crucial role in managing the flow of work and ensuring the smooth execution of the project. Agile methodologies, such as Scrum, rely on visual tools like Kanban boards or sprint backlogs to track and manage dependencies effectively.

Dependency constraints can be of different types, including mandatory dependencies, discretionary dependencies, and external dependencies. Mandatory dependencies indicate tasks that must be completed in a specific order due to logical or technical constraints. Discretionary dependencies, on the other hand, allow flexibility and enable teams to choose the order in which certain tasks are performed. External dependencies occur when certain tasks or deliverables rely on external factors, such as stakeholder approvals or vendor dependencies.

Managing dependency constraints requires constant communication, collaboration, and coordination among team members, stakeholders, and other project stakeholders. By identifying and understanding these constraints early on, project managers can mitigate risks, optimize resource allocation, and ensure the timely delivery of project milestones and objectives.

Dependency Mapping

Dependency Mapping is a crucial practice in Agile Process and Project Management disciplines that involves identifying and understanding the relationships and dependencies between various tasks, activities, or deliverables within a project. It is used to create a visual representation or documentation of the dependencies, helping teams and stakeholders to effectively plan, prioritize, and manage work.

By mapping dependencies, project teams can gain insights into the sequence, order, and relationships between different tasks. This allows them to identify critical paths, potential bottlenecks, and areas of risk or dependency conflicts. With this information, teams can make informed decisions about task prioritization, resource allocation, and scheduling, ultimately ensuring efficient project execution and successful delivery.

Dependency Sequencing

Dependency sequencing is a critical component of the Agile Process and Project Management disciplines. It refers to the order in which tasks or activities should be performed based on their dependencies or relationships with other tasks. In Agile, project tasks are broken down into smaller, manageable units called user stories or features, which are prioritized and scheduled for implementation.

When managing an Agile project, it is important to identify the dependencies between different tasks or user stories. These dependencies can be of different types, such as finish-to-start (where one task must be completed before another can begin), start-to-start (where two tasks can start simultaneously), or finish-to-finish (where two tasks must be completed at the same time).

Deployment Plan

A deployment plan refers to a document or a set of guidelines that outlines the systematic and organized approach to implementing a software application or system into the live production environment. It plays a crucial role in the Agile process and project management disciplines.

In the context of Agile, a deployment plan is developed and followed to ensure a smooth transition from the development phase to the operational phase. It includes various activities and tasks that need to be executed to deploy the software effectively. The plan may cover areas such as infrastructure setup, code deployment, database configuration, testing, quality assurance, user training, and data migration.

Documentation

Agile Process: Agile Process refers to a method used in project management for the purpose of delivering high-quality products or services in an efficient and flexible manner. It is an iterative approach that allows teams to work collaboratively, adapt to changes, and respond to customer needs effectively. The Agile Process is based on the values and principles outlined in the Agile Manifesto. It promotes close collaboration between cross-functional teams, continuous feedback, and frequent and incremental delivery of working software or solutions. The key elements of the Agile Process include: 1. Iterative Development: The project is divided into small iterations called sprints, usually lasting from one to four weeks. Each sprint includes the activities of planning, designing, coding, testing, and reviewing. 2. Continuous Feedback: Regular feedback is sought from stakeholders, including customers, to ensure that the product or service meets their requirements. This feedback is used to make necessary modifications or improvements in subsequent sprints. 3. Flexibility and Adaptability: Agile teams prioritize responding to changes in customer needs and market dynamics, rather than following a rigid plan. They embrace change and adjust their course accordingly to deliver the most valuable outcome. 4. Cross-functional Collaboration: Agile teams comprise individuals with various skill sets, such as developers, testers, designers, and business analysts. They work together, share ideas, and collaborate closely throughout the project, fostering creativity and innovation. Agile Process management requires effective communication, transparency, and self-organization within the team. It emphasizes continuous improvement and learning from both successes and failures. In summary, the Agile Process is an iterative project management approach that allows teams to deliver high-quality products or services by embracing change, promoting collaboration, and focusing on customer satisfaction. Project Management: Project Management refers to the practice of planning, organizing, and controlling resources and activities to achieve specific project goals within defined constraints. It involves the application of knowledge, skills, tools, and techniques to meet project requirements and deliver desired outcomes. The key elements of Project Management include: 1. Planning: Defining project objectives, scope, deliverables, timelines, and resource requirements. It involves creating a detailed project plan that outlines the tasks, dependencies, and responsibilities of team members. 2. Organizing: Forming project teams and assigning roles and responsibilities to individuals. This includes establishing communication channels, developing a project structure, and setting up appropriate governance mechanisms. 3. Controlling: Monitoring project progress, tracking performance, and taking corrective actions to ensure that the project stays on track. This involves regularly measuring actual progress against planned progress, identifying deviations, and implementing necessary adjustments. 4. Risk Management: Identifying potential risks and uncertainties that may impact project success, and developing strategies to mitigate or address them. This includes proactive risk identification, analysis, response planning, and monitoring. 5. Stakeholder Management: Engaging and managing project stakeholders to ensure that their needs, expectations, and concerns are addressed. This involves effective communication, stakeholder analysis, and building relationships to gain support and cooperation. Project Management brings structure, discipline, and accountability to the project execution process. It provides a framework for effective decision-making, resource allocation, and risk mitigation. Through proper planning, organizing, and controlling, project managers ensure the successful completion of projects on time, within budget, and meeting the defined quality standards. In conclusion, Project Management is a disciplined approach that enables the successful execution and delivery of projects by applying knowledge, skills, tools, and techniques to achieve project goals and meet stakeholder expectations.

Earned Schedule (ES)

Earned Schedule (ES) is a performance measurement technique that combines elements of Earned Value Management (EVM) with Agile methodology in the context of project management disciplines. It provides a more accurate and proactive approach to tracking a project's progress and forecasting its completion, specifically in Agile projects.

ES is based on the concept of earned value, which measures the value of work completed against the planned value of work at a specific point in time. Instead of just focusing on cost and schedule variances like traditional EVM, ES incorporates Agile principles to assess the earned value based on the completed user stories or backlog items. This allows for a more realistic and meaningful representation of progress in Agile projects.

Earned Value Analysis (EVA)

Earned Value Analysis (EVA) is a key performance measurement technique utilized in Agile Process and Project Management disciplines. It provides a quantitative assessment of project progress by determining the value of work completed in relation to the planned budget and schedule.

In Agile Project Management, EVA allows project managers to track and assess the actual progress of the project, enabling them to identify any deviations from the original plan and take necessary corrective actions. This analysis technique measures three crucial project parameters: planned value (PV), earned value (EV), and actual cost (AC).

Planned value (PV) refers to the estimated cost of completing the planned work at any given point in time, while earned value (EV) represents the measure of work actually completed and approved by the product owner or customer. Lastly, actual cost (AC) reflects the total cost incurred in completing the work at a specific point in time.

By comparing these three parameters, EVA provides project managers with valuable insights into the project's performance and budget utilization. It helps them evaluate whether the project is on track, over budget, or ahead of schedule. Additionally, project managers can calculate key performance indicators such as Schedule Performance Index (SPI) and Cost Performance Index (CPI) using EVA.

EVA serves as a powerful tool for project forecasting and risk management by highlighting early warning signs of potential budget and schedule deviations in Agile projects. By monitoring and analyzing these indicators, project teams can make informed decisions and take necessary actions to ensure project success.

Earned Value (EV)

Earned Value (EV) is a key performance indicator used in Agile Process and Project Management disciplines to measure the progress and performance of a project. It provides insights into the value delivered by the project team based on the work completed compared to the planned targets.

EV is calculated by multiplying the actual percentage of work completed by the total budget of the project. This helps in determining the value of the work accomplished and the corresponding cost incurred. It enables project managers to assess if the project is on track and progressing as planned, allowing them to take timely corrective actions if needed.

Earned Value Index (EVI)

The Earned Value Index (EVI) is a project management metric used in Agile processes to measure the efficiency and progress of a project in terms of cost and schedule. It is a quantitative indicator that compares the value of work actually completed to the value of work that was planned to be completed at a specific point in time.

EVI is calculated by dividing the Earned Value (EV) by the Planned Value (PV). The EV represents the estimated value of completed work, while the PV represents the estimated value of work that was scheduled to be completed at a specific time. By comparing the EV to the PV, the EVI provides insights into whether a project is over or under budget and whether it is ahead or behind schedule.

Earned Value Management (EVM)

Earned Value Management (EVM) is a technique used in Agile Process and Project Management disciplines to assess and measure project performance. It involves integrating project scope, schedule, and cost objectives to provide an accurate measure of project progress.

In the Agile context, EVM focuses on tracking the value delivered by the project throughout its lifecycle. It provides insights into whether the project is on track to deliver the expected value within the allocated resources. EVM helps Agile teams in making informed decisions and taking appropriate actions to ensure the project's success.

Economic Order Quantity (EOQ)

Economic Order Quantity (EOQ) is a management methodology used in the Agile Process and Project Management disciplines to determine the optimal order quantity of items based on cost considerations. It enables organizations to find the balance between carrying costs and ordering costs, ensuring efficient inventory management.

EOQ takes into account factors such as the cost of holding inventory, the cost of placing an order, and the demand for the item. By calculating the EOQ, organizations can minimize costs associated with inventory and ordering, ultimately increasing profitability.

Effective Communication

Effective communication in the context of Agile Process and Project Management disciplines refers to the clear and efficient exchange of information, ideas, and feedback among team members and stakeholders. It is a crucial aspect of successful project execution and collaboration.

In Agile, communication plays a pivotal role, as it enables team members to stay aligned, share progress updates, address challenges, and make informed decisions. It fosters transparency, trust, and a shared understanding of project goals and expectations. Effective communication ensures that everyone involved has access to the right information at the right time, promoting collaboration and enabling timely adjustments as needed.

Efficiency

Efficiency in the context of Agile Process and Project Management disciplines refers to the ability to maximize output while minimizing waste and unnecessary effort. It involves utilizing resources, time, and energy in the most effective and productive manner to achieve desired results.

In Agile methodologies, efficiency is a key principle that focuses on delivering value to the customer through continuous improvement and responding to change. It emphasizes the importance of eliminating activities that do not add value and ensuring that each task contributes to the overall goal of the project. Agile teams strive to work collaboratively, effectively communicate, and prioritize their work to ensure efficient delivery of high-quality products or services.

Effort Driven Scheduling

Effort Driven Scheduling is an approach used in Agile Process and Project Management disciplines to allocate resources and plan project timelines based on the effort required for each task. It involves assigning resources to tasks according to their capacity and availability. This scheduling technique takes into consideration the amount of effort needed to complete a task and adjusts the schedule accordingly.

In Agile Process, projects are typically managed in iterations or sprints. Effort Driven Scheduling helps in determining the number of tasks that can be accomplished within a specific time period. The focus is on ensuring that the team can complete the work based on their available capacity and the effort required for each task. This approach helps in managing expectations and preventing over-commitment.

Effort Estimation Techniques

Effort Estimation Techniques in the context of Agile Process and Project Management disciplines refer to the methods used to estimate the amount of work, time, and resources required to complete a task or project within an Agile framework. These techniques are essential for Agile teams to plan, prioritize, and allocate resources effectively.

One common technique used in Agile is Story Points, which is a relative estimation method based on the complexity, effort, and uncertainty of a user story. The team assigns story points to each user story during the backlog refinement process, considering factors such as complexity, dependencies, and effort needed. This technique simplifies the estimation process and allows for flexibility in adjusting estimates as the project progresses.

Another widely used technique is Planning Poker, which involves the entire Agile team participating in an estimation session. Each team member anonymously provides their estimate for a user story using a set of predefined values (e.g., 1, 2, 3, 5, 8, 13), representing the effort required. The team discusses the differences and reasons behind each estimate before reaching a consensus. Planning Poker fosters collaboration and ensures that different perspectives are considered in the estimation process.

The Delphi Technique is another technique used in Agile, where multiple experts provide independent estimates for a task or project. These estimates are then consolidated anonymously, and the experts are provided with the collective estimate. The process is repeated until a consensus is reached. The Delphi Technique helps eliminate bias and provides more accurate estimates by leveraging the collective knowledge and expertise of the team.

Effort Estimation

Effort estimation is the process of approximating the amount of work required to complete a specific task or project within the Agile Process and Project Management disciplines. It involves analyzing the scope of the project, understanding the requirements, and evaluating various factors that may influence the effort required.

In the Agile Process, effort estimation is typically done based on the user stories, which are concise descriptions of the project requirements from the user's perspective. These user stories are evaluated by the team during the planning phase to determine the level of complexity and effort involved in implementing them.

The effort estimation process in Agile involves breaking down the project into smaller tasks or work items known as backlog items or sprint tasks. Each backlog item is evaluated individually, and an estimation is assigned based on factors such as the size, complexity, and dependencies of the task.

Estimation techniques commonly used in Agile include relative sizing, planning poker, and t-shirt sizing. Relative sizing involves comparing the effort required for one task to another and assigning a relative value. Planning poker involves team members independently estimating the effort required and then discussing and reaching a consensus. T-shirt sizing involves assigning sizes like extra-small, small, medium, large, or extra-large to backlog items based on their effort.

Effort estimation in Agile is not a one-time activity but an iterative process. As the project progresses and more information becomes available, estimations may be refined and adjusted. Regular re-estimation helps the team in managing expectations, tracking progress, and making informed decisions to ensure successful project completion.

Emotional Intelligence (EI)

Emotional Intelligence (EI) refers to a set of skills that enables individuals to recognize, understand, and manage their own emotions, as well as the emotions of others. In the context of Agile Process and Project Management disciplines, EI plays a crucial role in enhancing communication, collaboration, and overall team dynamics.

Agile methodology emphasizes the importance of individuals and interactions over processes and tools. Effective communication and collaboration are critical for the success of Agile teams, and EI provides the foundation for building strong relationships and fostering trust among team members.

Emotional Intelligence

Emotional intelligence in the context of Agile Process and Project Management refers to the ability to identify, understand, and manage one's own emotions, as well as the emotions of others, in order to effectively collaborate, communicate, and problem-solve within an Agile environment.

Agile Process and Project Management methodologies emphasize the importance of self-organizing teams, constant collaboration, and adaptive planning. In such environments, emotional intelligence plays a crucial role in fostering teamwork, building strong relationships, and promoting a positive work culture.

Individuals with high emotional intelligence are able to accurately perceive and interpret the emotions of themselves and others. This enables them to effectively manage their own emotions and respond appropriately to the emotions of team members. By recognizing and addressing emotions in a constructive manner, project managers and team members can navigate conflicts, resolve issues, and maintain motivation and engagement.

Emotional intelligence also supports effective communication within Agile teams. Individuals with high emotional intelligence are able to express their ideas, opinions, and concerns in a clear, assertive, and respectful manner. They are also skilled listeners, capable of understanding and empathizing with the perspectives of others. This fosters open and honest communication, encourages active participation, and enhances collaboration.

In summary, emotional intelligence is a valuable skill set for Agile Process and Project Management professionals. It enables individuals to navigate the challenges and complexities of Agile environments, build strong relationships, and promote a collaborative and productive work culture.

End-User Training Plan

An end-user training plan in the context of Agile Process and Project Management disciplines is a structured outline that details the steps and activities required to train end-users on the use of a particular software or system. It is a comprehensive document that helps ensure that end-users have the necessary knowledge and skills to effectively utilize the product or service.

The training plan typically includes information such as the objectives of the training, the target audience, the training materials and resources required, the training schedule, and the evaluation methods to assess the effectiveness of the training.

End-User Training

End-User Training in the context of Agile Process and Project Management disciplines refers to the process of educating and preparing end-users for the effective and efficient use of a software product or system developed within an Agile framework.

During Agile development, software is developed and delivered incrementally, often in short iterations called sprints. This iterative approach allows for frequent feedback and collaboration between the development team and end-users. However, this also means that end-users need to be trained on new features and functionalities as they are added or modified throughout the development process.

Enterprise Environmental Factors (EEFs)

Enterprise Environmental Factors (EEFs) refer to the internal and external factors that can influence and impact the management of Agile processes and projects within an organization. These factors play a crucial role in shaping the project environment and can have a significant influence on project decisions and outcomes.

Internally, EEFs can include organizational culture, structure, and governance. The organization's values, norms, and practices can shape the adoption and implementation of Agile methodologies. The structure of the organization, such as the hierarchy, departments, and reporting relationships, can impact how Agile teams are formed and managed. Governance processes, such as project approval and decision-making mechanisms, can also affect Agile projects.

Externally, EEFs can encompass factors such as market conditions, industry standards, and regulatory requirements. Market conditions, such as customer demands and competitive pressures, can influence project priorities and scope. Industry standards and best practices can guide Agile implementation and ensure adherence to quality and compliance. Regulatory requirements, such as data privacy or safety regulations, can shape project constraints and deliverables.

Overall, EEFs provide the context in which Agile projects operate and help project managers and teams make informed decisions. Understanding and effectively managing these factors is essential for successful Agile process and project management, as they can both enable and constrain project activities and outcomes.

Enterprise Project Management (EPM)

Enterprise Project Management (EPM) is a comprehensive approach to managing and organizing projects within an organization, specifically in the context of Agile Process and Project Management disciplines.

EPM is designed to address the unique challenges and complexities that arise in managing projects at the enterprise level. It focuses on aligning project objectives with the overall goals and strategies of the organization, ensuring maximum efficiency and effectiveness in project execution.

EPM incorporates Agile principles and practices, which emphasize flexibility, collaboration, and continuous improvement. It enables organizations to adapt to changing requirements, market conditions, and stakeholder expectations, allowing for faster delivery of value and improved project outcomes.

In an Agile EPM framework, project management is decentralized, with self-organizing, cross-functional teams working in short iterations or sprints. These teams collaborate closely with stakeholders, including business leaders, customers, and end-users, to ensure that project deliverables meet their evolving needs and expectations.

EPM in the Agile context also emphasizes the importance of transparency and visibility. It promotes the use of visual management tools, such as Kanban boards and burn-down charts, to provide real-time updates on project progress and identify potential bottlenecks or areas for improvement.

Overall, EPM in the Agile Process and Project Management disciplines provides organizations with a structured and adaptable approach to managing projects at the enterprise level. It combines the benefits of Agile practices with a focus on aligning projects with organizational goals, delivering value, and enabling continuous improvement.

Enterprise Risk Management (ERM)

Enterprise Risk Management (ERM) refers to the systematic process of identifying, assessing, and managing risks within an organization. ERM takes into account all types of risks that may affect the achievement of organizational objectives, including financial, operational, strategic, and compliance risks.

In the context of Agile Process and Project Management disciplines, ERM plays a critical role in ensuring that risks are proactively identified and addressed throughout the project lifecycle. The Agile approach emphasizes adaptability, flexibility, and continuous improvement, which requires a comprehensive understanding of potential risks and the ability to mitigate them effectively.

By implementing ERM within the Agile framework, organizations can establish a structured and integrated approach to risk management. This involves conducting regular risk assessments, defining risk response strategies, and monitoring risk mitigation efforts. ERM helps project teams to identify potential obstacles or uncertainties early on and develop contingency plans to ensure project success.

Moreover, ERM emphasizes the importance of collaboration and communication within project teams. It encourages open dialogue among team members, stakeholders, and management to share and address concerns, prioritize risks, and make informed decisions. This promotes transparency, trust, and accountability, enabling teams to respond rapidly to emerging risks and changes in project requirements.

In summary, ERM is essential in the Agile process and project management disciplines as it enables organizations to effectively identify, assess, and address risks in a dynamic and iterative manner. By integrating ERM within the Agile framework, organizations can enhance their risk management capabilities, improve project outcomes, and ultimately achieve their strategic objectives.

Epics And Themes

An Epic in the context of Agile Process and Project Management disciplines refers to a large body of work that needs to be broken down into smaller, more manageable tasks. It represents a high-level user functionality or business requirement that can't be completed in a single sprint or iteration. Epics are typically defined at the early stages of a project or during the project planning phase.

Themes, on the other hand, are broader concepts or objectives that tie together multiple related Epics. They provide an overall direction or focus for the project and help align Epics towards achieving a common goal. Themes are defined at a higher level than Epics and are typically based on business or strategic objectives.

Escalation Process

An escalation process in the context of Agile Process and Project Management disciplines refers to a structured approach put in place to address and resolve issues or concerns that cannot be resolved at the team level. It is a methodical way to ensure that problems are escalated to the appropriate level of management or leadership for resolution.

The escalation process typically starts when a team encounters a significant obstacle or problem that they are unable to resolve on their own within a reasonable time frame. This could be a roadblock that is impacting the progress of the project, a critical decision that needs to be made, or a conflict that cannot be resolved at the team level.

When such an issue arises, the team members are responsible for identifying and documenting the problem, and then escalating it to the appropriate person or group. This escalation could be within the team itself, to a higher-level team or department, or even to the project sponsor or steering committee if necessary.

The escalation process ensures that there is a clear path for issues to be raised and resolved in a timely manner. It helps to prevent problems from lingering or escalating into larger issues that could derail the project. By promptly addressing and resolving problems, the escalation process helps to maintain the progress and momentum of the project.

Estimation Techniques

Estimation techniques in the context of Agile Process and Project Management disciplines refer to the methods used to predict the time, effort, and resources required for completing a task or project. These techniques help in determining the scope and schedule of the project, as well as identifying potential risks and challenges.

One commonly used estimation technique in Agile is called Planning Poker. This technique involves a team of experts coming together to estimate the effort required for each task. Each team member is given a set of cards representing different levels of effort, such as 1, 2, 3, 5, 8, 13, etc. The team discusses the requirements and complexities of the task and then privately selects a card that represents their estimate. After everyone has chosen a card, the team members reveal their estimates simultaneously. If there is a large difference in estimates, the team discusses the reasons behind their choices and repeats the process until a consensus is reached. Planning Poker allows for collaborative decision-making, takes into account various perspectives, and helps in aligning the team's understanding of the task.

Expert Judgment

Expert Judgment is a valuable technique employed in both Agile Process and Project Management disciplines. It involves seeking advice and guidance from subject matter experts or individuals who have significant experience and knowledge in a specific domain or field.

In Agile Process, Expert Judgment plays a crucial role in decision-making, problem-solving, and risk assessment. As Agile teams aim to deliver incremental value, they often encounter complex challenges that require expertise beyond their own capabilities. By consulting with experts, teams can gain valuable insights and perspectives to make informed decisions and overcome obstacles more efficiently.

Similarly, in Project Management, Expert Judgment is utilized to enhance the effectiveness and quality of project planning, execution, and control. Project managers seek input from experts to validate assumptions, estimate resources, assess project risks, and develop strategies for successful project completion. Expert Judgment helps to ensure that project plans are comprehensive, accurate, and aligned with industry best practices.

By leveraging Expert Judgment, Agile teams and project managers can tap into the knowledge and expertise of professionals who have faced similar challenges in the past. This collective wisdom assists in mitigating risks, optimizing decision-making, and enhancing the overall success of Agile projects and traditional project management endeavors.

Expert Resource

Agile Process Management is a discipline that focuses on the iterative and incremental delivery of projects, with the goal of maximizing customer value and adapting to changing requirements. It is based on the Agile Manifesto, which emphasizes collaboration, self-organization, and flexibility.

Agile Project Management is a subset of Agile Process Management that specifically applies to managing and delivering projects. It relies on adaptive planning, continuous feedback, and frequent iterations to ensure that projects remain on track and deliver high-quality outcomes.

External Stakeholders

External stakeholders are individuals, groups, or organizations that are not directly involved in the Agile process or project management, but have an interest or are affected by the outcomes of the project. These stakeholders may include customers, suppliers, competitors, government agencies, and community organizations.

External stakeholders play a vital role in the success of an Agile project, as they provide valuable input, support, and resources. They can influence the project through their requirements, feedback, and expectations. Understanding and managing the needs and expectations of external stakeholders is crucial for project success.

Feasibility Assessment Report

A feasibility assessment report is a formal document prepared in the context of Agile Process and Project Management disciplines. It aims to evaluate the potential viability and practicality of a proposed project or idea. This assessment is conducted to determine whether the project is worth pursuing and to identify any potential challenges or limitations that may arise during its execution.

The report typically includes an analysis of various factors such as technical feasibility, economic viability, operational feasibility, and schedule feasibility. In terms of technical feasibility, the report assesses whether the necessary technology and resources are available to implement the project successfully. Economic viability considers the financial aspects of the project, such as the potential return on investment and cost-benefit analysis.

Operational feasibility evaluates whether the project aligns with the organization's strategic objectives and whether it can be integrated smoothly into existing systems and processes. Schedule feasibility assesses the project's timeline and whether it can be completed within the desired timeframe.

The feasibility assessment report serves as a tool for decision-making, enabling stakeholders to make informed choices regarding the project's continuation or termination. It provides a comprehensive evaluation of the project's feasibility, highlighting its strengths, weaknesses, opportunities, and potential risks.

Feasibility Assessment

A feasibility assessment, in the context of Agile Process and Project Management disciplines, refers to the evaluation of the practicality and viability of a project or initiative. It is carried out to determine if the project is achievable within the given constraints such as time, resources, budget, and technological capabilities.

The assessment typically involves conducting a thorough analysis of various factors and considerations that may impact the successful implementation of the project. These include the availability of necessary skills and expertise, potential risks and challenges, market demand, regulatory compliance, and alignment with organizational goals and objectives.

The Agile approach to feasibility assessment emphasizes frequent and ongoing evaluation throughout the project lifecycle. Instead of conducting a single assessment at the beginning of the project, Agile teams continuously reassess the feasibility of their goals and objectives, adapting as necessary to changing circumstances or emerging challenges.

The feasibility assessment is integral to the Agile process as it helps the team make informed decisions and prioritize their efforts. By identifying potential roadblocks or limitations early on, the team can adjust their plans and strategies accordingly, ensuring a higher probability of project success.

Feasibility Report

The feasibility report is a formal document that assesses the practicality and viability of a project or a process in the Agile Process and Project Management disciplines. It is an essential tool utilized by project managers to evaluate the overall potential success of an initiative before committing resources and efforts to its execution.

Within the Agile framework, the feasibility report serves as a means to determine if the project aligns with the organization's strategic goals, if it can be realistically completed within the given time and budget constraints, and if it possesses the necessary resources and expertise to be successfully implemented. The report typically includes an analysis of various factors, including the technical, economic, legal, and operational aspects of the project or process.

Feasibility Study

A feasibility study is a systematic analysis and evaluation of a proposed project or solution to determine its viability, effectiveness, and potential for success. It is a crucial step in the project management process, especially within the Agile methodology, as it helps project teams assess the feasibility and viability of a project idea before investing significant time, effort, and resources.

The feasibility study in Agile project management focuses on gathering and analyzing information, conducting research, and evaluating various factors to determine if the proposed project aligns with the organization's goals, objectives, and strategic direction. It involves assessing technical, economic, legal, operational, and scheduling aspects to identify risks, challenges, and opportunities.

Throughout the feasibility study, Agile project teams collaborate with stakeholders, including business owners, sponsors, subject matter experts, and customers, to gather requirements, understand their expectations, and ensure alignment with the project's vision. This iterative and collaborative approach enables teams to gather feedback and make necessary adjustments to the project scope, deliverables, and timelines.

The final outcome of a feasibility study in Agile project management is a comprehensive report that outlines the findings, recommendations, and potential risks associated with the proposed project. This report serves as a decision-making tool, enabling stakeholders to make informed choices about proceeding with the project, modifying its scope, or abandoning it altogether.

Feature Flags

A feature flag is a technique used in Agile Process and Project Management disciplines to enable the controlled release of new features or functionality within a software application. It serves as a toggle or switch that allows developers to turn on or off specific features, configurations, or experiments without the need for redeployment or code changes.

By using feature flags, development teams can introduce new features to a select group of users or environments, using the concept of progressive deployment. This approach allows for continuous delivery and faster feedback loops, as changes can be tested and monitored in real-time. It also provides a way to mitigate risks associated with deploying unproven or unstable features, allowing teams to safely roll back or disable new functionality if necessary.

Financial Modeling

Financial modeling is a process of creating a mathematical representation or simulation of a financial situation or decision-making process. It involves using various tools and techniques to analyze and predict the financial performance and outcomes of a project or organization.

In the context of Agile Process and Project Management disciplines, financial modeling plays a crucial role in supporting decision-making and resource allocation. It helps Agile teams and project managers estimate the financial impact of different scenarios, understand the financial feasibility of their projects, and make well-informed decisions based on financial insights.

Financial Reporting Tools

Financial reporting tools are software applications that are used in the context of Agile Process and Project Management disciplines to gather, track, analyze, and report financial data and information. These tools provide a streamlined and efficient way to manage financial activities and ensure accurate and timely reporting.

Within Agile Process and Project Management, financial reporting tools play a crucial role in providing visibility into the financial performance of projects and helping stakeholders make informed decisions. These tools enable project managers to track project costs, monitor budget utilization, and assess the financial impact of various project activities. They also facilitate the generation of financial reports, including balance sheets, income statements, cash flow statements, and other financial metrics.

Financial Reporting

Financial reporting in the context of Agile Process and Project Management disciplines refers to the systematic process of collecting, analyzing, and presenting financial information related to the progress and performance of a project or a set of projects, in a structured and concise manner.

Agile Process and Project Management methodologies emphasize adaptability, collaboration, and continuous improvement. The focus is on delivering value to customers through iterative and incremental development. Financial reporting plays a crucial role in supporting decision-making, ensuring transparency, and tracking the financial health of the project.

The primary purpose of financial reporting in Agile Project Management is to provide stakeholders with a clear understanding of the project's financial status, including costs, budget allocations, and forecasts. This enables stakeholders to make informed decisions regarding resource allocation, risk management, and project prioritization. Financial reporting also helps identify potential cost overruns, discrepancies, or variances from the planned budget, allowing for timely corrective actions to be taken.

Furthermore, financial reporting in Agile Project Management facilitates communication and collaboration among project teams and stakeholders. It provides a common language for discussing financial matters and ensures that all parties involved have access to up-to-date financial information. This promotes transparency, trust, and alignment within the project, enhancing overall project success.

Fishbone Diagram

A fishbone diagram, also known as a cause-and-effect diagram or Ishikawa diagram, is a visual tool utilized in Agile Process and Project Management disciplines to identify and analyze the potential causes contributing to a problem or effect. It helps teams to understand the root causes and brainstorm possible solutions for improvement.

The diagram represents a skeletal structure shaped like a fishbone, where the "head" indicates the problem or effect being investigated, and the "bones" represent the main categories of potential causes or factors influencing the problem. The main categories typically include People, Processes, Policies, Environment, and Equipment – often referred to as the 5P's – but can vary depending on the specific context of the project or process being analyzed.

Float

Float refers to the amount of time a task or activity can be delayed without impacting the overall project schedule. In Agile Process and Project Management, float is an important concept used to manage and allocate time effectively to deliver projects on time.

Float is calculated by determining the difference between the earliest start and finish dates and the latest start and finish dates of a task or activity. The earliest dates represent the earliest point at which the task can start or finish, considering any dependencies or constraints. On the other hand, the latest dates represent the latest point at which the task can start or finish without delaying the project.

Having a positive float indicates that a task can be delayed without impacting the project's critical path or the overall completion date. This provides flexibility for the project team in managing any changes or unexpected events that may occur during the project's execution. Float can be used strategically to prioritize tasks, as tasks with less float are more critical and require more attention to ensure they are completed on time.

However, if float becomes zero or negative, it means that the task is on the critical path and any delay to it will directly impact the overall project schedule. In such cases, careful attention and effective management are required to mitigate risks and prevent delays that could impact the project's success.

Force Majeure

Force Majeure is a term used in Agile Process and Project Management disciplines to refer to an unforeseeable event or circumstance that is beyond the control of the project team and prevents them from fulfilling their obligations or achieving their goals. It is often referred to as an "act of God" and is typically associated with events such as natural disasters, political unrest, or legal or regulatory changes.

When a Force Majeure event occurs, it can have a significant impact on the project timeline, scope, and resources. It may result in delays, budget overruns, or even the complete cancellation of the project. In Agile methodologies, which prioritize adaptability and flexibility, the project team needs to be prepared to adjust their plans and expectations in response to Force Majeure events.

Functional Decomposition

Functional Decomposition is a technique used in Agile Process and Project Management disciplines to break down a complex system or project into smaller, more manageable and cohesive parts. It involves taking the main system or project and dividing it into its constituent functions or features, which can then be further divided into sub-functions or sub-features, and so on. This process is repeated until the functions or features become small enough to be easily understood and implemented.

The goal of functional decomposition is to simplify the development or management of a project by breaking it down into manageable pieces that can be worked on independently. This allows teams to focus on specific functions or features without being overwhelmed by the complexity of the entire system or project.

Functional Manager

A functional manager, in the context of Agile Process and Project Management disciplines, refers to an individual responsible for overseeing a specific functional area or department within an organization. They are typically experts or specialists in their respective domains and have a deep understanding of the specific processes, practices, and technologies used in their area of expertise.

In an Agile environment, the functional manager plays a crucial role in ensuring the successful implementation and execution of Agile methodologies. They provide guidance and support to Agile teams, facilitate cross-functional collaboration, and ensure alignment between individual team goals and overall organizational objectives.

Functional Requirements Document (FRD)

A Functional Requirements Document (FRD) is a formal document that outlines the detailed specifications and requirements for a software application or system. It serves as a comprehensive guide that helps the development team understand what needs to be built and ensures that the final product meets the expectations of the stakeholders.

In the context of Agile Process and Project Management disciplines, the FRD plays a crucial role in promoting collaboration and transparency. It provides a clear definition of the features, functionalities, and user interactions required in the software, which helps the development team prioritize and plan their work effectively. By breaking down the requirements into smaller, manageable pieces, the FRD enables Agile teams to work in short, iterative cycles known as sprints.

Functional Requirements Traceability Matrix (RTM)

A Functional Requirements Traceability Matrix (RTM) is a document that is widely used in Agile Process and Project Management disciplines. It serves as a tool to ensure that all functional requirements of a project are validated and testable, while tracking their progress throughout the development life cycle.

The RTM maps each functional requirement to the corresponding test case(s) that verify its implementation. This creates a traceability link, allowing efficient tracking and management of requirements. The Agile process emphasizes collaboration and adaptability, and the RTM helps teams stay organized by providing a clear view of the progress and coverage of functional requirements.

Functional Requirements

A functional requirement in the context of Agile Process and Project Management disciplines refers to a specific behavior or functionality that a system, product, or software application must possess in order to meet the needs of its users or stakeholders. It focuses on the capabilities and features of the system rather than how it is implemented.

Functional requirements are typically defined based on the user stories or product backlog items generated during Agile development. These requirements help guide the development team in building the necessary functionality and allow stakeholders to evaluate and provide feedback on the progress of the project.

Functional Specification

A functional specification is a formal document that outlines the specific features, functions, and requirements of a software product or system. It serves as a blueprint for development teams, stakeholders, and clients, providing a clear understanding of what the product should deliver and how it should function.

In the context of Agile Process and Project Management disciplines, a functional specification takes on a slightly different role compared to traditional waterfall methodologies. In Agile, the focus is on delivering working software quickly and continuously, allowing for flexibility and adaptability throughout the development process. Therefore, the functional specification in Agile becomes a living document that evolves and is refined collaboratively throughout the project.

Gantt Chart

A Gantt Chart is a visual representation of a project timeline that provides a concise and clear overview of the project schedule, tasks, and their respective durations. It is widely used in Agile Process and Project Management disciplines to effectively plan, coordinate, and track the progress of projects.

The Gantt Chart consists of a horizontal timeline and vertical bars representing different tasks or activities. Each bar corresponds to a specific task and displays its start and end dates. The length of the bar reflects the duration of the task, allowing project managers to quickly identify potential bottlenecks or dependencies between activities.

Gap Analysis Report

A gap analysis report, within the context of Agile Process and Project Management disciplines, is a formal document that assesses the current state of a project or process and identifies the gaps or discrepancies between the existing situation and the desired or expected state.

Agile project management emphasizes the iterative development and continuous improvement of products or services, making gap analysis an essential tool in understanding the areas of improvement and guiding decision-making processes. The report typically includes an analysis of the project's objectives, scope, and requirements, as well as an assessment of the current progress and performance metrics.

During the gap analysis process, project managers identify the gaps or discrepancies by comparing the current state of the project to the desired outcome. This involves evaluating various factors such as budget, resources, time, team competency, stakeholder expectations, and other relevant variables. Gaps can manifest in areas such as functionality, quality, efficiency, communication, and compliance.

The gap analysis report serves as a foundation for developing strategies and actionable plans for closing the identified gaps and achieving the project's goals. It provides insights into the necessary improvements and helps allocate resources effectively. The report may also outline the potential risks, opportunities, and challenges associated with the identified gaps.

By conducting a thorough gap analysis, Agile project managers can better understand the project's current state, identify areas of improvement, and align their actions with the desired outcomes. This process promotes continuous improvement and enables more effective decision-making and resource management.

Gap Analysis

A gap analysis is a formal process used in Agile Process and Project Management disciplines to identify the difference or "gap" between a company's current performance or state and its desired performance or state. It involves conducting a thorough examination of existing processes, practices, systems, and resources to determine areas of improvement and areas where the company falls short of its objectives.

The gap analysis is performed by comparing the company's current state to its goals or benchmarks. This comparison is done across various areas, such as organizational structure, team dynamics, project management practices, communication strategies, and technological infrastructure. The goal is to identify gaps or discrepancies between what is currently in place and what is required to achieve the desired performance or state.

Once the gaps are identified, the Agile Process and Project Management team can develop strategies and action plans to bridge those gaps. This may involve implementing process improvements, adopting new tools or methodologies, enhancing communication channels, providing additional training, reallocating resources, or making organizational changes.

By conducting a gap analysis, organizations can gain valuable insights into areas that need improvement and can make informed decisions on how to best address those gaps. It helps teams align their efforts with the organization's overall goals and objectives, ensuring that they are working towards a common vision.

Gap Filling

Agile Process:

The Agile process is a project management approach that focuses on flexibility, collaboration, and delivering value to the customer in a continuous and incremental manner. It involves breaking down complex projects into smaller iterations called sprints, which typically last between one to four weeks. The Agile process embraces change and welcomes feedback from stakeholders throughout the project's lifecycle.

Agile project teams are self-organizing and cross-functional, meaning that they consist of individuals with different expertise who work together to deliver a product or service. Daily stand-up meetings, known as scrums, are held to facilitate communication and ensure that everyone is aligned with the project goals. The project's progress is regularly reviewed during sprint reviews, where stakeholders provide feedback and suggest changes.

By following the Agile process, project teams are able to adapt quickly to changes in requirements, scope, and technology. This allows for faster delivery of value to the customer and greater customer satisfaction. The iterative nature of the Agile process also enables a continuous improvement cycle, where lessons learned from each sprint are incorporated into future iterations.

Overall, the Agile process provides a framework for managing projects that encourages collaboration, flexibility, and customer-centricity. It promotes transparency, empowers teams to make decisions, and fosters a culture of continuous learning and improvement.

Go-Live

Go-Live refers to the final stage in the Agile Process and Project Management disciplines, where a project or product is ready for deployment or launch. It marks the moment when the developed solution is made available to end users or customers, either in a production environment or a live system.

In Agile, Go-Live is significant because it represents the culmination of all the iterations and sprints that have been completed throughout the project. It is the point where the deliverables are considered to be in a state that can be released to users for their use or consumption.

Group Decision-Making Techniques

Group decision-making techniques are processes or methodologies used in the Agile Process and Project Management disciplines to facilitate effective and efficient decision-making within a group or team. These techniques enable teams to consider multiple perspectives, gather and evaluate information, and reach consensus or make informed decisions collaboratively.

One commonly used group decision-making technique in these disciplines is brainstorming. In a brainstorming session, team members generate ideas and solutions to a problem or challenge without any judgment or criticism. This technique encourages creativity and allows for a diverse range of ideas to be shared. Once all ideas are collected, the team can then evaluate and prioritize them based on feasibility, impact, or other criteria.

Another technique is the use of multi-voting. This technique involves each team member voting on a pre-determined set of options or ideas. It allows the team to focus on the most preferred options quickly and efficiently. This technique is particularly useful when there are many options to choose from and when consensus is required.

In addition, the Delphi method is often employed. This technique involves gathering input from each team member individually, usually through questionnaires or surveys. The responses are then compiled, analyzed, and shared with the group anonymously. This allows for unbiased input and encourages thorough consideration of different viewpoints.

Overall, these group decision-making techniques in Agile Process and Project Management aim to promote collaboration, foster innovation, and ensure that decisions are based on collective knowledge and expertise. By employing these techniques, teams can make informed and effective decisions that align with project goals and objectives.

Group Decision-Making

Group decision-making in the context of Agile Process and Project Management disciplines refers to the collaborative process of making decisions within a group or team. It involves the active participation and contribution of multiple individuals to arrive at a consensus or make a joint decision.

In Agile methodologies, such as Scrum, groups play a critical role in decision-making as they are self-organizing and cross-functional. The decision-making process is typically iterative and involves regular discussions and feedback to ensure the best possible outcome. Agile teams rely on continuous communication and collaboration to collectively solve problems, prioritize tasks, and plan project activities.

Groupthink

Groupthink is a phenomenon that can occur within Agile Process and Project Management disciplines, where team members prioritize consensus and conformity over critical thinking and independent decision-making.

In the context of Agile, Groupthink can manifest itself when team members excessively rely on the opinions and ideas of others, leading to a lack of diverse perspectives and innovative solutions. This can hinder the effectiveness of the Agile process and project management by stifling creativity and limiting the exploration of alternative approaches.

Human Resource Constraints Analysis

A Human Resource Constraints Analysis is a process in Agile Process and Project Management disciplines that involves identifying and assessing the limitations and restrictions related to the availability and allocation of human resources for a specific project or initiative. It aims to evaluate whether the project team has the necessary skills, expertise, and capacity to complete the project successfully within the given timeframe and resource constraints.

This analysis is performed by the project manager or Agile team, in collaboration with the HR department or resource management team, to determine potential resource bottlenecks or gaps that may hinder the project's progress. It includes evaluating factors such as the number of available resources, their skill sets, their availability during different project phases, and any imminent resource shortages.

The Human Resource Constraints Analysis helps in making informed decisions about resource allocation, planning for potential resource shortages or fluctuations, and identifying possible solutions to mitigate any identified constraints. It also aids in estimating the project's timeline and identifying risks associated with resource availability or competency gaps.

By conducting this analysis early in the project lifecycle, Agile teams can proactively address resource constraints and take appropriate actions such as hiring additional resources, reallocating existing resources, or providing training to bridge competency gaps. This analysis encourages effective resource management, enhances project planning, and facilitates successful project execution within the defined constraints.

Human Resource Constraints

Human resource constraints refer to the limitations or restrictions in the availability, allocation, or capacity of human resources within the context of Agile Process and Project Management disciplines. In an Agile environment, where work is typically done in teams and projects are delivered in short iterative cycles, human resources play a crucial role in ensuring the success of the projects.

These constraints can arise due to various factors, such as limited availability of skilled personnel, competing project priorities, or organizational policies. When human resource constraints exist, it means that there may be inadequate or insufficient resources to effectively meet the demands of a project or initiative.

Human Resource Management Plan

A Human Resource Management Plan in the context of Agile Process and Project Management disciplines refers to the document or strategy that outlines how the organization's human resources will be managed and utilized throughout the project. This plan encompasses various aspects such as recruitment, selection, onboarding, training, development, performance evaluation, and retention of project team members.

The Human Resource Management Plan is specifically tailored to the unique characteristics and requirements of Agile projects, which emphasize collaboration, flexibility, and quick adaptation to changes. The plan aims to ensure that the right individuals with appropriate skill sets are available at the right time to contribute to the project's success.

Human Resource Planning

Human Resource Planning is the strategic process of identifying and acquiring the right personnel with the necessary skills, knowledge, and expertise to meet the project requirements and effectively support the Agile process and project management disciplines. It involves forecasting future human resource needs, assessing the available resources, and developing strategies to ensure the availability of a competent workforce.

In the context of Agile process and project management, Human Resource Planning plays a vital role in ensuring that the project team is appropriately staffed and capable of delivering the project objectives. It involves understanding the project requirements, identifying the skills and competencies needed, and aligning the available team members with the appropriate roles and responsibilities. This helps in optimizing the utilization of resources, improving team productivity, and enhancing project outcomes.

Human Resources

Human Resources (HR) plays a vital role in Agile Process and Project Management disciplines. HR is responsible for the management and development of an organization's most important asset, its people. In the context of Agile Process and Project Management, HR deals with a variety of tasks and responsibilities.

Firstly, HR is involved in the recruitment and selection process, ensuring that the right individuals with the necessary skills and experience are brought into the Agile teams. HR works closely with the hiring managers and team leads to understand the specific requirements of each Agile project and identify candidates who possess the technical expertise, as well as the collaborative and adaptive mindset required in an Agile environment.

Secondly, HR plays a significant role in the development and training of Agile teams. This includes identifying the training needs of team members and coordinating the provision of relevant training programs. HR also ensures that Agile team members have access to ongoing learning resources and opportunities for professional growth, helping them to continually enhance their skills and capabilities.

Lastly, HR is responsible for creating and fostering a positive organizational culture and work environment that embraces Agile values and principles. HR supports the implementation of Agile practices by facilitating effective communication and collaboration across teams, promoting transparency and trust, and ensuring that team members have the necessary support and resources to thrive in an Agile setting.

Impact Analysis Report

Impact analysis is a crucial activity performed in the Agile process and project management disciplines. It refers to the process of identifying the potential effects and implications that a proposed change or enhancement may have on various aspects of a project. The purpose of conducting an impact analysis is to assess the scope and magnitude of the change and determine how it can affect the project, including its timeline, budget, resources, and overall success.

An impact analysis involves analyzing the dependencies, interconnections, and relationships between the affected components, systems, processes, and stakeholders. It helps project managers and teams evaluate the risks, challenges, and opportunities associated with the proposed change. By conducting a thorough impact analysis, the project team can make informed decisions and develop appropriate strategies to mitigate any negative consequences and maximize the positive outcomes of the change.

Impact Analysis

Impact Analysis, in the context of Agile Process and Project Management disciplines, refers to the systematic evaluation of the potential consequences and effects that a proposed change or modification may have on various aspects of a project. It entails assessing the ripple effects of the change on the project's scope, resources, timeline, budget, and stakeholders.

The purpose of conducting an Impact Analysis is to provide a comprehensive understanding of the implications of a change, helping project teams make informed decisions and guiding them in planning and managing the change effectively. By considering all the potential impacts, the project team can evaluate the risks, benefits, and feasibility of implementing the change, making it an essential practice in Agile environments where flexibility and adaptability are crucial.

During an Impact Analysis, the project team identifies and analyzes the dependencies, interrelationships, and interdependencies between different project components, such as requirements, tasks, deliverables, and stakeholders. This analysis enables them to assess how a change in one component or area may affect the others and the overall project objectives.

Through an Impact Analysis, the project team can anticipate and address potential risks, such as delays, resource constraints, conflicts, or increased costs, resulting from the proposed change. It assists in prioritizing the changes based on their impact, urgency, and alignment with project goals and empowers the team to make informed decisions about whether to accept, modify, or reject a proposed change.

Implementation

Agile Process is a project management approach that focuses on delivering high-quality results by dividing the project into small, manageable increments called iterations. It emphasizes collaboration, adaptive planning, and continuous improvement throughout the project lifecycle. In Agile Process, requirements and solutions evolve through the collaborative effort of self-organizing, cross-functional teams. It promotes flexibility, transparency, and rapid response to change by encouraging stakeholders' involvement and providing regular feedback.

Project Management disciplines in Agile are the practices and techniques used to effectively plan, execute, and control projects within the Agile framework. It encompasses various methodologies such as Scrum, Kanban, and Lean, which provide specific guidelines and processes for managing projects using an Agile approach. Project Management disciplines in Agile include activities like defining project goals, creating a product backlog, conducting sprint or iteration planning, monitoring progress through daily stand-up meetings, reviewing and improving deliverables in sprint or iteration reviews, and retrospectives.

Inception Phase

In the context of Agile Process and Project Management disciplines, the Inception Phase refers to the initial stage of a project where the project's concept, objectives, and feasibility are explored and defined. It is the first step in the project lifecycle and sets the foundation for everything that follows.

During the Inception Phase, the project team collaborates with stakeholders to identify the project's goals, requirements, and constraints. This involves conducting market research, analyzing the competitive landscape, and understanding the needs of the end users. The team establishes a clear vision for the project and creates a preliminary plan outlining the key deliverables, timeline, and budget.

The Inception Phase also involves identifying and evaluating potential risks and dependencies that may impact the project's success. Risk mitigation strategies are developed to minimize potential obstacles and ensure that the project remains on track. Additionally, the team defines the project's scope and establishes a baseline to measure progress and manage any changes that may arise during the subsequent phases.

The Inception Phase is characterized by a high level of collaboration and communication between the project team, stakeholders, and sponsors. It is crucial to gather input from all relevant parties to ensure that the project aligns with their expectations and requirements. By the end of the Inception Phase, the team should have a comprehensive understanding of the project's objectives, risks, constraints, and feasibility, providing a solid foundation for the next phase of the project.

Incident Report

The incident report is a formal document that is used in Agile Process and Project Management disciplines to record and document any incidents or issues that occur during the course of a project. It provides a clear and concise summary of the incident, including details such as the date and time it occurred, the individuals involved, the impact it had on the project, and any actions taken to resolve the issue.

The purpose of the incident report is to ensure that all stakeholders are aware of any incidents or issues that may impact the project, and to facilitate effective communication and problem-solving. It serves as a historical record of the project, allowing for analysis and learning to improve future projects.

Incremental Development

Incremental development is a software development approach that is used within the Agile process and project management disciplines. It entails the gradual development and delivery of a product through the completion of iterative and incremental cycles.

In the Agile context, incremental development focuses on breaking down a project into smaller, more manageable increments or iterations. Each increment aims to deliver a working and usable subset of the overall product, allowing for continuous feedback and improvement.

This approach promotes flexibility and adaptability, as it allows for the incorporation of changing requirements and priorities throughout the project. It enables the development team to respond to customer feedback, market demands, and evolving business needs effectively.

Furthermore, incremental development in Agile emphasizes collaboration and communication between the development team and stakeholders. Regular meetings and reviews enable the team to gather feedback and insights, ensuring that the end product aligns with the desired goals and objectives.

By breaking down the development process into smaller increments, the risk associated with complex projects is reduced. Issues or challenges that arise within each increment can be addressed and resolved promptly, without significantly impacting the overall project timeline.

Overall, incremental development in the Agile process and project management disciplines is an iterative approach that allows for continuous improvement and adaptation. It ensures that the final product meets customer expectations by incorporating feedback and managing changing requirements effectively.

Influence Diagrams

An influence diagram is a graphical representation of the relationships between different variables or factors that can potentially influence a decision or outcome in the context of Agile Process and Project Management disciplines. It is used to analyze and understand the cause-and-effect relationships among these variables, allowing project managers to make more informed decisions based on the potential impacts of different factors.

The influence diagram consists of nodes and arrows, where nodes represent the variables or factors, and arrows represent the influence or impact that one variable has on another. The direction of the arrows indicates the causal relationship between variables, with the arrow pointing from the influencing variable to the influenced variable.

Information Radiator (Info Radiator)

An Information Radiator, also known as an Info Radiator, is a visual representation of important project information that is displayed prominently in a team's workspace. It serves as a communication tool to provide real-time status updates and key metrics to all stakeholders, fostering transparency and enabling quick decision-making.

The purpose of an Info Radiator in the context of Agile Process and Project Management disciplines is to create a shared understanding among team members and stakeholders about the project's progress, priorities, and potential issues. It helps to align everyone's expectations and keeps everyone informed and engaged, reducing the need for formal status meetings and constant status report requests.

Information Radiator

An information radiator is a visual display that provides real-time and transparent information about a project or process. It is a widely used tool in Agile Process and Project Management disciplines to promote transparency, collaboration, and communication within a team or organization.

The main purpose of an information radiator is to make information easily accessible and understandable to everyone involved in the project or process. By displaying key metrics, progress updates, and status indicators on a visible and easily readable display, team members can quickly and effortlessly stay informed about the project's current state.

Information radiators typically take the form of physical charts, whiteboards, or digital screens, placed in a central location where team members can easily see them. They often include visual representations, such as charts, graphs, or diagrams, to provide information in a format that is easily comprehensible at a glance.

The use of information radiators in Agile Project Management is grounded in the principle of transparency, which is a core value of Agile methodologies. By making information openly available and visible to all team members, it fosters a shared understanding of the project's progress, goals, and challenges. It provides a common point of reference that encourages collaboration, discussion, and problem-solving within the team.

Information radiators play a vital role in Agile Process and Project Management by fostering transparency, facilitating communication, and promoting collaboration. It creates a shared understanding among team members, helps identify issues and bottlenecks early on, and allows for timely adjustments and interventions to keep the project on track. Overall, an information radiator contributes to the success of Agile projects by ensuring that vital project information is readily available and understood by the entire team.

Inspection

Inspection is a formal process within the Agile Process and Project Management disciplines that involves the careful examination and evaluation of artifacts, documents, or deliverables to identify defects, errors, or areas for improvement. It is a systematic and structured approach used to validate and verify the quality and correctness of work products produced during the Agile development process.

During an inspection, a group of individuals, often referred to as the inspection team, come together to review and analyze the selected artifacts. The team typically consists of members with diverse roles and expertise, including developers, testers, business analysts, and stakeholders. The artifacts that are subject to inspection may include software code, design documents, user stories, requirements specifications, or any other relevant deliverables.

The inspection process follows a predefined set of steps, which typically include planning, preparation, inspection, and resolution. During the planning phase, the goals and objectives of the inspection are established, and the scope and criteria for inspection are defined. The preparation phase involves selecting the artifacts to be inspected, providing relevant background information, and setting up a suitable environment for the inspection. The inspection phase is where the actual examination and evaluation of the artifacts take place. The inspection team thoroughly examines the artifacts, looking for defects, inconsistencies, or non-compliance with defined standards or best practices. Any identified issues are documented and recorded for further action. The resolution phase involves addressing and resolving the identified issues, which may include rework, clarification, or refinement of the artifacts.

Integrated Change Control

Integrated Change Control in the context of Agile Process and Project Management refers to the process of managing and evaluating proposed changes within a project in a systematic and controlled manner. It involves the identification, evaluation, and approval or rejection of changes to project scope, schedule, and resources.

In Agile methodologies, change is considered inevitable and often desirable. The Integrated Change Control process ensures that changes are properly assessed for their impact on the project and that they align with the project objectives and overall strategic direction. This process helps in maintaining project governance and ensuring that changes are implemented in a controlled way, without causing unnecessary disruptions or delays.

Integration Management Plan

Integration Management Plan is a critical component of Agile Process and Project Management disciplines. It refers to a comprehensive document that outlines the approach, processes, and tools to effectively integrate various components and deliverables of an Agile project.

The Integration Management Plan focuses on defining the strategy to coordinate and synchronize the work across different Agile teams and disciplines, ensuring that the project goals and objectives are achieved. It involves identifying the dependencies, understanding the interdependencies between Agile teams, and establishing effective communication and collaboration channels.

The plan outlines the integration management approach, including the processes and techniques for integrating Agile processes, tools, and methodologies. It defines the roles and responsibilities of team members involved in the integration process, ensuring a clear division of work and accountability.

The Integration Management Plan also addresses the management of changes and updates throughout the Agile project. It outlines the procedures for handling change requests, evaluating their impacts, and incorporating them into the project scope. This ensures that any modifications or adjustments to the project do not disrupt the overall integration and synchronization efforts.

In summary, the Integration Management Plan in the context of Agile Process and Project Management disciplines serves as a guiding document for effectively integrating various components and deliverables, ensuring successful project outcomes. It provides a roadmap, communication channels, and processes for coordinating the work across Agile teams, managing dependencies, and handling changes in an integrated and efficient manner.

Integration Management

Integration Management is a crucial aspect of Agile Process and Project Management disciplines. It refers to the coordination and consolidation of all the various elements, processes, and components involved in a project, ensuring that they work together effectively and seamlessly.

In an Agile context, Integration Management involves identifying, defining, and overseeing the integration of various Agile practices and techniques, such as Scrum, Kanban, and Lean methodologies, into a cohesive and streamlined project management framework. This allows for the efficient coordination and synchronization of activities and deliverables across multiple teams and stakeholders, ultimately leading to the successful completion of the project.

Integration Testing Plan

Integration testing is a vital component of the Agile process and Project Management disciplines. It focuses on the collaboration and integration of different software components or modules to ensure that they work together effectively. The primary goal of integration testing is to identify and resolve any issues or defects that may arise when the individual components are combined.

In an Agile development environment, integration testing is typically performed continuously throughout the software development lifecycle. As new features or updates are implemented, they are integrated and tested with the existing components to ensure seamless functionality. This iterative approach enables developers to catch and address any integration issues early on, allowing for faster and more efficient troubleshooting.

Integration Testing

Integration testing is a crucial element within the Agile Process and Project Management disciplines. It refers to the testing of individual software components or modules as a collective unit to ensure that they properly integrate and function together. This type of testing is performed to detect any defects or issues that may arise when different modules are integrated, allowing for early identification and resolution of problems.

Integration testing is typically carried out after unit testing, where individual components are tested in isolation. It aims to validate the interactions and dependencies between various components of the software system. The purpose is to uncover any inconsistencies or errors that may arise due to the integration of different modules.

In an Agile environment, integration testing is performed iteratively throughout the development process. Each new module or increment is integrated with the existing system, and the appropriate tests are executed to ensure seamless integration. Integration tests are often automated and included in the continuous integration pipeline to detect integration issues as early as possible.

Successful integration testing ensures that the software system functions as a cohesive unit, rather than merely a collection of individual components. It verifies that data flows correctly between modules, interfaces are correctly implemented, and the system behaves as expected when different components interact.

Integration testing is a critical aspect of project management in an Agile context, facilitating the early detection and resolution of integration issues. By addressing these issues promptly, the development team can maintain a high level of software quality and reduce the risk of bugs or failures during later stages of the project.

Issue Escalation

Issue Escalation in the context of Agile Process and Project Management disciplines refers to the process of raising an issue to a higher level of authority or management when it cannot be resolved at its current level. It is a formal approach to ensure that unresolved issues are addressed appropriately and in a timely manner.

When working in an Agile environment, issue escalation becomes crucial as it allows teams to quickly overcome obstacles and ensure the smooth progress of the project. It helps identify roadblocks or bottlenecks that can hinder the team's ability to deliver the desired outcomes. By escalating the issue, the team ensures that it receives the necessary support and attention from the relevant stakeholders or individuals who have the authority or resources to resolve it.

In Agile, issue escalation is typically carried out by following established communication channels and protocols. Team members raise the issue with their immediate supervisor or Scrum Master, who then assesses its severity and impact on project progress. If it is determined that the issue cannot be resolved within the team or at the current level, it is escalated to higher levels of management or the project sponsor.

The purpose of issue escalation is to prevent delays, address risks, and maintain project momentum. It allows for prompt decision-making and resolution of critical issues, ensuring the team can stay focused on its objectives and deliver value to the customer. By providing a formal process for issue escalation, Agile methodologies promote transparency, collaboration, and accountability across the project team and stakeholders.

Issue Log

Issue Log is a document or artifact that is used in the Agile Process and Project Management disciplines to track and manage issues or problems that arise during the course of a project. It serves as a central repository for capturing, documenting, and monitoring issues throughout the project lifecycle.

The purpose of an Issue Log is to provide a structured mechanism for identifying, recording, and resolving issues in a timely manner. It allows project teams to track and prioritize issues, assign ownership, and monitor their progress towards resolution. Issues can range from technical problems and defects to process or resource-related challenges.

Issue Resolution Process

An issue resolution process is a systematic approach used in Agile project management disciplines to address and resolve any problems, obstacles, or conflicts that may arise during the course of a project. It is a set of predefined steps and procedures that enables project teams to effectively manage and resolve issues in a timely and efficient manner.

The first step in the issue resolution process is to identify and document the issue. This involves clearly defining the problem, its impact on the project, and any relevant details or context. Once the issue has been properly documented, it is important to prioritize it based on its urgency and impact on project objectives.

Once the issue has been identified and prioritized, the next step is to analyze the root cause of the issue. This involves conducting a thorough investigation to understand the underlying factors that have contributed to the problem. It may require gathering additional information, conducting interviews, or analyzing data to determine the cause.

Once the root cause has been identified, the project team can then develop and implement a plan for resolving the issue. This may involve collaborating with stakeholders, developing alternative solutions, and evaluating potential risks and benefits.

After the plan has been implemented, it is important to monitor the progress and ensure that the issue is being resolved according to the plan. This involves tracking the status of the resolution, communicating updates to relevant stakeholders, and making any necessary adjustments or refinements.

In conclusion, the issue resolution process in Agile project management disciplines is a structured approach that enables project teams to effectively address and resolve problems or conflicts that arise during the course of a project. By following a systematic approach, project teams can minimize the impact of issues on project objectives and ensure successful project delivery.

Issue Resolution

Issue resolution in the context of Agile Process and Project Management disciplines refers to the process of addressing and resolving problems, conflicts, or obstacles that occur during a project's lifecycle. It involves identifying, analyzing, and finding solutions to issues that could potentially impact the project's schedule, budget, quality, or scope.

Agile methodologies, such as Scrum, emphasize continuous improvement and the ability to quickly adapt to changes. Issue resolution is an integral part of Agile project management as it allows teams to address challenges and impediments promptly, ensuring the project stays on track and aligns with the stakeholders' expectations.

Issue

An Agile Process is a project management approach that emphasizes flexibility, collaboration, and iterative development to deliver high-quality products or services.

Agile Project Management is a discipline that uses the Agile Process to manage complex projects, allowing for adaptability and continuous improvement while promoting customer satisfaction and team engagement.

Issues Log

An issues log is a key tool used in the Agile Process and Project Management disciplines to track and manage problems or concerns that arise during the course of a project. It provides a central repository for documenting and monitoring issues, ensuring they are promptly addressed and resolved.

The issues log is typically maintained by the project manager or a designated team member, and it captures important details such as the issue description, its impact on the project, the person responsible for resolving it, and the target resolution date. By documenting issues in a structured manner, the log enables the project team to have a clear understanding of the problem, its severity, and the necessary steps to address it.

The issues log serves several purposes within Agile Project Management. Firstly, it helps in identifying potential risks and challenges that may affect project delivery. By logging and categorizing various issues, the project team can proactively mitigate risks and develop contingency plans to minimize their impact. Secondly, the log facilitates effective communication and collaboration among project stakeholders. It provides a transparent view of ongoing issues, keeping the team updated and allowing for timely discussions and decision-making. Lastly, the log acts as a historical record, allowing the team to learn from past issues and improve their future project management practices.

Overall, an issues log is an essential tool within Agile Process and Project Management, assisting in the identification, resolution, and prevention of issues and thereby contributing to the successful delivery of projects.

Iteration

Iteration, in the context of Agile Process and Project Management disciplines, refers to a time-boxed development cycle where a small, specific set of tasks are completed by a cross-functional team. It is a fundamental concept in Agile methodologies such as Scrum and Kanban, emphasizing regular review and adaptation to ensure continuous improvement.

An iteration typically consists of several phases, including planning, execution, review, and retrospective. During the planning phase, the team defines the specific goals and tasks they aim to complete within the iteration. This helps create a clear scope and focus, allowing for better time management and progress tracking.

The execution phase involves the team actively working on the defined tasks in a collaborative and iterative manner. The team follows a short-term plan and regularly synchronizes their efforts, allowing for constant feedback and adjustments. The tasks chosen for an iteration are typically prioritized based on their value and need, ensuring that the most important work is accomplished first.

Once the defined tasks are completed, the team enters the review phase. Here, they assess the work completed during the iteration and evaluate whether it meets the intended objectives. This review helps identify areas of improvement, potential issues, and potential adjustments needed for the subsequent iterations.

The retrospective phase follows the review and focuses on process improvement. The team reflects on their own performance and identifies ways to enhance their productivity, communication, and collaboration. This allows the team to adapt and continuously improve their working practices, enabling them to deliver higher quality and more valuable outputs with each subsequent iteration.

Kanban Board

A Kanban board is a visual tool used in Agile project management to manage and track the progress of work items in a project. It provides a clear and easily understandable way to visualize the flow of work from start to finish, allowing team members to have a shared understanding of the project status and identify any bottlenecks or delays that may arise.

The Kanban board consists of columns representing different stages or phases of the project, such as "To Do," "In Progress," and "Done." Each work item is represented by a card or sticky note that is moved across the board as it progresses through the stages. This visual representation of the workflow facilitates communication, collaboration, and transparency within the project team.

By using a Kanban board, teams can visually manage their work, set priorities, and ensure a smooth flow of tasks. It helps in preventing overloading team members with excessive work and assists in identifying potential issues or blockers early on. Team members can easily see what tasks are in progress, which tasks are completed, and what tasks are still pending.

In addition to tracking the progress of work items, a Kanban board can also include other useful information such as due dates, assignees, and any dependencies between tasks. This allows team members to have a comprehensive view of the project status and make informed decisions on task prioritization and resource allocation.

Kanban Card

A Kanban card is a visual representation of a work item in Agile process and project management disciplines. It is typically used in the Kanban methodology, which focuses on visualizing and limiting work in progress to improve efficiency and flow of work.

A Kanban card contains key information about a specific task or work item, such as its name, description, priority, assigned team member, and status. It serves as a single unit of work that moves through various stages of completion on a Kanban board.

The Kanban card is often displayed on a physical or digital board, where it can be easily seen by the entire team. As work progresses, the card is moved from one column to another to represent its current status, such as backlog, in progress, or done.

One of the key benefits of using Kanban cards is that they provide a clear visual representation of the team's work and its progress. By having a visual overview of all the tasks on the Kanban board, the team can quickly see which tasks are in progress, which are completed, and which are blocked or delayed.

Furthermore, Kanban cards promote transparency and collaboration within the team. They enable team members to easily communicate and share information about specific tasks by attaching additional notes or documents to the card. This helps team members stay aligned and make informed decisions about their work.

In summary, a Kanban card is a visual tool that represents a work item in Agile project management. It helps teams track and manage their work in a transparent and collaborative manner, leading to improved efficiency and productivity.

Kanban System

A Kanban system is a visual project management tool and methodology that supports the Agile process by providing a clear and transparent way of managing and monitoring the flow of work. It is designed to help teams prioritize and track tasks, improve efficiency, and optimize workflow.

In the context of Agile project management, a Kanban system is based on the principles of Lean Manufacturing, which emphasizes continuous improvement and waste reduction. It uses a Kanban board, which is a visual representation of the project's workflow, divided into different stages or columns. Each column represents a specific stage of the work, such as backlog, to-do, in progress, testing, and done.

The Kanban board is typically divided into swimlanes, which can be used to categorize tasks by different criteria, such as priority, team members, or project milestones. Each task is represented by a card, which contains relevant information, such as task description, owner, due date, and any dependencies or blockers.

The Kanban system operates on the principles of limiting work in progress (WIP) and visualizing work. By setting WIP limits, teams can prevent overloading and bottlenecks, leading to a smoother and more efficient workflow. Progress is visualized by moving cards across the columns on the Kanban board, giving everyone involved a clear overview of the project's status.

Overall, the Kanban system helps Agile teams manage their work effectively, improve collaboration and communication, and continuously adapt and optimize their processes based on real-time data and insights.

Kanban

Kanban is a visual framework that focuses on incrementally improving the way work is done by optimizing the flow of work within a system. It is primarily used in Agile Process and Project Management disciplines to enhance collaboration, efficiency, and transparency.

In the context of Agile, Kanban facilitates the implementation of the Agile principles, fostering continuous delivery of value through iterative and incremental work cycles.

Key Performance Indicator (KPI) Dashboard

A Key Performance Indicator (KPI) Dashboard is a visual representation of important metrics and indicators that help measure the performance and progress of an Agile Process or Project Management discipline. It provides an at-a-glance overview of the key aspects of the project or process, allowing stakeholders to quickly assess its performance and make data-driven decisions.

The KPI Dashboard typically includes various KPIs or measurements that are relevant to the specific objectives and goals of the Agile Process or Project Management discipline. These indicators can be categorized into different areas, such as productivity, quality, efficiency, customer satisfaction, and financial performance.

Key Performance Indicator (KPI) Metrics

Key Performance Indicators (KPIs) are quantifiable metrics utilized in Agile Process and Project Management disciplines to measure the performance and progress of a project or team. KPIs provide objective and measurable data that enable organizations to assess their effectiveness in achieving desired outcomes and delivering value.

In Agile Process and Project Management, KPIs focus on evaluating key areas such as project progress, team performance, and customer satisfaction. These metrics aid in monitoring the overall health of the project and serve as indicators of success or areas needing improvement.

Key Performance Indicator (KPI)

A Key Performance Indicator (KPI) in the context of Agile Process and Project Management disciplines is a quantifiable measure used to evaluate the success or performance of a project, team, or individual in achieving specific goals or objectives. KPIs are essential tools for monitoring and controlling the progress and quality of work within an Agile project, while also providing valuable insights for decision-making and continuous improvement.

Unlike traditional project management approaches, Agile methodologies emphasize frequent iterations and adaptability. KPIs in Agile focus on measuring the effectiveness of Agile practices and the delivery of value to stakeholders. These KPIs are often related to Agile principles, such as customer satisfaction, team performance, cycle time, throughput, and the quality of the delivered product or service.

KPIs in Agile are typically defined collaboratively by the project team and stakeholders during project planning or at the start of each iteration. They should be simple, measurable, and aligned with the project's objectives. Examples of Agile KPIs include customer satisfaction ratings, team velocity, burn-down or burn-up charts, defect rate, cycle time, lead time, and business value delivered. These KPIs provide real-time feedback on the progress and help the Agile team to identify areas for improvement or potential risks.

It is important to regularly review and analyze the KPIs to gain insights into the project's performance and make informed decisions. KPIs also facilitate transparency and accountability within Agile teams and contribute to a culture of continuous learning and improvement. By tracking and evaluating KPIs, Agile projects can stay on track, adapt to changes effectively, and deliver value to stakeholders in a timely and efficient manner.

Key Success Factors (KSFs)

Key Success Factors (KSFs) refer to the critical variables or elements that are essential for the success of a project or process within the Agile Process and Project Management disciplines. These factors are the key drivers that determine the achievement of project objectives, deliverables, and outcomes in an Agile environment.

Agile Process and Project Management focus on iterative and incremental development approaches, emphasizing collaboration, adaptability, and customer-centricity. The KSFs within this context comprise various aspects critical for success, including but not limited to:

1. Effective Communication: Open and transparent communication channels among team members, stakeholders, and customers are vital for sharing ideas, progress, and feedback regularly. It enables the team to quickly adapt to changing requirements and resolve issues promptly.

2. Continuous Planning and Prioritization: Regular planning sessions ensure that the team is aligned with project goals and can prioritize tasks effectively based on business value. It allows for adaptability in responding to evolving needs and delivering high-impact features or functionality earlier.

3. Cross-functional Collaboration: A collaborative environment where individuals with diverse skill sets work together fosters innovation, creativity, and problem-solving. It enables the Agile team to leverage the collective expertise to deliver quality outcomes.

4. Customer Engagement and Involvement: Close collaboration with the customer throughout the development process helps in understanding their needs, expectations, and feedback. Regular involvement of the customer ensures that the delivered product meets their requirements and provides value.

5. Empowered and Self-organizing Teams: Agile teams are self-organizing and empowered to make decisions, plan, and execute work independently. This autonomy fosters creativity, productivity, and accountability within the team.

Overall, the identified KSFs facilitate the successful implementation of Agile Process and Project Management methodologies, ensuring efficient delivery, customer satisfaction, and the ability to respond to changes effectively.

Kick-Off Meeting

A kick-off meeting is a formal gathering that marks the beginning of a project in Agile Process and Project Management disciplines. During this meeting, the project team, stakeholders, and key individuals come together to establish a shared understanding of the project objectives, scope, deliverables, and timelines.

The primary purpose of a kick-off meeting is to align all participants on the project's goals and ensure everyone is on the same page. This meeting sets the foundation for the entire project and helps to establish clear communication channels, roles, and responsibilities, as well as identify potential risks and issues.

Key agenda items in a kick-off meeting typically include:

- Introductions: All project participants introduce themselves, providing a brief background and their roles in the project.

- Project overview: The project manager provides an overview of the project, including the objectives, scope, and expected outcomes.

- Roles and responsibilities: The project team members and stakeholders discuss their roles and responsibilities, clarifying expectations and identifying any gaps.

- Communication plan: The team establishes a clear communication plan, defining how and when project updates, meetings, and progress reports will be shared.

- Project timeline and milestones: The project manager presents the project timeline, including key milestones and deadlines. This helps to create a shared understanding of the project's schedule.

- Risk assessment: The team identifies potential risks and issues that may impact the project, and discusses mitigation strategies and contingency plans.

- Questions and clarifications: Participants have an opportunity to ask questions, seek clarifications, and address any concerns they may have regarding the project.

A well-executed kick-off meeting fosters a collaborative environment, promotes team cohesion, and ensures that everyone involved is aligned and committed to the project's success. It also helps to establish strong communication channels, which are essential for effective project management and agile processes.

Knowledge Transfer

Knowledge Transfer refers to the process of sharing information, skills, expertise, and experience from one individual or group to another within an Agile process or project management discipline. It involves transferring knowledge in a structured and systematic manner to ensure a smooth transition and optimal use of knowledge across the project lifecycle.

In Agile, knowledge transfer is essential for promoting collaboration, continuous learning, and efficient project execution. It enables team members to leverage the collective knowledge and insights gained from past experiences to make informed decisions, improve performance, and deliver high-quality outcomes.

Lead Time

Lead time in the context of Agile Process and Project Management refers to the time it takes for a project or task to move from the initial request or requirement to its completion. It is a key metric used to measure the efficiency and effectiveness of the project delivery process.

In Agile methodologies, lead time is particularly important because it provides insights into the speed and responsiveness of the team. It helps determine how quickly the team can deliver value to the stakeholders. Lead time encompasses various stages of the project, including requirements gathering, planning, development, testing, and deployment.

Leadership Styles Assessment

In Agile Process and Project Management disciplines, leadership styles refer to the patterns of behavior and actions exhibited by leaders when collaborating with team members to accomplish project goals. These styles are influenced by the principles and values of Agile methodologies, which prioritize flexibility, self-organization, and iterative development.

The first leadership style commonly observed in Agile environments is the Servant Leadership style. Servant leaders focus on enabling and supporting their team members to perform at their best. They prioritize the needs and development of their team, ensuring that they have the resources, guidance, and autonomy necessary to succeed. Servant leaders also foster a collaborative and inclusive work culture, promoting active participation from all team members and valuing their diverse perspectives.

The second leadership style frequently seen in Agile settings is the Transformational Leadership style. Transformational leaders inspire and motivate their teams by articulating a compelling vision and purpose for the project. They embody the values and principles of Agile through their enthusiasm, energy, and passion. These leaders encourage innovation, experimentation, and continuous improvement, creating an environment that encourages team members to take risks and think creatively to overcome challenges.

Leadership Styles

Agile process and project management disciplines require effective leadership styles to ensure the successful execution and delivery of projects. Leadership styles refer to the approach and behavior of a leader in guiding and motivating a team towards their goals.

In the context of Agile process and project management, there are three commonly recognized leadership styles:

1. Servant Leadership: This style emphasizes the leader's focus on serving the needs of the team members and stakeholders. A servant leader acts as a facilitator, removing obstacles, and empowering team members to make decisions. They prioritize collaboration, open communication, and trust within the team, enabling self-organization and promoting a culture of continuous improvement.

2. Transformational Leadership: A transformational leader inspires and motivates the team by articulating a compelling vision and encouraging creativity and innovation. They create a positive and supportive environment, promoting individual growth and development. Transformational leaders nurture strong relationships with their team members and promote collective ownership and shared responsibility for the project's success.

3. Lean Leadership: This style focuses on driving efficiency and eliminating waste in project management processes. A lean leader ensures streamlined processes, reduces bottlenecks, and fosters a culture of continuous improvement. They encourage collaboration, empower teams to take ownership of their work, and strive for delivering value to the customer in the most efficient way.

Lessons Learned Database

A Lessons Learned Database is a repository or collection of organized information that captures and documents the valuable insights, experiences, and knowledge gained throughout the course of an Agile Process or Project Management discipline. It serves as a living document that allows teams to reflect on their past projects, identify what worked well, and learn from their mistakes or areas of improvement.

The primary purpose of establishing a Lessons Learned Database is to promote continuous learning and improvement within an organization. By capturing and sharing lessons learned, teams can avoid repeating the same mistakes and leverage successful practices for future projects. The database acts as a knowledge-sharing platform, facilitating the dissemination of best practices, methodologies, and innovative solutions across different teams and projects.

Lessons Learned Register

A Lessons Learned Register is a formal document used in Agile Process and Project Management disciplines to capture and store valuable insights gained from past experiences and projects. It serves as a repository of knowledge to help teams and practitioners improve their performance, make informed decisions, and avoid repeating mistakes.

The Lessons Learned Register is typically created and maintained throughout the project lifecycle, with inputs from team members, stakeholders, and other relevant parties. It documents both positive and negative lessons, focusing on key takeaways, best practices, and areas for improvement.

Lessons Learned Repository

A Lessons Learned Repository is a centralized database or collection of information that captures and stores valuable lessons learned throughout the Agile Process and Project Management disciplines. It serves as a knowledge base that allows teams to learn from past experiences and apply these insights to improve future project outcomes.

Within the Agile Process, which emphasizes iteratively delivering value to customers, the Lessons Learned Repository plays a critical role in facilitating continuous improvement. It enables teams to reflect on their practices, identify areas for enhancement, and share key learnings with others. By documenting and accumulating lessons learned, teams can avoid repeating mistakes, capitalize on successful strategies, and foster a culture of learning and innovation.

Lessons Learned Workshop

A Lessons Learned Workshop is a collaborative session conducted within the Agile Process and Project Management disciplines to capture, analyze, and consolidate knowledge gained from a completed project or iteration. The goal of this workshop is to identify both successful practices and areas for improvement to enhance future projects and optimize team performance.

During the workshop, team members engage in open and honest discussions, sharing their individual experiences, insights, and lessons learned throughout the project. This knowledge is then analyzed and categorized, enabling the identification of patterns, trends, and recurring issues. The workshop facilitator encourages participation from all team members, ensuring that a variety of perspectives are considered and valuable lessons are uncovered.

The Lessons Learned Workshop aligns with the Agile principles of continuous improvement and reflection. It fosters a culture of learning and adaptation, enabling teams to iterate and refine their processes, methodologies, and techniques. By leveraging the collective knowledge and experiences of the team, organizations can avoid repeating mistakes, capitalize on successful practices, and drive the evolution of their project management approaches.

Lessons Learned

Lessons learned in the context of Agile Process and Project Management disciplines refer to the knowledge and insights gained throughout the course of a project or a specific iteration within the Agile framework. These lessons are derived from both successes and failures experienced during the project, and are used to improve future performance and decision-making.

The process of capturing and analyzing lessons learned involves various activities, such as documenting experiences, evaluating outcomes, identifying root causes of issues, and deriving actionable recommendations. By capturing and leveraging these lessons, organizations can enhance their ability to adapt, learn, and continuously improve their project management practices.

Management Reserve Allocation

Management Reserve Allocation is a practice used in Agile Process and Project Management disciplines to allocate a portion of the project budget and schedule for unforeseen risks and opportunities that may arise during the project execution.

Agile projects are inherently flexible and adaptive to change, making them well-suited to handle unexpected risks and opportunities. However, it is essential to have a system in place to account for these unpredictable events, as they can impact the project's timeline, budget, and overall success. The Management Reserve Allocation serves as a contingency fund that can be utilized to address these unforeseen circumstances.

Management Reserve

A Management Reserve is a dedicated portion of a project's budget or time that is set aside specifically for unanticipated events or risks that may arise during the course of the project. In the context of Agile Process and Project Management disciplines, the Management Reserve is an essential tool for effectively managing and mitigating risks that can impact project timelines and budgets.

This reserve is typically established during the project planning phase, where the project team, stakeholders, and relevant decision-makers identify potential risks and uncertainties that may affect the project's progress. The Management Reserve is then allocated to address these unforeseen risks and uncertainties, providing a safety net to accommodate unforeseen events, changes in requirements, or other challenges that may arise throughout the project lifecycle.

Unlike contingency reserves, which are typically built into individual tasks or work packages, the Management Reserve is a separate allocation that is managed at the project level. It allows for flexibility and adaptability, enabling project managers to respond effectively to unexpected events without compromising the project's overall objectives or delivery timelines. The amount of Management Reserve allocated will vary depending on the project's complexity, size, and level of uncertainty.

By setting aside a Management Reserve, project managers can proactively address risks and uncertainties, minimizing the impact of potential disruptions on project schedules, budgets, and deliverables. It provides a buffer that allows for quick decision-making and appropriate course corrections, ensuring that the project remains on track and successfully achieves its objectives.

Management By Exception

Management by Exception is a concept widely used in Agile Process and Project Management disciplines. It refers to a management approach where managers only intervene or take action when there are deviations from the expected or desired outcomes. Instead of closely monitoring and controlling every aspect of the project, managers focus on identifying exceptions or deviations from the plan and then address those specific issues.

In the context of Agile Process and Project Management, Management by Exception aligns perfectly with the Agile principles of self-organization and trust. It empowers the team members to take ownership of their work and make decisions independently, while the manager's role is to provide guidance and support when specific exceptions arise.

Management By Objectives (MBO)

Management by Objectives (MBO) is a goal-oriented management approach that is commonly used in both Agile Process and Project Management disciplines. MBO focuses on setting clear and specific objectives for individuals or teams, and aligning these objectives with the overall goals of the organization or project. The key principle behind MBO is that employees or team members are motivated and perform better when they have a clear understanding of what is expected of them and how their work contributes to the larger objectives.

In an Agile Process, MBO can be applied by breaking down the project objectives into smaller, manageable tasks or user stories. These objectives are then assigned to specific team members, who have the autonomy to decide how to achieve the objectives. Regular check-ins and feedback sessions are conducted to ensure that the team is on track and to make any necessary adjustments to the objectives. This iterative and collaborative approach allows for flexibility and adaptability, which are essential in an Agile environment.

Market Analysis

Market analysis, within the context of Agile Process and Project Management disciplines, refers to the examination and evaluation of the market forces and dynamics that can impact the success of a project or initiative. It involves assessing the needs, preferences, and behaviors of customers, as well as evaluating the competitive landscape and industry trends.

In Agile Process and Project Management, market analysis plays a crucial role in guiding decision-making and shaping project outcomes. By understanding the market forces at play, project managers can make informed choices about product features, pricing strategies, target markets, and marketing campaigns.

Market analysis typically involves gathering and analyzing data from various sources, such as market research reports, customer surveys, competitor analysis, and industry studies. This data is then used to identify market opportunities, assess potential risks, and develop strategies to effectively position a product or service in the market.

Market analysis also helps project managers track and monitor market trends and customer feedback throughout the project lifecycle. By staying attuned to market shifts and customer needs, project teams can adapt their plans and strategies in a timely manner, ensuring that products or services align with market demands and stay competitive.

Market Research Survey

An Agile Process is a project management approach that emphasizes flexibility, collaboration, and iterative development. It is a framework that allows for the adaptation of project requirements and changes in priorities throughout the project lifecycle.

Agile Process is characterized by its incremental nature, where work is split into smaller, manageable pieces called iterations or sprints. Each iteration typically lasts for a fixed duration, often two to four weeks, during which a specific set of project deliverables is completed. This iterative approach enables early and continuous delivery of valuable and functional product increments.

Agile Process promotes frequent communication and collaboration between the project team and stakeholders. It encourages face-to-face interactions, emphasizes teamwork, and values individuals and interactions over stringent processes and tools.

Agile Project Management is the application of Agile principles and practices in managing projects. It involves the use of Agile frameworks such as Scrum, Kanban, or Lean to guide the project team in planning, executing, and delivering project outcomes.

Agile Project Management focuses on creating a flexible project environment that can respond effectively to changes and uncertainties. It replaces traditional linear project planning with adaptive planning, where requirements evolve through collaboration and feedback.

The primary goal of Agile Project Management is to ensure the delivery of high-quality products that meet customer needs and expectations. It achieves this by fostering continuous improvement, frequent inspection, and adaptation of project processes and deliverables.

Market Research

Market research is a systematic process of collecting, analyzing, and interpreting data about a specific market or target audience. It aims to provide valuable insights and information to support decision-making in Agile Process and Project Management disciplines.

In Agile Process, market research plays a crucial role in understanding customer needs and preferences. By gathering data on customer behavior, market trends, and competitor analysis, Agile teams can make informed decisions during product development and prioritization of features. Market research helps identify target customers, their pain points, and how the product can address their needs effectively.

In Project Management, market research helps in identifying the viability and potential success of a project. It assesses market demand, competition, and customer preferences to determine the feasibility of the project's goals and objectives. Market research provides valuable insights into market trends, customer behavior, and potential risks that may impact the project's success.

This information enables project managers to make informed decisions regarding project scope, timelines, budgeting, and resource allocation.

In both Agile Process and Project Management, market research serves as a foundation for effective strategic planning and decision-making. It provides valuable data-driven insights, allowing teams to align their product or project with customer needs, industry standards, and market demands. By incorporating market research into their processes, Agile teams and project managers can increase the chances of delivering successful and impactful outcomes.

Market Share

Market share refers to the portion or percentage of a particular market that is controlled or held by a company or product. It is a measure of a company's success and competitiveness in the market, indicating its ability to attract and retain customers compared to its competitors. In the context of Agile Process and Project Management disciplines, market share can be used as a metric to evaluate the effectiveness of projects and the overall success of the Agile approaches and methodologies being employed.

Agile project management focuses on delivering value to customers in shorter iterations or sprints, allowing for flexibility and adaptability in response to changing customer needs and market conditions. By analyzing the market share of a particular product or solution developed using Agile methods, project managers can assess the impact of their projects on the market, identify areas for improvement, and make informed decisions about future iterations or releases.

Maturity Model

A maturity model is a structured framework that allows organizations to assess and improve their current state of maturity in a specific discipline. In the context of Agile process and project management, a maturity model provides a roadmap for organizations to measure their level of Agile adoption and identify areas for improvement.

The Agile maturity model typically consists of a series of predefined stages or levels, each representing a different level of Agile maturity. These levels may range from initial or ad-hoc Agile practices to optimized and fully matured Agile processes. Organizations can use the maturity model to benchmark their Agile practices against industry standards and best practices.

Milestone Chart

A milestone chart is a visual representation of significant events or milestones in a project, presented in a tabular or graphical format. It serves as a valuable tool in project management, particularly in the Agile process, to track and communicate project progress, dependencies, and key deadlines.

In the Agile methodology, which emphasizes adaptability and collaboration, milestones are typically time-based events that mark the completion of specific project deliverables or the achievement of significant objectives. These milestones are crucial for establishing a project timeline, allocating resources, and ensuring that the project stays on track.

A milestone chart provides a clear overview of the project's major milestones, their expected completion dates, and any dependencies or predecessors. It allows the project team and stakeholders to visualize the project's progress and identify any bottlenecks or areas requiring attention.

In an Agile project, the milestone chart is often combined with other visual planning tools, such as a Gantt chart or Kanban board, to provide a comprehensive view of the project's status and progress. It helps Agile teams stay focused, prioritize tasks, and adjust their plans as needed to meet project goals and deliver value to the stakeholders.

Milestone Payment

A milestone payment, in the context of Agile Process and Project Management disciplines, refers to a pre-defined payment that is made upon the successful completion of a specific deliverable or milestone within a project. It serves as a key indicator of progress and allows for the allocation of funds accordingly.

In Agile project management, milestones are often used as checkpoints to track the development and implementation of various features or functionalities. They help ensure that projects are on track and progressing as planned. Each milestone represents a significant achievement or completion of a specific task or set of tasks within a project. Therefore, milestone payments are made as a way to acknowledge these significant accomplishments.

Milestone Reporting

Milestone Reporting refers to the process of monitoring and communicating progress, achievements, and key events at important stages of an Agile project. It plays a crucial role in Agile process and project management methodologies by providing visibility and transparency into the project's status and milestones.

At various points throughout the project lifecycle, milestones are set to mark significant progress or the completion of critical tasks. Milestone Reporting involves capturing and documenting these milestones, along with any associated key performance indicators (KPIs), to track the project's progress. It helps project managers and stakeholders to assess if the project is on track, identify any potential risks or issues, and make data-informed decisions.

The key aspects of Milestone Reporting include identifying appropriate milestones, defining expected objectives and deliverables for each milestone, and establishing clear metrics and measures to evaluate progress. It also involves gathering relevant data, analyzing it, and preparing concise and informative reports that highlight the achievements, challenges, and upcoming milestones.

Milestone Reporting acts as a communication tool to keep all stakeholders informed about the project's progress and to align their expectations. It helps foster collaboration, facilitate decision-making, and ensure that everyone is on the same page regarding the project's status and direction.

In conclusion, Milestone Reporting is an integral part of Agile project management. It enables continuous monitoring, assessment, and communication of project milestones, thereby supporting effective decision-making and successful project outcomes.

Milestone Trend Analysis

Milestone Trend Analysis is a technique used in the Agile Process and Project Management disciplines to track and analyze the progress of a project at key milestone points. It involves comparing the actual progress and performance against planned targets or milestones to identify trends, patterns, and potential risks.

The main purpose of conducting milestone trend analysis is to gain insights into the project's overall health, identify any potential deviations from the planned path, and take proactive measures to address them. By regularly monitoring key milestones and analyzing trends, project managers can effectively manage and control the project's progress.

Milestone

An Agile process is an iterative and incremental approach to project management that focuses on flexibility, collaboration, and continuous improvement. It emphasizes adaptive planning, rapid delivery, and frequent customer feedback.

In the Agile framework, projects are divided into small, manageable increments called iterations or sprints. During each iteration, cross-functional teams collaborate closely to plan, develop, test, and deliver a working product increment. The development process is dynamic, as requirements and priorities can change throughout the project, and teams must be able to respond quickly to these changes.

Agile project management relies on regular communication and collaboration among team members, stakeholders, and customers. This open and transparent approach enables teams to gather feedback and make adjustments early and often, ensuring that the final product meets customer expectations.

Key principles of Agile project management include self-organizing teams, continuous delivery, and a focus on delivering value to the customer. The emphasis is on empowering teams to make decisions, adapt to new information, and deliver high-quality results.

Agile processes are particularly suited to complex and uncertain projects, where requirements may evolve over time or are not fully known at the start. By providing flexibility and adaptability, Agile project management allows teams to embrace change and deliver successful outcomes in a rapidly changing business environment.

Mind Mapping

Mind Mapping is a visual tool used in the context of Agile Process and Project Management disciplines. It involves the creation of a diagram that represents ideas, concepts, or tasks. The central idea or theme is placed in the center of the map, and related ideas branch out from it, forming a hierarchical structure. The purpose of mind mapping is to stimulate creative thinking, generate ideas, organize thoughts, and enhance understanding. It allows project teams to brainstorm and explore potential solutions, make connections between different aspects of a project, and identify dependencies and relationships. In the Agile Process, mind mapping can be used during the planning and initiation stages. It helps to identify and prioritize project requirements, define user stories, and break down tasks into smaller, manageable units. By visualizing the project scope and its components, teams can gain clarity and alignment, enabling them to deliver value incrementally and respond to changing requirements effectively. Mind mapping also supports collaboration and communication within Agile teams. It provides a common understanding of the project goals, objectives, and deliverables. It allows team members to contribute their ideas and perspectives, facilitating discussions, and fostering creativity. The visual nature of mind maps makes them easy to share and understand by all stakeholders, enabling effective decision-making and ensuring everyone is on the same page. Overall, mind mapping is a versatile tool that enhances project management in Agile contexts. It promotes creativity, organization, and collaboration, facilitating the successful delivery of projects in iterative and adaptable environments.

Mitigation Plan

An Agile Mitigation Plan is a documented strategy that outlines the proactive steps and measures to address and minimize potential risks and issues in an Agile project. It is an essential component of Agile Project Management, aimed at promoting adaptability, flexibility, and continuous improvement.

The Agile Mitigation Plan is developed collaboratively by the project team, including the product owner, Scrum master, and development team. It focuses on identifying risks and uncertainties that may hinder the project's progress and success. The plan then defines specific actions and contingency plans to be undertaken in response to these risks.

Unlike traditional project management approaches, an Agile Mitigation Plan is iterative and dynamic, aligning with the principles of Agile methodology. It embraces change and encourages teams to regularly review, revise, and update the plan as new risks emerge or existing risks evolve.

The key components of an Agile Mitigation Plan include:

- Risk Identification: Identifying potential risks and issues that may impact the project's scope, timeline, or quality.

- Risk Analysis: Assessing the likelihood and impact of each identified risk to prioritize mitigation efforts.

- Risk Response Planning: Defining specific actions and countermeasures to address and minimize the impact of identified risks.

73

- Risk Monitoring and Control: Regularly monitoring the project for new risks, assessing their significance, and adjusting mitigation actions as necessary.

By incorporating an Agile Mitigation Plan into the project management process, Agile teams can identify and address risks promptly, ensuring the project's overall success and enabling continuous delivery of valuable products or services.

Mitigation Strategies Plan

A mitigation strategies plan in the context of Agile Process and Project Management disciplines refers to a comprehensive set of actions and measures put in place to identify and address potential risks and challenges that may arise during the course of a project. The plan serves as a proactive approach to minimize the negative impact of these risks and ensure the successful completion of the project.

The mitigation strategies plan involves several key steps. First, it requires a thorough risk assessment, where potential risks and their potential impact on the project are identified and analyzed. This is followed by the development of specific mitigation strategies that outline how each risk will be addressed and controlled. These strategies may include alternative approaches, contingency plans, or specific actions to prevent the risk from occurring or to mitigate its impact if it does occur.

Throughout the project, the mitigation strategies plan is continuously monitored and updated as new risks emerge or existing risks evolve. This ensures that the project team remains proactive in identifying and managing potential threats. The plan also includes clear communication channels to keep all stakeholders informed of the mitigation strategies in place and any updates to the plan.

By having a well-defined mitigation strategies plan, Agile teams can effectively manage risks and uncertainties, allowing them to maintain project timelines, budgets, and quality targets. The plan fosters a proactive mindset, enabling the team to quickly respond to unforeseen events and minimize their impact on project outcomes. Ultimately, a mitigation strategies plan promotes project success by ensuring that risks are handled efficiently and effectively throughout the Agile process.

Mitigation Strategies

Mitigation strategies in the context of Agile Process and Project Management disciplines refer to proactive measures taken to identify, analyze, and address potential risks and issues that may impact the successful execution of a project. These strategies aim to minimize the negative impact of risks and ensure that projects stay on track and meet their objectives.

Agile methodologies emphasize the importance of adaptability and flexibility to respond to changing requirements and uncertainties. Therefore, mitigation strategies in this context involve continuous monitoring and evaluation of risks throughout the project lifecycle. This enables project teams to identify risks early on, assess their potential impact, and implement appropriate actions to mitigate or eliminate them.

One common mitigation strategy in Agile is frequent and open communication among project team members and stakeholders. This allows the early identification and resolution of issues, encourages collaborative problem-solving, and ensures everyone is aligned towards project goals.

Another mitigation strategy is the use of iterative and incremental development cycles. By breaking down project deliverables into smaller, manageable chunks, teams can quickly identify and address any potential risks or issues that may arise. This not only helps to reduce the overall impact of risks but also enables teams to adapt and adjust their plans based on changing requirements or market conditions.

Furthermore, Agile teams often employ techniques such as risk assessment workshops, retrospectives, and regular project reviews to identify potential risks and determine appropriate mitigation actions. These activities facilitate the identification of lessons learned, promote

74

continuous improvement, and help teams to continuously refine their mitigation strategies throughout the project.

Mitigation

Mitigation is a disciplined and proactive approach undertaken in Agile Process and Project Management disciplines to anticipate, identify, evaluate, and manage the risks that may arise throughout the project lifecycle. It involves designing and implementing strategies and measures to minimize the adverse impact and likelihood of identified risks.

In the context of Agile Process and Project Management, mitigation is an essential practice that aims to ensure the successful delivery of projects within the defined scope, timelines, and budget. It involves an ongoing process of risk identification and evaluation, followed by the development and implementation of appropriate risk response plans.

Mitigation activities typically begin by identifying potential risks and their associated impacts on the project objectives. This process involves analyzing historical project data, conducting interviews, and engaging subject matter experts to gather insights and information. Once the risks are identified, they are assessed in terms of their likelihood and severity. This evaluation enables project managers and teams to prioritize risks based on their potential impact and likelihood of occurrence.

After prioritizing risks, mitigation strategies and actions are developed. These strategies can include activities such as risk avoidance, risk acceptance, risk transfer, or risk reduction. Risk avoidance involves taking proactive measures to eliminate or minimize the likelihood of risks occurring. Risk acceptance, on the other hand, acknowledges that certain risks cannot be completely mitigated and focuses on developing contingency plans to address them if they arise. Risk transfer involves transferring the management of specific risks to external parties, such as insurance companies or third-party vendors. Risk reduction strategies aim to minimize the impact and likelihood of risks through various actions, such as implementing additional quality controls, conducting more frequent testing, or enhancing communication and collaboration within the project team.

In summary, mitigation in Agile Process and Project Management disciplines is a systematic approach to identify, assess, and manage risks throughout the project lifecycle. It involves the development and implementation of strategies and actions to minimize the impact and likelihood of risks, ensuring project success.

Monitoring And Controlling

Monitoring and controlling in the context of Agile Process and Project Management disciplines refer to the ongoing activities and processes that aim to track, assess, and regulate the progress and performance of a project or process. It involves continuously monitoring and evaluating the project and making necessary adjustments to ensure that it is on track and aligned with the project objectives and desired outcomes.

The monitoring and controlling phase typically involves the following key activities:

- Tracking and measuring project progress: This includes collecting and analyzing data on key project parameters such as scope, schedule, budget, and quality. It helps in identifying any deviations from the planned targets and taking appropriate actions to address them.

- Performance assessment and reporting: Regularly assessing the performance of the project team and individual team members is crucial to ensure that they are meeting their respective goals and delivering the required outcomes. It involves providing feedback, guidance, and coaching to enhance performance and address any performance gaps.

- Risk management: Identifying and evaluating potential risks and taking proactive measures to mitigate their impact on the project's success is an essential part of monitoring and controlling. It includes establishing risk mitigation strategies and contingency plans to handle any unexpected events or challenges.

- Change management: As projects progress, changes in requirements, scope, or objectives may arise. Monitoring and controlling involve effectively managing these changes by evaluating their impact, assessing the risks associated with them, and implementing them in a controlled manner without compromising the project's overall goals and objectives.

Motivation Theories Application

Motivation Theories Application in the context of Agile Process and Project Management disciplines involves the practical utilization of various psychological theories and concepts to enhance and maintain the motivation levels of team members throughout the project lifecycle. Agile methodologies, characterized by iterative and collaborative approaches, require a high level of engagement and commitment from team members.

One widely applied theory is Herzberg's Two-Factor Theory, which suggests that certain factors, known as motivators, contribute to job satisfaction, while other factors, referred to as hygiene factors, only prevent dissatisfaction. In Agile Project Management, motivators can include meaningful work, autonomy, and opportunities for personal and professional growth. To apply this theory, project managers can assign responsibilities that align with team members' interests and strengths, allow them to make decisions concerning their work, and provide opportunities for skills development.

Another relevant theory is Self-Determination Theory, which emphasizes the importance of three psychological needs: autonomy, competence, and relatedness. In the Agile context, autonomy can be fostered by empowering team members to make decisions about their work and allowing flexible working arrangements. Competence can be enhanced by providing regular feedback, training opportunities, and recognition of achievements. Relatedness can be promoted through team-building activities, fostering a sense of collaboration and creating a supportive work environment.

Additionally, the Expectancy Theory, proposed by Victor Vroom, suggests that individuals are motivated to exert effort when they believe their efforts will lead to desired outcomes. In Agile Project Management, project managers can apply this theory by aligning individual goals with project objectives, clarifying expectations, and providing resources and support necessary for success.

Motivation Theories

Theories of motivation explain why individuals behave in certain ways and what drives them to achieve their goals. In the context of Agile Process and Project Management disciplines, understanding motivation theories can help project managers create an environment that encourages team members to perform at their best and achieve project objectives.

One well-known theory is Maslow's Hierarchy of Needs. According to this theory, individuals have a set of hierarchical needs that must be met in a specific order. In an Agile project management setting, project managers can use this theory to identify and address the needs of team members. For example, providing a safe and inclusive work environment can fulfill the need for belongingness and social interaction, while offering opportunities for skill development can fulfill the need for self-esteem and achievement.

Another relevant theory is Herzberg's Two-Factor Theory, which distinguishes between hygiene factors and motivators. Hygiene factors are the basic requirements for job satisfaction, such as fair compensation and comfortable working conditions. Motivators, on the other hand, include factors like recognition, responsibility, and growth opportunities. By understanding this theory, project managers can focus on both addressing hygiene factors and providing motivators to keep team members engaged and satisfied in their roles.

Motivation

Motivation can be defined as the driving force that compels individuals or teams to take action and achieve their goals. In the context of Agile Process and Project Management disciplines, motivation plays a crucial role in ensuring the successful implementation and completion of projects.

In Agile, where projects are typically divided into short iterations called sprints, motivation plays a key role in keeping the team focused and committed. It is essential for the team members to be motivated to do their best work and to continuously improve throughout the project. Motivated team members are more likely to proactively seek solutions to problems, collaborate effectively, and deliver high-quality results.

Multi-Criteria Decision Analysis (MCDA)

Multi-Criteria Decision Analysis (MCDA) is a systematic approach used in Agile Process and Project Management disciplines to evaluate and prioritize multiple options based on a set of predefined criteria. It involves a structured decision-making process that incorporates both quantitative and qualitative factors to provide a comprehensive assessment of various alternatives.

In the context of Agile Process and Project Management, MCDA helps teams in making informed decisions by considering multiple criteria that are relevant to the project objectives. These criteria could include factors such as cost, time, risk, quality, customer satisfaction, technical feasibility, and resource availability.

The MCDA process typically involves the following steps:

1. Identification of Decision Criteria: The first step is to define and identify the criteria that will be used to evaluate the different options. These criteria should align with the project goals and priorities.

2. Weighting of Criteria: Once the criteria are identified, the next step is to assign weights to each criterion based on their relative importance. This allows the decision-makers to prioritize the criteria according to their significance.

3. Evaluation of Alternatives: After assigning weights to criteria, the alternatives or options under consideration are evaluated against each criterion. The evaluation can be done using different techniques such as scoring models, cost-benefit analysis, or performance metrics.

4. Aggregation and Analysis of Results: The results from the evaluation are then aggregated and analyzed to determine the overall performance of each alternative. This analysis helps in identifying the most suitable option that aligns with the project objectives and criteria.

Overall, MCDA provides a structured framework for teams to evaluate and prioritize alternatives in a systematic and transparent manner, ensuring that decisions are based on a thorough analysis of multiple criteria.

Negotiation Skills

Negotiation skills are essential in the context of Agile Process and Project Management disciplines. It refers to the ability to engage in a strategic discussion with stakeholders, team members, and other relevant parties to reach a mutually beneficial agreement or resolution.

In Agile Process, negotiation skills are crucial during the planning and execution stages. The Agile approach encourages collaboration and flexibility, which often leads to diverse perspectives and conflicting viewpoints. Project managers need to effectively negotiate with team members to align their goals, assign tasks, and set realistic expectations. Negotiation skills also come into play when resolving conflicts, managing scope changes, or making trade-off decisions between quality, cost, and time.

Similarly, in Project Management disciplines, negotiation skills help in coordinating resources, managing schedules, and ensuring project success. Project managers need to negotiate with stakeholders to define project objectives, gather requirements, and secure necessary support. They also negotiate with suppliers to secure favorable contracts, resolve issues related to project constraints, and manage risks effectively.

Effective negotiation skills enable project managers to build strong relationships, ensure transparency, and foster a collaborative environment. It allows them to balance the needs and expectations of various stakeholders while ensuring project deliverables are met. By leveraging negotiation skills, project managers can navigate complexities, resolve conflicts, and enhance project outcomes in line with Agile principles and project management best practices.

Negotiation Techniques Workshop

A negotiation techniques workshop in the context of Agile Process and Project Management disciplines is a training session designed to enhance the skills and knowledge of individuals involved in negotiation within an Agile environment. The workshop aims to provide participants with the necessary tools and strategies to effectively negotiate and resolve conflicts that may arise during Agile projects.

The workshop typically covers a range of negotiation techniques and principles that are relevant to Agile Project Management, such as collaborative problem-solving, win-win solutions, and consensus building. Participants will learn how to identify and understand different negotiation styles, as well as how to adapt their approach based on the specific circumstances of the project.

Through practical exercises and case studies, participants will have the opportunity to apply and practice the negotiation techniques discussed during the workshop. This will enable them to develop their negotiation skills and gain confidence in dealing with challenging situations that may arise within an Agile project team.

Overall, the negotiation techniques workshop in the Agile Process and Project Management disciplines provides participants with valuable insights and strategies to effectively navigate the complex dynamics of Agile projects. By enhancing their negotiation skills, participants will be better equipped to manage conflicts, facilitate effective communication, and ultimately contribute to the successful delivery of Agile projects.

Negotiation Techniques

Negotiation techniques in the context of Agile Process and Project Management disciplines involve the effective communication and collaboration between the project team and stakeholders to reach mutually beneficial agreements and resolve conflicts.

The Agile approach emphasizes flexibility, adaptability, and continuous improvement. In this context, negotiation techniques play a crucial role in ensuring that the project team and stakeholders are aligned in their goals and expectations. These techniques help facilitate open and constructive discussions, promote transparency and trust, and enable effective decision-making.

Negotiation

Negotiation in the context of Agile Process and Project Management disciplines refers to the act of coming to a mutual agreement or compromise between stakeholders involved in the project. It is a key skill that project managers and team members must possess in order to efficiently manage resources, navigate conflicts, and achieve project goals.

Agile methodologies focus on flexibility, collaboration, and delivering value to the customer. Negotiation plays a crucial role in this process, as it enables teams to adapt to changing requirements, prioritize tasks, and ensure stakeholder satisfaction. By engaging in effective negotiations, project managers can address conflicts, resolve disagreements, and make decisions that align with the project objectives.

Network Diagram

A network diagram is a visual representation of the dependencies and relationships between various tasks or activities in a project. It illustrates how different tasks are interconnected and how they influence each other.

In the context of Agile Process and Project Management, a network diagram is often used to plan and organize project activities in a structured and logical manner. It helps teams to understand the sequence of tasks and their dependencies, enabling them to identify potential roadblocks and optimize the project timeline.

Operational Readiness

Operational Readiness in the context of Agile Process and Project Management disciplines refers to the state of preparedness of a system or organization to effectively and efficiently handle the operations and maintenance activities after the completion of a project or implementation of a new process.

It involves ensuring that all necessary resources, tools, and documentation are in place to support the ongoing operations and maintenance of the system or process. This includes having a well-defined operational plan, clear roles and responsibilities, and the necessary training and support for the team members involved.

Operational Readiness also involves conducting thorough testing and validation of the system or process to identify and address any potential issues or gaps before it is deployed or implemented. This includes evaluating the system's performance, reliability, scalability, and security to ensure that it meets the defined operational requirements and can effectively support the desired business outcomes.

Furthermore, Operational Readiness encompasses the establishment of appropriate monitoring and measurement mechanisms to continuously assess the system's performance and identify any areas of improvement or optimization. It also involves implementing effective change management practices to handle any future changes or updates to the system or process in a controlled and efficient manner.

Operations And Maintenance (O&M)

Operations and Maintenance (O&M) in the context of Agile Process and Project Management refers to the ongoing activities and activities that are necessary to ensure the smooth functioning of a software system or project after it has been developed and delivered to the end users. It encompasses the various tasks and processes involved in managing, supporting, and maintaining the software application or system throughout its lifecycle.

O&M activities in Agile Process and Project Management are centered around the principles of continuous improvement and collaboration. They involve monitoring and analyzing system performance, identifying and fixing issues or bugs, enhancing the system based on user feedback and evolving requirements, and ensuring the system remains stable, secure, and up-to-date.

O&M activities can include but are not limited to:

1. Software installation, configuration, and deployment

2. System monitoring and performance evaluation

3. Troubleshooting and fixing software defects, bugs, or errors

4. Applying patches and updates to address security vulnerabilities or add new features

5. Providing user support and training

6. Conducting regular system backups and disaster recovery planning

7. Conducting system audits and ensuring compliance with relevant regulations or standards

8. Evaluating and implementing system improvements and optimizations based on user feedback and changing business needs

The O&M activities are critical for ensuring the long-term success and sustainability of a software project or system. By continuously monitoring and maintaining the system, organizations can effectively address issues, adapt to changing requirements, and deliver high-quality and reliable software solutions to their users.

Operations And Maintenance Plan (O&M)

An Operations and Maintenance Plan (O&M) in the context of Agile Process and Project Management disciplines is a document that outlines the activities, tasks, and responsibilities required to ensure the smooth operation and effective maintenance of a product or system.

The O&M plan serves as a roadmap for the ongoing support and management of the product or system throughout its lifecycle. It provides clear guidelines and procedures for the operational personnel, such as administrators, IT support teams, or maintenance technicians, to follow in order to maintain and optimize the product or system's performance.

The O&M plan typically includes information on the various aspects of the product or system, such as hardware, software, infrastructure, and data management. It details the specific maintenance tasks and their frequency, such as software updates, hardware upgrades, system backups, or security audits.

Furthermore, the O&M plan may also contain information on incident management, problem resolution, and change management processes. This ensures that any issues or problems that arise during the operation of the product or system are promptly addressed and resolved, minimizing disruptions and downtime.

In an Agile environment, the O&M plan may be more flexible and adaptable compared to traditional project management approaches. It may take into account the iterative and incremental nature of Agile development, which requires continuous monitoring and improvement of the product or system based on user feedback and changing requirements.

In summary, an Operations and Maintenance Plan in Agile Process and Project Management disciplines is a comprehensive document that provides guidance and instructions for the ongoing operation and maintenance of a product or system. It ensures that the product or system remains reliable, secure, and optimized throughout its lifecycle.

Organizational Change Management (OCM)

Organizational Change Management (OCM) is a discipline within Agile Process and Project Management that focuses on enabling and facilitating the successful implementation of organizational changes. OCM recognizes that change is a constant and essential part of any organization's growth and adaptation to the dynamic business environment.

OCM involves a systematic approach to understanding, planning, and implementing changes within an organization, including changes to processes, technologies, structures, and strategies. It aims to minimize resistance and maximize adoption and sustainment of the changes by the individuals and teams affected.

In the context of Agile Process and Project Management, OCM plays a critical role in ensuring that the agile values and principles are adopted and embedded throughout the organization. It involves effectively communicating the change vision and rationale to all stakeholders, including employees, customers, and partners, to gain their buy-in and commitment.

OCM also involves assessing and addressing the impacts of the changes on individuals, teams, and the organization as a whole. This includes identifying and mitigating potential barriers and resistance to change, providing training and support to enhance skills and capabilities, and fostering a culture of continuous learning and improvement.

Overall, OCM in the context of Agile Process and Project Management is a holistic and proactive approach to managing and guiding organizational changes, ensuring their successful implementation and long-term sustainability. It recognizes that people are at the heart of any change, and their support and engagement are essential for achieving the desired outcomes.

Organizational Culture Assessment

An organizational culture assessment is a systematic evaluation of the beliefs, values, norms, and behaviors that exist within an organization. In the context of Agile Process and Project Management disciplines, this assessment focuses on understanding the cultural aspects that either enable or hinder the successful implementation of Agile practices.

Agile methodologies prioritize collaboration, continuous learning, and adaptability. Therefore, an organization's culture plays a crucial role in determining its ability to embrace and sustain Agile practices. A culture assessment helps identify the existing cultural characteristics and assess their alignment with Agile principles.

Through various data collection methods, such as surveys, interviews, and observations, the assessment evaluates the following cultural dimensions:

Collaboration and Communication: Assessing the extent to which individuals and teams actively collaborate, share information openly, and communicate effectively. This dimension helps identify any barriers to effective collaboration and communication within the organization.

Empowerment and Autonomy: Evaluating the level of empowerment given to teams and individuals, and their autonomy in decision-making. This dimension helps identify whether the organizational culture supports self-organizing teams and promotes employee empowerment.

Learning and Adaptability: Assessing the organization's openness to learning from failures, experimentation, and continuous improvement. This dimension helps identify whether the culture encourages innovation, learning, and adaptation to changing market or project requirements.

Leadership and Support: Evaluating leadership behaviors and practices that support Agile implementation. This dimension helps identify whether the leadership is providing the necessary support, coaching, and guidance to enable Agile teams to thrive.

The findings from the culture assessment can be used to identify areas for improvement, develop strategies to align the culture with Agile values, and foster a culture of continuous learning and improvement that supports Agile Process and Project Management.

Organizational Culture

Organizational culture refers to the shared values, beliefs, norms, and behaviors that characterize an organization. In the context of Agile process and project management disciplines, organizational culture plays a crucial role in the successful adoption and implementation of Agile methodologies. Agile processes focus on collaboration, adaptability, and continuous improvement. Therefore, an organizational culture that fosters and supports these values is essential for Agile success. Agile methodologies encourage self-organizing teams, frequent communication, and empowerment. Thus, an organization with a culture that promotes autonomy, trust, open communication, and knowledge sharing is more likely to embrace and benefit from Agile practices. In Agile project management, cross-functional teams work together closely to deliver incremental value. An organizational culture that values teamwork, collaboration, and interdepartmental cooperation facilitates efficient Agile project management. Agile processes also prioritize transparency, feedback, and continuous learning. Therefore, a culture that embraces transparency, encourages constructive feedback, and values a learning mindset is conducive to effective Agile project management. Moreover, Agile methodologies emphasize adaptability and flexibility to change. An organizational culture that embraces change, encourages innovation, and values experimentation is more likely to thrive in Agile adoption. In contrast, a culture that resists change, values stability over agility, and punishes failure can hinder the successful implementation of Agile methodologies. In conclusion, organizational culture plays a significant role in Agile process and project management disciplines. A culture that values collaboration, open communication, autonomy, trust, transparency, feedback, learning, adaptability, and innovation is essential for the successful adoption and implementation of Agile methodologies.

Organizational Process Assets (OPAs)

Organizational Process Assets (OPAs) refer to the set of internal resources and knowledge that an organization possesses and utilizes to execute projects in an Agile process and project management discipline. These assets include processes, procedures, templates, historical data, lessons learned, and other forms of organizational knowledge that guide the planning, execution, monitoring, and control of projects.

In the Agile context, OPAs are essential for promoting efficiency, consistency, and standardization within project teams. They serve as a repository of best practices and lessons learned from past projects, aiding in decision-making and reducing risks. OPAs also provide a basis for establishing and improving Agile processes and methodologies within the organization.

Organizational Structure

An organizational structure refers to the framework that defines how an organization is arranged and how its tasks, roles, and responsibilities are allocated, coordinated, and controlled to achieve its goals. In the context of Agile Process and Project Management disciplines, organizational structure plays a crucial role in facilitating effective communication, collaboration, and decision-making within Agile teams.

Agile organizations typically adopt a flat and decentralized organizational structure, commonly known as a cross-functional team structure. This structure emphasizes self-organizing and cross-functional teams, where individuals from different functional areas work together to deliver value to the customer. The Agile teams are empowered to make decisions, plan and prioritize their work, and determine how to best achieve their objectives within the boundaries defined by the broader organizational goals and Agile principles.

PERT Chart

Pert Chart, short for Program Evaluation and Review Technique Chart, is a project management tool utilized in Agile Process and other project management disciplines. It is a graphical representation that provides a visual overview of tasks, their dependencies, and the timeline of a project.

The Pert Chart is essential for project planning, scheduling, and decision-making. It helps project managers and teams to understand the flow of work, identify critical steps, and estimate the time needed to complete each task. By visualizing the dependencies among various activities, it enables stakeholders to prioritize and allocate resources effectively.

Pareto Analysis

Pareto Analysis, also known as the 80/20 rule, is a decision-making tool used in Agile Process and Project Management disciplines. It is named after Italian economist Vilfredo Pareto, who observed that 80% of the effects often come from 20% of the causes. The principle behind Pareto Analysis is that by identifying and focusing on the significant few, rather than the trivial many, one can optimize resources and achieve better outcomes.

In the context of Agile Process and Project Management, Pareto Analysis helps in prioritizing work and identifying the most impactful tasks or issues. It involves the following steps:

1.

Define the problem or goal: To begin with, the team needs to clearly define the problem or goal they want to address using Pareto Analysis.

2.

Gather data: The next step is to collect relevant data associated with the problem or goal. This data can include metrics, customer feedback, or any other relevant information.

3.

Analyze the data: The team should analyze the collected data to identify patterns and the distribution of causes. This analysis allows them to determine the significant few causes that contribute to the majority of the effect.

4.

Identify the vital few: Based on the Pareto principle, the team can identify the vital few causes that have the most impact on the problem or goal. These causes should be the focus of improvement efforts.

By applying Pareto Analysis, Agile teams can optimize their efforts by focusing on the most critical tasks or issues. This ensures that the team's resources are utilized effectively, leading to improved project outcomes and overall productivity.

Pareto Chart Analysis

A Pareto Chart is a visual representation of data that helps identify the most significant factors or causes contributing to a problem or issue. It provides a clear and concise analysis of the frequency or occurrence of these factors, allowing project managers in Agile Process and Project Management disciplines to prioritize improvement efforts effectively.

In Agile, Pareto charts are commonly used in the context of problem-solving and process improvement. They help teams identify the root causes of issues or bottlenecks affecting project performance or product quality. By visually presenting data in descending order of importance, Pareto charts allow project teams to focus their attention on the vital few factors that are responsible for the majority of problems.

Pareto Chart

A Pareto Chart is a visual representation tool used in Agile Process and Project Management disciplines to identify and prioritize the most significant factors contributing to a problem or project outcome. It is based on the Pareto principle, also known as the 80/20 rule, which states that roughly 80% of the effects come from 20% of the causes.

The Pareto Chart consists of both a bar graph and a line graph. The bar graph displays the frequency or occurrence of various factors, arranged in descending order. The most important factors are represented by the tallest bars on the left, gradually decreasing in height towards the right. The accompanying line graph represents the cumulative percentage of the total factors. This line typically starts at zero and rises diagonally towards the right side of the chart. The point at which it intersects the line corresponding to 80% represents the threshold for identifying the most significant factors.

Pareto Principle (80/20 Rule)

The Pareto Principle, also known as the 80/20 Rule, is a concept widely applied in the context of Agile Process and Project Management disciplines. It states that roughly 80% of the effects come from 20% of the causes, meaning that a small number of factors usually contribute to a large majority of the results or outcomes.

In Agile Process and Project Management, the Pareto Principle can be used as a guideline to prioritize efforts and resources. By identifying the vital few factors that have the most significant impact on the project's success, teams can focus their energy on those aspects and achieve maximum value within a limited timeframe.

For example, during the planning phase of an Agile project, the team can conduct a Pareto analysis to determine which features or requirements will deliver the most value to the end-users. By identifying the 20% of features that will address 80% of the user's needs, the team can prioritize their development efforts and allocate resources accordingly.

Moreover, the Pareto Principle can also be applied to identify and mitigate risks in Agile projects. By analyzing historical data, the team can identify the 20% of risks that are responsible for 80% of the project's potential negative impacts. This enables them to proactively address those risks and minimize their effects on the project's overall performance.

Pareto Principle

The Pareto Principle, also known as the 80/20 rule, is a widely recognized concept in Agile Process and Project Management disciplines. It states that roughly 80% of the effects are derived from 20% of the causes or inputs. This principle can be applied to various aspects of Agile methodologies, such as planning, prioritization, and problem-solving, to maximize efficiency and focus on the most significant factors.

In the context of Agile Process and Project Management, the Pareto Principle helps identify and prioritize the critical tasks or features that contribute the most value to a project. By focusing on the vital few inputs, teams can effectively allocate resources, minimize waste, and maximize productivity. It allows Agile teams to make data-driven decisions and tackle the most influential aspects first, ensuring that the majority of the benefits are achieved with minimal effort.

Peer Review

Agile Process:

Agile Process is a project management approach that emphasizes flexibility, collaboration, and continuous improvement. It enables teams to deliver value to stakeholders through incremental and iterative development cycles.

Agile Process prioritizes customer satisfaction by embracing changing requirements throughout the project life cycle. It promotes adaptive planning, allowing teams to respond quickly to changing market conditions, customer needs, and technological advancements.

The key principles of Agile Process include actively involving the customer and stakeholders in the development process, delivering working software frequently, welcoming changes even in the late stages of the project, promoting self-organizing teams, encouraging face-to-face communication, and regularly reflecting on how to improve efficiency and effectiveness.

By breaking down complex projects into smaller manageable tasks, Agile Process enables teams to deliver incremental value to customers quickly. It promotes transparency among team members, ensuring everyone has a clear understanding of project goals, roles, and responsibilities.

Through the use of Agile Process, project managers and teams can foster a collaborative environment that empowers individuals and promotes a sense of ownership and shared responsibility. They can continuously inspect and adapt their processes, making necessary adjustments to deliver high-quality results that meet customer expectations.

Overall, Agile Process is a project management framework that values flexibility, adaptability, collaboration, and continuous improvement to deliver customer-centric solutions efficiently and effectively.

Performance Metrics

Performance metrics, in the context of Agile Process and Project Management disciplines, refer to quantifiable measures used to evaluate the progress, effectiveness, and efficiency of a project or process. These metrics provide objective insights into various aspects of the project or process, enabling teams to make data-driven decisions and adjustments to improve performance and achieve desired outcomes.

Agile teams typically use a combination of leading and lagging performance metrics to assess both the current state and predict future trends. Leading metrics focus on leading indicators, which are early indicators that provide insights into future performance. Examples of leading metrics in Agile project management may include tracking the number of user stories completed per sprint or the velocity of the team. These metrics help teams identify potential roadblocks, bottlenecks, or opportunities for improvement before they impact overall project performance.

Lagging metrics, on the other hand, measure historical performance and are useful for evaluating the results achieved. They usually include metrics such as on-time delivery, customer satisfaction ratings, or defects per unit of work. Lagging metrics provide an assessment of the overall success of a project or process and can help teams identify areas for improvement or celebrate achievements.

Performance Reporting Metrics

Performance Reporting Metrics in the context of Agile Process and Project Management disciplines refer to the quantitative and qualitative measures used to assess and communicate the progress, efficiency, and effectiveness of an Agile project. These metrics provide valuable insights into the project's performance, allowing project managers to make data-driven decisions, identify areas of improvement, and ensure project success.

Agile Performance Reporting Metrics typically include key performance indicators (KPIs) that measure various aspects of the project, such as team productivity, stakeholder satisfaction, quality of deliverables, and overall project progress. These metrics can be categorized into three main areas:

1. Time and Resource Metrics: These metrics focus on the project's adherence to deadlines, the utilization of resources, and the efficiency of development cycles. Examples of such metrics include Cycle Time, Lead Time, Velocity, and Burn-down Rate.

2. Quality Metrics: These metrics assess the quality of the project's deliverables and the effectiveness of the team's development processes. They include metrics such as Defect Density, Code Coverage, Test Coverage, and Customer Satisfaction.

3. Stakeholder Metrics: These metrics measure the satisfaction and engagement level of project stakeholders, including customers, end-users, and team members. They provide insights into the project's alignment with stakeholder expectations and include metrics like Net Promoter Score, Stakeholder Feedback, and User Satisfaction.

By analyzing and interpreting these performance reporting metrics, Agile project managers can monitor project progress, identify bottlenecks, address issues promptly, and continuously improve the project's overall performance. They provide a basis for data-driven decision-making and help in refining Agile methodologies for future projects.

Performance Reporting

Performance reporting in the context of Agile Process and Project Management disciplines refers to the systematic and regular assessment of project progress and outcomes. It involves collecting, analyzing, and presenting relevant information to stakeholders to provide visibility into the project's performance against predetermined goals and objectives.

The purpose of performance reporting is to enable informed and data-driven decision-making, facilitate communication, and promote transparency among project team members, management, and other stakeholders. It helps to identify potential issues, track the project's adherence to the planned schedule and budget, and assess the overall quality of deliverables.

Agile performance reporting typically includes key metrics, such as the velocity of work completed, burn-up or burn-down charts, and cumulative flow diagrams. These metrics provide insights into the progress of individual sprints and the overall project, enabling project teams to effectively plan and adapt their work to achieve desired outcomes.

Furthermore, performance reporting in Agile Process and Project Management involves frequent and informal communication methods, such as daily stand-up meetings and retrospective sessions, to ensure timely feedback and continuous improvement. It focuses on collaboration, enabling team members to share information, address challenges, and align their efforts to meet project objectives.

To successfully execute performance reporting in the Agile context, project managers and team members need to establish clear metrics, establish a cadence for reporting, and use visual tools to present data in a simple and understandable manner. Additionally, promoting a culture of transparency and trust among stakeholders is essential for effective performance reporting and decision-making.

Phase Gate Review

A Phase Gate Review is a formal evaluation process that occurs at key points throughout the Agile Process and Project Management disciplines. It is used to assess the progress, quality, and viability of a project as it moves from one phase to the next.

During a Phase Gate Review, a cross-functional team consisting of project stakeholders, subject matter experts, and senior management evaluates various aspects of the project, such as deliverables, timeline, budget, risks, and resources. The purpose of this evaluation is to ensure that the project is on track, aligned with business objectives, and has a high likelihood of success.

Phase Gate

A Phase Gate is a structured milestone review and decision-making process that is essential for effective project management in Agile. It acts as a control mechanism to evaluate the progress, quality, and viability of a project at critical stages or phases throughout its lifecycle.

In Agile project management, the Phase Gate process consists of predetermined checkpoints, often referred to as gates, where the project team, stakeholders, and management review the project's deliverables, risks, and objectives. By conducting these reviews at specific intervals, the project's progress and alignment with the overall business strategy can be assessed, enabling informed decision-making and course correction if required.

During each phase gate review, the project team provides detailed documentation, including project plans, requirements, design, and test cases. This documentation serves as evidence of completion and readiness for the next phase. The project's performance against defined metrics, such as cost, schedule, and quality, is also measured and evaluated during the phase gate process.

Phase gates create transparency and accountability throughout the project, enabling stakeholders to make well-informed decisions based on accurate and up-to-date information. These gates help mitigate project risks by identifying potential issues, bottlenecks, or deviations from the project plan early on, allowing timely corrective actions to be taken.

By incorporating the phase gate process into Agile project management, teams can ensure that projects progress in a controlled and measurable manner, with a focus on delivering value to the customer and achieving business objectives.

Phase Review Meeting

A Phase Review Meeting is a formal meeting conducted within the Agile Process and Project Management disciplines to evaluate the progress and performance of a project at the end of a specific phase. It serves as a platform for stakeholders, including the project team, sponsors, and other relevant parties, to review the work completed during the phase and make informed decisions regarding the project's next steps.

During a Phase Review Meeting, the project team presents the outcomes, deliverables, and results achieved in the phase, providing a comprehensive overview of the accomplishments, challenges, and potential risks encountered. The stakeholders analyze the presented information, assess the project's adherence to timelines, scope, and quality, and determine whether the project should proceed to the next phase or make adjustments based on the insights gained from the review.

The primary objectives of the Phase Review Meeting include identifying any deviations from the initial project plan, addressing and resolving issues and concerns, and ensuring the project aligns with the organization's strategic goals and objectives. The meeting also serves as an opportunity to validate the project's trajectory, assess resource allocation, and facilitate effective communication among stakeholders.

At the end of the Phase Review Meeting, stakeholders collaboratively make decisions regarding the project's continuation, modification, or termination. This decision-making process takes into consideration the risks, benefits, constraints, and feedback obtained during the review, enabling informed adjustments and improvements to the project's direction moving forward.

Phase Review

The phase review is a key component in the Agile Process and Project Management disciplines. It is a structured review process that takes place at the end of each phase or iteration of a project. The purpose of the phase review is to assess the progress of the project and make informed decisions about the next steps.

During the phase review, the project team and stakeholders come together to evaluate the outcomes of the completed phase or iteration. They review the deliverables, compare them against the project objectives, and determine if they meet the desired requirements and quality standards. The phase review also involves assessing the project timeline, budget, and resources to ensure they align with the overall project plan.

Based on the findings of the phase review, the project team can make informed decisions about the next phase or iteration. They may decide to proceed as planned, make adjustments to the project plan, or even terminate the project if it is no longer feasible or aligned with the organization's goals. The phase review provides an opportunity to identify any issues or risks early on and take corrective actions before they escalate.

In conclusion, the phase review plays a vital role in the Agile Process and Project Management disciplines. It enables the project team and stakeholders to assess the progress, outcomes, and alignment of the project at the end of each phase or iteration. By conducting thorough phase reviews, organizations can ensure the successful execution of their projects and deliver the desired outcomes.

Portfolio Analysis

The portfolio analysis is a critical component of Agile Process and Project Management disciplines. It involves evaluating and assessing the organization's portfolio of projects to gain insights into their collective performance, alignment with business goals, and resource utilization. This analysis is essential for effective decision-making and optimizing the overall project portfolio.

Agile process and project management teams use portfolio analysis to prioritize projects, allocate resources, and identify areas of improvement. It helps them understand the health and progress of each project and make informed decisions to ensure successful outcomes. By analyzing the portfolio, teams can identify projects that are at risk or not aligned with organizational objectives and take appropriate actions.

Post-Implementation Review (PIR)

A Post-Implementation Review (PIR) is a formal assessment conducted in the Agile Process and Project Management disciplines to evaluate the success and effectiveness of a project after its completion and implementation. It serves as a review mechanism to gather feedback and insights on the outcomes of the project, assess its alignment with the project's objectives, and identify areas for improvement.

The purpose of a PIR is to provide an opportunity to reflect on the overall performance of the project team, assess whether the project met its intended goals and objectives, and identify any discrepancies or deviations from the original plan. The review process involves conducting a thorough analysis of the project's deliverables, resources utilized, timeline adherence, and stakeholder satisfaction.

During the PIR, the project team, stakeholders, and other relevant parties participate in discussions, share their perspectives, and provide feedback on various aspects of the project. This feedback is essential in identifying strengths and weaknesses, lessons learned, and areas that require further attention in future projects.

The findings and insights obtained from a PIR can be used to enhance future project planning, develop best practices, and optimize resource allocation. Additionally, the review process enables the project team to celebrate successes, acknowledge team members' contributions, and foster a culture of continuous improvement.

Post-Implementation Support Plan

A post-implementation support plan in the context of Agile Process and Project Management disciplines refers to a comprehensive strategy put in place to provide assistance and guidance after the completion of a software implementation or project. It ensures that the implemented solution continues to function effectively, meets the users' requirements, and addresses any issues or challenges that may arise.

This support plan involves a set of activities and processes that are tailored to the specific needs of the project and organization. It typically includes regular monitoring and evaluation of the solution's performance, identification and resolution of any bugs or errors, continuous improvement of the software, and ongoing user training and support.

Post-Implementation Support

Post-Implementation Support refers to the activities and processes performed after the deployment of a software project in order to ensure its successful operation and user satisfaction. In the context of Agile Process and Project Management disciplines, this support encompasses a range of tasks that aim to address any issues or concerns that arise after the implementation phase. One aspect of Post-Implementation Support is monitoring and troubleshooting. This involves closely observing the software performance, identifying any issues, and actively seeking solutions to address them. It may include analyzing system logs, conducting tests, and gathering feedback from users to identify and resolve any technical glitches or bugs. Another important aspect of Post-Implementation Support is facilitating user adoption and training. Agile projects often involve frequent iterations and deployments, and ensuring that end-users understand and effectively use the software is crucial for achieving project success. This support may involve providing training sessions, creating user manuals or documentation, and offering ongoing assistance and guidance to end-users. Additionally, Post-Implementation Support involves gathering user feedback and continuously improving the software. Agile methodologies emphasize collaboration and adaptability, and this support phase provides an opportunity to receive input from end-users, gather their suggestions or recommendations, and incorporate them into future iterations or updates of the software. Overall, Post-Implementation Support plays a critical role in ensuring a smooth transition from the implementation to the operational phase of a software project. It helps to address any challenges that may arise and ensures that the software meets the needs and expectations of its users. By actively monitoring, troubleshooting, facilitating user adoption, and gathering feedback, this support phase enables continuous improvement and ensures the long-term success of the software project.

Process Improvement Plan

A process improvement plan in the context of Agile Process and Project Management disciplines refers to a structured and systematic approach to enhance the effectiveness, efficiency, and quality of the processes and practices used within an Agile project or organization. It involves identifying areas for improvement, defining specific improvement goals, implementing targeted changes, and evaluating the results to ensure continuous improvement.

The process improvement plan is based on the principles of Agile, which emphasizes collaboration, continuous learning, and adaptability. It aims to create an environment that fosters innovation, transparency, and continuous improvement of the processes and practices used in Agile project management.

Process Improvement

Process improvement is a continuous and iterative approach within Agile Process and Project Management disciplines that focuses on identifying, analyzing, and enhancing existing processes to optimize efficiency, productivity, and overall performance.

In Agile, process improvement is an integral part of the iterative development cycles and is driven by the principles of transparency, inspection, and adaptation. It aims to identify areas of improvement and implement changes that align with the Agile values and principles.

Process improvement in Agile involves several key activities. Firstly, it requires a thorough analysis of the current processes to understand their strengths, weaknesses, and potential bottlenecks. This analysis is often done through techniques like value stream mapping, root cause analysis, and process metrics.

Based on the analysis, process improvement teams collaborate closely with stakeholders to identify and prioritize improvement opportunities. These opportunities are then translated into actionable plans and experiments that can be implemented incrementally. Agile frameworks like Scrum provide specific ceremonies, such as sprint retrospectives, where teams reflect on the previous iteration and discuss potential improvements.

Throughout the process improvement journey, teams continuously monitor the implemented changes and gather feedback to assess their impact. This feedback helps in making data-driven decisions and adjustments to the process. Regular inspection and adaptation ensure that the process remains aligned with the evolving needs of the project and organization.

In conclusion, process improvement within Agile Process and Project Management disciplines is an ongoing effort to enhance existing processes through analysis, experimentation, and adaptation. By embracing a continuous improvement mindset, Agile teams strive for efficiency, effectiveness, and customer satisfaction.

Process Performance Metrics

Process Performance Metrics are quantitative measures used to assess the effectiveness and efficiency of a process in Agile Process and Project Management disciplines. These metrics provide valuable insights into the performance of the process and help in identifying areas for improvement.

In Agile, the focus is on delivering value to the customer in a iterative and incremental manner. Therefore, process performance metrics play a crucial role in monitoring and evaluating the progress of the project. They enable teams to track and analyze various aspects of the process to ensure that it is aligned with the project objectives and is delivering the desired outcomes.

Procurement Management Plan

A procurement management plan in the context of Agile Process and Project Management disciplines is a document that outlines the strategies, processes, and procedures for acquiring goods and services needed for a project. It serves as a roadmap for all procurement activities throughout the project lifecycle, ensuring that the project team has the necessary resources to deliver the desired outcomes.

The procurement management plan within Agile focuses on the iterative and incremental nature of the project, adapting to changing project requirements and priorities. It incorporates Agile principles such as collaboration, flexibility, and continuous improvement, enabling the project team to make timely and informed procurement decisions.

Procurement Management

Procurement Management is the process of planning, sourcing, and acquiring the necessary goods, services, and resources required for a project or organization. In the context of Agile Process and Project Management, procurement management plays a crucial role in ensuring that the project team has access to the right resources at the right time.

The Agile approach emphasizes the importance of collaboration, flexibility, and adaptability. Therefore, procurement management in Agile projects involves a more dynamic and iterative approach compared to traditional project management methodologies. Instead of relying on predefined requirements and long-term contracts, Agile procurement management focuses on ongoing communication and continuous refinement of project needs.

Procurement Statement Of Work (SOW)

A Procurement Statement of Work (SOW) is a formal document in the context of Agile Process and Project Management disciplines that outlines the requirements, deliverables, and expectations of a procurement process. It serves as a contractual agreement between the buyer and the vendor, providing a clear understanding of the scope of work, project objectives, and desired outcomes.

The Procurement SOW typically includes a detailed description of the goods, services, or works being procured, along with specific performance criteria, quality standards, and timelines. It may also outline the procurement process, including evaluation criteria, supplier selection criteria, and any specific terms and conditions that must be met.

Procurement

Procurement in the context of Agile Process and Project Management disciplines refers to the process of acquiring goods, services, or resources from external suppliers or vendors to support the project's development and meet the team's needs. It involves identifying the necessary requirements, evaluating potential suppliers, negotiating contracts, and managing the ongoing relationship with the selected suppliers.

In an Agile environment, procurement is approached with a flexible and adaptive mindset. Rather than following traditional procurement methods that involve detailed upfront planning and fixed contracts, Agile procurement focuses on collaboration, responsiveness, and continuous improvement. The Agile procurement process is iterative and allows for adjustments based on changing project needs and requirements.

Project Appraisal

A project appraisal is a systematic and structured process used in the Agile Process and Project Management disciplines to assess the feasibility, viability, and potential benefits of a project before it is initiated. It involves evaluating the project's objectives, scope, timeline, resources, risks, and costs to determine its overall value and potential for success.

During the project appraisal, the project team and stakeholders analyze various aspects of the project, such as its goals and requirements, to ensure alignment with the organization's strategic objectives and priorities. They assess the project's feasibility by considering factors like technical feasibility, resource availability, and potential risks. This evaluation helps in identifying any potential obstacles or challenges that may arise during project execution.

The project appraisal also involves conducting a detailed cost-benefit analysis to determine the anticipated benefits and returns on investment. This analysis considers both tangible and intangible benefits, such as increased revenue, improved customer satisfaction, and enhanced brand reputation. It also factors in the project's estimated costs, including labor, materials, technology, and any potential risks or uncertainties that may impact the financial outcomes.

Based on the findings of the appraisal, a decision is made whether to proceed with the project, modify its scope, or terminate it altogether. The appraisal serves as a valuable tool for project selection and prioritization, helping organizations make informed decisions about resource allocation and investment. By evaluating the project's potential impact and value, the appraisal minimizes the chances of undertaking projects that do not align with the organization's goals or do not offer sufficient benefits for the effort and resources invested.

Project Artifact Repository

A project artifact repository, in the context of Agile Process and Project Management disciplines, is a centralized location or system that stores and organizes various artifacts created during the project lifecycle. An artifact can be any tangible or intangible item that is produced or used during the project, such as documents, code, designs, test cases, user stories, and so on.

The repository serves as a valuable resource for project teams, providing a secure and structured space to store, access, and manage artifacts. It acts as a single source of truth, ensuring consistency and traceability of project deliverables. By having a centralized repository, team members can easily collaborate, share, and retrieve artifacts, fostering transparency and efficiency in the project lifecycle.

Project Artifact

Project Artifact refers to any tangible or intangible deliverable produced during the course of a project, which captures important information or documents a specific aspect of the project. Within the context of Agile Process and Project Management disciplines, project artifacts play a crucial role in facilitating effective collaboration, communication, and progress tracking.

In Agile methodologies, such as Scrum or Kanban, project artifacts are used to provide transparency and promote visibility across the team. The artifacts serve as a means to capture and communicate project requirements, progress, and outcomes. They often take the form of documents, charts, diagrams, or digital tools to ensure that information is easily accessible and understood by all stakeholders.

Common examples of project artifacts in Agile practices include: - User Stories: These concise descriptions of desired functionalities are used to define and prioritize requirements and guide the development process. - Product Backlog: This artifact represents a dynamic list of all desired features, enhancements, and bug fixes, serving as a roadmap for the development team. - Sprint Backlog: This artifact contains a subset of the product backlog, outlining the specific tasks and user stories that the team commits to completing within a sprint. - Burndown Chart: This visual representation tracks the team's progress over time, illustrating the remaining work against the planned timeline. - Retrospective Notes: These documents capture the team's reflections and lessons learned after each sprint, facilitating continuous improvement and knowledge sharing.

Overall, project artifacts in Agile Process and Project Management disciplines play a vital role in fostering collaboration, transparency, and accountability. They serve as a tangible representation of the project's progress and requirements, enabling effective decision-making and ensuring the successful delivery of valuable outcomes.

Project Baseline

"Project Baseline" refers to an essential component of Agile Process and Project Management disciplines. It is the initial reference point that establishes the foundation for the project. In Agile, a project baseline is an important artifact used to track and measure progress against the original plan. A project baseline consists of various elements, including the project scope, schedule, cost, and quality. It represents the agreed-upon starting point against which actual project performance is measured. It aids in understanding how the project is progressing, identifying deviations from the initial plan, and facilitating informed decision-making. Within Agile, the project baseline is often created during the initial planning phase and serves as a point of reference throughout the project lifecycle. It provides a clear picture of the project's objectives, deliverables, timelines, and resources needed to complete it. The primary purpose of establishing a project baseline is to provide a benchmark for assessing and managing changes. As the project progresses, changes to scope, schedule, or resources may occur, and the baseline acts as a reference point to evaluate these changes. By comparing actual progress against the baseline, teams can identify areas of concern, measure performance, and make necessary adjustments to ensure project success. Maintaining a project baseline in Agile helps in managing expectations, ensuring transparency, and promoting collaboration within the project team. It serves as a common understanding between stakeholders and team members, enabling effective communication and alignment of goals. In conclusion, a project baseline in Agile Process and Project Management disciplines represents the initial reference point that encompasses the scope, schedule, cost, and quality of a project. It provides a benchmark for assessing progress, managing changes, and ensuring successful project delivery.

Project Charter

A project charter is a formal document that provides a clear description of the project's objectives, scope, deliverables, and stakeholders. It serves as the foundation for the project by outlining the project's purpose and aligning it with the organization's overall goals.

In the context of Agile Process and Project Management disciplines, the project charter takes on a slightly different role. Agile methodologies, such as Scrum, emphasize flexibility, collaboration, and iterative development. Therefore, the project charter is often less detailed and static compared to traditional project management approaches.

Instead of a lengthy document, the Agile project charter is usually a concise statement that captures the project's high-level goals and the key success criteria. It describes the project's vision in a way that enables the Agile team to align their efforts and make informed decisions throughout the project's lifecycle.

The Agile project charter may include a brief description of the project's scope, identifying the major features or functionalities that are expected to be developed. It may also outline the project's timeline and budgetary constraints. However, the emphasis is on flexibility and adaptability, allowing for changes in requirements and priorities as the project progresses.

Furthermore, the Agile project charter typically identifies the project's key stakeholders, including the product owner, Scrum Master, and development team. It also establishes the initial prioritization of the project's backlog, ensuring that the team focuses on delivering the highest value features first.

In summary, the Agile project charter is a concise document that acts as a guiding principle for the Agile team. It communicates the project's vision, goals, and initial planning, while allowing for flexibility and adaptability as the team embraces Agile methodologies.

Project Closeout Checklist

A project closeout checklist is a tool used in Agile Process and Project Management disciplines to ensure that all necessary tasks and activities are completed before officially closing a project.

The checklist serves as a systematic guide for project managers and team members to follow, ensuring that no essential actions or documentation are overlooked. It helps ensure that all loose ends are tied up and all deliverables and requirements have been met.

Project Closeout Phase

The Project Closeout Phase in the context of Agile Process and Project Management disciplines refers to the final stage of a project where all its remaining activities, tasks, and deliverables are completed and finalized. This phase encompasses the necessary steps to formally bring the project to a close and ensure that all project objectives and scope have been achieved.

During this phase, the project team conducts a thorough review of the project to assess its overall success, analyze lessons learned, and identify opportunities for improvement in future projects. The team also ensures that all project documentation, such as final reports, documentation of completed tasks, and project artifacts, are properly archived and stored for future reference.

In the Agile Process, the Project Closeout Phase may also involve conducting a retrospective to evaluate the team's performance and identify areas for improvement in Agile practices and processes. This retrospective allows the team to reflect on their experience and feedback, enabling them to continuously improve their work and enhance their overall performance in future projects.

Overall, the Project Closeout Phase is a critical stage in project management as it marks the official end of the project and ensures that all loose ends are tied up, all deliverables are completed, and all necessary documentation is compiled for reference. It serves as a final opportunity for the project team to assess their achievements, gather lessons learned, and improve their future project management endeavors.

Project Closure Phase

The Project Closure Phase is the final stage of the project where the team completes all the necessary activities to officially close the project. In the context of Agile Process, project closure involves evaluating the project's success and delivering a retrospective of the team's performance. This phase ensures that all project objectives have been met and provides an opportunity to reflect on lessons learned and identify areas for improvement.

In Agile Project Management disciplines, the Project Closure Phase includes the following key activities:

1. Final Deliverables: The team ensures that all project deliverables have been completed and meet the agreed-upon criteria for acceptance. This includes documentation, software, and any other artifacts produced during the project.

2. Stakeholder Communication: The team communicates with all stakeholders to inform them of the project's closure. This includes providing a summary of the project's outcomes, sharing lessons learned, and acknowledging the contributions of team members and stakeholders.

3. Post-Implementation Review: The team conducts a comprehensive review of the project to evaluate its success and identify areas for improvement. This review includes assessing whether project objectives were achieved, examining the effectiveness of Agile practices used, and identifying any challenges or issues encountered during the project.

4. Knowledge Transfer: The team ensures that knowledge gained throughout the project is captured and shared with relevant stakeholders. This may involve documenting processes, creating training materials, and organizing knowledge-sharing sessions.

5. Celebration and Closure: The team celebrates the successful completion of the project, recognizing the efforts and achievements of individuals and the team as a whole. This signifies the formal closure of the project and sets the stage for future endeavors.

Project Closure Report

A project closure report is a formal document that summarizes the overall outcome and experiences gained from executing a project within the context of the Agile Process and Project Management disciplines.

It provides a comprehensive account of the completed project, including the objectives, scope, deliverables, timeline, and key milestones achieved. The report also evaluates the project's success against predefined metrics and identifies any deviations or challenges encountered during its execution.

Additionally, the closure report assesses the effectiveness of the Agile process in achieving project goals, highlighting the methodologies and techniques utilized. It outlines the lessons learned, best practices, and recommended improvements for future projects.

Furthermore, the report documents the project team's performance, including their roles, responsibilities, and contributions. It recognizes individual and collective achievements, highlighting areas where performance exceeded expectations and acknowledging any notable contributions or challenges faced by team members.

Overall, the project closure report serves as a valuable reference for future projects and provides stakeholders with a comprehensive overview of the project's success, challenges, and outcomes within the Agile Process and Project Management disciplines.

Project Closure

Project closure refers to the formal process of ending a project in the Agile Process and Project Management disciplines. It involves conducting various activities to ensure that all project deliverables are completed, documented, and handed over to the relevant stakeholders.

During project closure, the Agile team conducts a thorough review and analysis of the project's success against the defined objectives and timeline. This includes assessing whether the project has achieved its intended goals, met the customer's expectations, and adhered to the Agile principles and practices.

The primary objectives of project closure in Agile are to evaluate the project's overall performance, identify and document lessons learned, and generate feedback for continuous improvement. This feedback is crucial for future projects and can help refine the organization's Agile practices and methodologies.

Additionally, project closure involves finalizing all financial aspects of the project, such as budget reconciliation and resource utilization. It also includes archiving project documentation, ensuring that all necessary information and artifacts are preserved for future reference.

Furthermore, project closure in Agile entails releasing project resources, both human and material, and assessing their performance during the project. This evaluation helps in recognizing team members' contributions and identifying areas where additional training or support may be needed.

Overall, project closure is a crucial step in the Agile Process and Project Management disciplines as it wraps up the project, captures valuable insights, and provides the groundwork for future projects.

Project Communication Plan Template

A project communication plan is a formal document that outlines how communication will be managed throughout the duration of a project. It serves as a reference for team members to understand the communication protocols and processes to follow. In the context of Agile Process and Project Management disciplines, a project communication plan plays a vital role in facilitating effective and efficient communication within the team and with stakeholders.

Agile projects emphasize the importance of open and transparent communication among team members, as well as with customers and other stakeholders. The communication plan in Agile projects focuses on ensuring that information flows freely and is shared in a timely manner. It defines the channels and frequency of communication, the roles and responsibilities of the project team, and the methods for resolving any communication issues that may arise.

Project Communication Plan

A project communication plan is a formal document that outlines the communication strategies and channels to be used throughout the duration of a project. In the context of Agile process and project management disciplines, the communication plan serves as a crucial tool to ensure effective and timely communication among all project stakeholders.

The Agile methodology emphasizes collaboration, flexibility, and continuous feedback. Therefore, the communication plan in an Agile project is designed to support these principles by promoting frequent and transparent communication. It establishes clear guidelines for how information will be shared, who should be involved in the communication, and which communication channels are most appropriate for different types of messages.

Project Constraints

Project constraints, within the context of Agile Process and Project Management disciplines, refer to the limitations or boundaries that impact the project's execution, scope, resources, and schedule. These constraints act as predefined factors that have a direct influence on how the project is planned, developed, and delivered.

There are typically three main types of project constraints:

- Time Constraints: These constraints focus on the duration and deadlines of the project. It includes fixed start and end dates, predefined milestones, and time availability of resources. Agile methods emphasize the importance of fixed iteration lengths to ensure constant delivery of value.

- Resource Constraints: These constraints revolve around the limited resources, such as budget, personnel, equipment, and materials, available for the project. Agile processes aim to optimize resource utilization by enabling self-organizing teams and minimizing dependencies.

- Scope Constraints: These constraints define the boundaries and requirements of the project. They include the features, functionalities, and deliverables that need to be included within the project scope. Agile methodologies encourage flexibility and iterative development, allowing scope adjustments based on customer feedback and changing market conditions.

Agile Project Management uses various techniques, such as backlog prioritization, iterative planning, and frequent stakeholder collaboration, to effectively manage these constraints and deliver successful outcomes. By continuously adapting and responding to change, Agile teams can mitigate the negative impact of constraints and maximize value creation within the given limitations.

Project Governance Framework

A Project Governance Framework is a structured set of policies, processes, and procedures that provide guidance and direction for managing projects in an Agile process and Project Management disciplines.

It defines the roles, responsibilities, and decision-making authority within the project management team, ensuring the project is aligned with organizational objectives and stakeholders' expectations.

The framework encompasses various key elements, including project governance structure, project lifecycle management, reporting and communication mechanisms, risk and issue management, decision-making processes, and performance measurement metrics.

Within an Agile context, the framework supports the principles of collaboration, self-organization, and iterative development. It promotes transparency, accountability, and adaptability to manage projects effectively in a dynamic and evolving environment.

The framework outlines the governance body's composition and their respective roles, such as the steering committee, product owner, scrum master, and project manager. It sets guidelines for effective communication, regular reviews, and feedback loops to ensure continuous improvement.

The Project Governance Framework also defines the project management processes, including planning, scheduling, prioritization, and resource allocation, to ensure efficient utilization of resources and timely delivery of project deliverables.

Overall, the Project Governance Framework allows organizations to establish a consistent and standardized approach to project management in Agile processes, enabling effective decision-making, risk mitigation, and successful project outcomes.

Project Governance Structure

The project governance structure in the context of Agile Process and Project Management disciplines refers to the framework and set of practices that ensure effective decision-making, accountability, and control in an Agile project. Agile projects emphasize collaboration, flexibility, and adaptability, and the governance structure must align with these principles. It provides guidance on how decisions are made, who is responsible for making them, and how project activities are monitored and controlled. The governance structure typically includes three key components: the project team, the project owner, and the project stakeholders. The project team consists of cross-functional members who work together to deliver the project objectives. The project owner is responsible for defining and prioritizing the project requirements and ensuring that the team stays focused on delivering value to the customer. The project stakeholders, including executives, customers, and other relevant parties, have an interest in the project and provide feedback and support throughout its lifecycle. The governance structure facilitates communication and collaboration among these three components. Regular meetings, such as daily stand-ups and sprint retrospectives, enable the team to discuss progress, identify issues, and make decisions collectively. The project owner acts as the central point of contact and provides guidance and direction to the team. The stakeholders are engaged through regular updates and involvement in key decision points. The Agile governance structure also includes mechanisms for monitoring and controlling the project. This may include visual boards, such as kanban or scrum boards, which provide visibility into the progress of the work. Regular reviews are conducted to assess the project's performance, identify areas for improvement, and make necessary adjustments. In summary, the project governance structure in Agile Process and Project Management disciplines establishes clear roles, responsibilities, and communication channels to ensure effective decision-making, accountability, and control in an Agile project. It promotes collaboration, flexibility, and adaptability, enabling the team to deliver value iteratively and incrementally.

Project Governance

Project Governance in Agile Process and Project Management disciplines refers to the framework and processes that ensure effective decision-making, accountability, and control over projects in an organization. It provides the structure and guidelines for managing projects, ensuring alignment with organizational objectives and strategies.

In an Agile environment, project governance focuses on enabling the iterative and collaborative nature of Agile methodologies while ensuring compliance with organizational policies, standards, and regulatory requirements. It encompasses the roles, responsibilities, and decision-making processes necessary to deliver successful projects.

Project Initiation Document (PID) Template

A Project Initiation Document (PID) is a formal document that defines the initial objectives, scope, and constraints of a project. It is an essential part of project management, providing a clear and concise overview of what the project aims to achieve, how it will be executed, and the resources required to successfully deliver it.

In the Agile process, the PID acts as a reference point and serves as a starting point for the project. It outlines the project's goals and objectives, identifies key stakeholders, defines the project's scope, and establishes the project team's roles and responsibilities. The PID also includes a high-level analysis of risks and assumptions, as well as a preliminary timeline and budget.

The PID is a dynamic document that evolves throughout the project's lifecycle. It serves as a communication tool between the project team, stakeholders, and other relevant parties. It is used to align everyone's expectations, provide clarity on the project's purpose and deliverables, and ensure there is a shared understanding of the project's requirements and constraints.

Overall, a well-written and comprehensive PID is crucial for successful project initiation. It helps minimize misunderstandings, sets realistic expectations, and provides a solid foundation for effective project planning and execution.

Project Initiation Document (PID)

A Project Initiation Document (PID) is a formal document that serves as a starting point for a project in the context of Agile Process and Project Management disciplines. It outlines the objectives, scope, deliverables, timeline, and budget of the project. The PID defines the project's vision, goals, and desired outcomes.

In an Agile environment, the PID is usually a lightweight document that provides the necessary information to get the project started. It is created collaboratively by the project team, including the project manager, product owner, and stakeholders.

The PID typically includes the following sections:

- Project Overview: This section provides a high-level description of the project, including its purpose and objectives.

- Scope: This section defines the boundaries and extent of the project. It outlines what will be included and excluded from the project.

- Deliverables: This section lists the tangible outputs that the project will produce. It clearly defines what will be delivered to the stakeholders.

- Timeline: This section outlines the project's timeline, including key milestones and delivery dates. It provides a roadmap for the project's execution.

- Budget: This section details the project's budget, including estimated costs and any financial constraints that need to be considered.

- Stakeholders: This section identifies the key stakeholders involved in the project and their roles and responsibilities.

The PID serves as a reference point throughout the project and is used to ensure that everyone involved is on the same page. It helps to align expectations and provides a common understanding of the project's objectives and constraints.

Overall, the PID is an essential document that plays a crucial role in the successful initiation and execution of a project in an Agile environment.

Project Integration

Project integration refers to the process of coordinating and consolidating various components of a project in order to ensure the smooth execution and delivery of the project's objectives. This process is an essential aspect of project management, particularly in the context of Agile methodology.

In the Agile process, project integration involves the seamless integration and collaboration of different teams, stakeholders, and project components to achieve a unified vision and goal. It encompasses the alignment of project goals, requirements, timelines, resources, and deliverables.

Project Justification

Project Justification is the process of evaluating and determining the rationale or validity of a project. In the context of the Agile Process and Project Management disciplines, project justification serves as a critical step in project initiation and planning.

Agile Process emphasizes the importance of delivering value to the customer and continuously adapting to changing requirements. Before initiating a project within the Agile framework, it is essential to ensure that the project is justified and aligned with the business objectives. Project justification helps in assessing the feasibility, viability, and potential benefits of the project.

Project Life Cycle Models

A project life cycle model refers to a framework that outlines the various stages or phases that a project undergoes from initiation to closure. It provides a structured approach to project management, enabling organizations to plan, execute, and control project activities systematically. In the context of Agile processes and project management disciplines, two commonly used project life cycle models are the Waterfall model and the Agile model.

The Waterfall model follows a sequential approach, where each phase of the project is completed before moving on to the next. It consists of distinct phases, including requirement gathering, design, development, testing, deployment, and maintenance. This model is commonly used when project requirements are well-defined and unlikely to change significantly. However, it can be inflexible and may not be suitable for projects where requirements are likely to evolve.

In contrast, the Agile model follows an iterative and incremental approach, where the project is

97

divided into smaller time-bound iterations called sprints. Each sprint typically lasts for 1-4 weeks and involves requirements gathering, design, development, testing, and review. The Agile model emphasizes collaboration, adaptability, and continuous improvement. It allows for changing requirements and encourages customer feedback throughout the project's lifecycle.

Project Life Cycle Phases

In the context of Agile Process and Project Management disciplines, the Project Life Cycle consists of a series of phases, each with its own set of activities and deliverables. These phases provide structure and guidance to teams, ensuring that projects are executed efficiently and successfully. While the number and names of these phases may vary depending on the specific methodology or framework used, they generally include the following: 1. Initiation: This phase involves defining the project's objectives, scope, and stakeholders. It includes activities such as conducting a feasibility study, creating project charters, and identifying high-level requirements. 2. Planning: During this phase, the team develops a comprehensive project plan that outlines the detailed tasks, resources, and schedule. It includes activities such as creating a work breakdown structure, estimating effort and cost, and identifying and mitigating risks. 3. Execution: This phase is where the actual work is done. Teams work collaboratively to complete the project tasks while continuously engaging with stakeholders for feedback and adjustments. 4. Monitoring and Controlling: Throughout the project, progress is monitored, and any deviations from the plan are identified and addressed. This phase involves activities such as tracking project metrics, conducting regular status meetings, and applying changes as necessary. 5. Closure: In this final phase, the project is formally completed and closed. It includes activities such as conducting post-project reviews, capturing lessons learned, and transitioning deliverables to the operations team. Each phase has its own specific objectives, inputs, outputs, and activities. The Agile approach emphasizes iterative and incremental development, allowing for flexibility and adaptability throughout the project life cycle.

Project Life Cycle

The project life cycle refers to the series of phases that a project goes through from its initiation to its closure. It is a framework that provides structure and guidance to project management teams, ensuring that projects are planned, executed, and delivered successfully.

In Agile Process, the project life cycle follows an iterative and incremental approach, with each iteration being referred to as a sprint. The project is divided into multiple sprints, each of which has a fixed duration and delivers a potentially shippable increment of the product. The Agile project life cycle consists of the following phases:

1. Initiation: In this phase, the project objectives, scope, and stakeholders are identified. A high-level plan is created, and the project team is formed.

2. Planning: The project plan is developed, including detailed requirements, tasks, and estimates. The team also defines the project's timeline, budget, and resources.

3. Execution: The project plan is put into action during this phase. The development team works on the project tasks, and regular communication and collaboration take place.

4. Monitoring and Control: The project's progress is monitored and measured against the plan. Issues and risks are identified and managed, ensuring that the project stays on track.

5. Closure: The project is formally closed, and the final product is delivered to the stakeholders. Lessons learned are captured for future reference, and the team celebrates the project's success.

The Agile project life cycle is highly flexible and adaptable, allowing for changes and adjustments to be made at each iteration. This approach enables continuous improvement and ensures that the project delivers value to the stakeholders.

Project Management Information System (PMIS)

A Project Management Information System (PMIS) is a software tool or system that is used to facilitate and enhance project management activities in the Agile Process and Project Management disciplines. It is designed to support project managers, team members, and other stakeholders by providing a centralized platform for planning, tracking, and evaluating project activities.

The primary goal of a PMIS in the Agile Process and Project Management disciplines is to improve communication, collaboration, and decision-making. It provides real-time visibility into project progress, status, and key performance indicators, such as budget, schedule, and resources. This enables project managers and team members to make informed decisions and adapt their plans and strategies accordingly.

Project Management Office (PMO)

A Project Management Office (PMO) is a centralized department within an organization that establishes and maintains project management standards, practices, and methodologies. In the context of Agile Process and Project Management disciplines, the PMO plays a crucial role in providing guidance, support, and oversight to Agile teams.

The primary function of a PMO in an Agile environment is to foster collaboration and ensure alignment with organizational strategies and goals. The PMO achieves this by facilitating the adoption and implementation of Agile methodologies, such as Scrum or Kanban, across projects and teams. It provides Agile training and coaching to stakeholders, helping them understand the principles and values that underpin Agile practices.

The PMO also acts as a knowledge hub for Agile best practices, enabling teams to learn from each other and continuously improve their Agile processes. It establishes frameworks for estimating, planning, and tracking Agile projects, promoting transparency and accountability. The PMO may develop standardized Agile templates, tools, and dashboards to facilitate communication, reporting, and decision-making at various levels of the organization.

Furthermore, the PMO serves as a governance body, ensuring that Agile projects adhere to organizational policies, procedures, and regulatory requirements. It provides project portfolio management oversight, helping prioritize and align Agile initiatives with business strategies. Additionally, the PMO may perform audits and reviews to identify areas for improvement and guide the implementation of lessons learned.

In summary, the PMO in an Agile context establishes and maintains project management standards, supports Agile teams through training and coaching, fosters collaboration and continuous improvement, provides governance and oversight, and ensures alignment with organizational strategies and goals.

Project Manager

Agile Process:

Agile process is a project management approach that emphasizes flexibility, adaptability, and collaboration in order to deliver high-quality software products. It is characterized by iterative and incremental project cycles which allow for frequent feedback and adjustments, ensuring that the final product meets the customer's requirements and expectations. Agile process aims to maximize customer value by continuously delivering functional software.

Project Management Disciplines:

Project management disciplines refer to the various methodologies and tools used to plan, execute, monitor, and control projects, ensuring that they are completed successfully. These disciplines encompass a wide range of activities, including project initiation, scope definition, resource allocation, risk management, and communication. Project management disciplines are designed to ensure that projects are delivered on time, within budget, and according to the desired quality standards. They provide a structured framework for managing projects, enabling project managers to effectively coordinate and align team efforts, mitigate risks, and respond to changes in project requirements.

Project Office

A Project Office, in the context of Agile Process and Project Management disciplines, refers to a centralized unit or team responsible for providing support and guidance to project teams. Its main objective is to ensure successful project execution by establishing and enforcing standard processes, procedures, and best practices across the organization.

The Project Office plays a crucial role in promoting consistency, efficiency, and transparency in project management. It serves as a hub for project-related information, fostering collaboration and communication among team members. It also acts as a central repository for project documentation, tools, and templates, enabling teams to access and leverage valuable resources.

Within the Agile framework, the Project Office adapts its practices to align with the principles and values of Agile methodologies. It embraces flexibility, adaptability, and a focus on delivering value to the customer. The Project Office supports Agile project teams by facilitating the use of Agile tools and frameworks such as Scrum or Kanban.

The Project Office also plays a critical role in enabling continuous improvement and learning within the organization. It collects and analyzes project data and metrics to identify areas for improvement and make data-driven decisions. It fosters a culture of feedback and learning, encouraging project teams to reflect on their performance and incorporate lessons learned into future projects.

Project Portfolio Management (PPM)

Project Portfolio Management (PPM) is a strategic approach that encompasses the Agile Process and Project Management disciplines. It involves the centralized management of multiple projects, programs, and product portfolios to ensure alignment with organizational strategies and objectives.

In an Agile context, PPM aims to optimize the value and impact of projects by prioritizing and managing the project portfolio based on business goals and customer needs. It provides a framework for decision-making, resource allocation, and communication across project teams, stakeholders, and senior executives.

Project Portfolio

A project portfolio in the context of Agile process and Project Management disciplines refers to a collection of projects or initiatives managed by an organization or team. It encompasses a strategic approach to managing and prioritizing multiple projects to achieve strategic goals and objectives.

The project portfolio provides a holistic view of all ongoing and proposed projects within the organization. It includes various project-related information such as project goals, timelines, resources, risks, and financials. The portfolio enables decision-makers to evaluate and prioritize projects based on their alignment with the organization's objectives, available resources, and potential benefits.

By using Agile principles and practices, project portfolio management allows organizations to adapt to changing priorities and uncertainties. Agile methodologies prioritize collaboration, flexibility, and iterative development, which help project managers and teams to respond quickly to changes in business needs and customer requirements.

Effective project portfolio management involves continuous monitoring and evaluation of projects to ensure alignment with business strategies, optimize resource utilization, and mitigate risks. It helps stakeholders to identify potential conflicts or dependencies between projects and facilitates informed decision-making regarding resource allocation, project prioritization, and risk mitigation strategies.

Overall, project portfolio management in the Agile context enables organizations to better manage their project portfolios, improve project success rates, and achieve business goals through adaptable planning, resource optimization, and alignment with strategic objectives.

Project Quality Metrics Dashboard

A Project Quality Metrics Dashboard is a visual tool used in Agile process and project management disciplines to measure, track, and communicate the quality metrics and performance of a project. It provides a centralized view of key quality indicators and metrics, allowing project teams to make data-driven decisions and take necessary actions to ensure project quality.

The dashboard typically includes various metrics such as defect density, test coverage, customer satisfaction, rework effort, and code complexity. These metrics are collected throughout the project lifecycle and are presented in a simple and intuitive format, usually in the form of charts, graphs, or tables.

The purpose of the Project Quality Metrics Dashboard is to provide stakeholders, including project managers, Scrum Masters, and development teams, with a clear and real-time understanding of the quality status of the project. It enables them to identify areas of improvement, measure the effectiveness of quality management activities, and assess the project's overall health and progress.

By regularly reviewing the quality metrics displayed on the dashboard, project teams can proactively address any quality-related issues and optimize their processes to deliver high-quality products or services. The dashboard serves as a communication tool, fostering transparency and collaboration among team members, and promoting a culture of continuous improvement.

In conclusion, the Project Quality Metrics Dashboard is an essential component of Agile project management, providing a visual representation of quality metrics to facilitate decision-making and foster a quality-conscious mindset within the project team.

Project Quality Metrics

Project Quality Metrics are quantitative and qualitative measures used to evaluate the performance of a project in terms of meeting predefined quality standards. In the context of Agile Process and Project Management disciplines, these metrics play a crucial role in continuously monitoring and improving the quality of software development projects.

In Agile, the focus is on delivering value to the customer through iterative development cycles. Project Quality Metrics help in assessing the effectiveness of these iterations by providing valuable insights into the quality of the software product being developed. These metrics help in identifying areas of improvement, detecting potential risks, and ensuring that the project meets the expected quality standards.

Project Reporting

Project Reporting refers to the process of documenting and communicating the progress, status, and outcomes of a project in a structured and transparent manner. It is an essential component of Agile Process and Project Management disciplines, providing stakeholders with valuable insights into the project's performance and helping to ensure alignment with business goals.

Agile Project Reporting emphasizes frequent and meaningful communication, enabling project teams to make data-driven decisions and adapt their approach based on real-time feedback. It involves capturing and sharing relevant information related to project scope, timelines, budget, risks, and quality. This information is typically presented through various reports and dashboards that are accessible to all relevant stakeholders.

Through Project Reporting, Agile teams can track and visualize progress, identify and address potential bottlenecks or issues, and foster collaboration and transparency. It enables stakeholders to have a clear understanding of the project's health and enables them to provide timely guidance and support.

Effective Project Reporting in Agile Process and Project Management disciplines should be concise, accurate, and easily understandable. It should focus on key performance indicators, such as burn-down charts, sprint velocity, and backlog status, to provide a holistic view of the project's progress. Additionally, it should facilitate open communication and encourage feedback and discussion to promote continuous improvement and learning within the project team.

In conclusion, Project Reporting plays a vital role in Agile Process and Project Management by enabling teams to track progress, identify and address issues, and facilitate collaboration and transparency. It ensures that stakeholders have the necessary information to make informed decisions and support the successful delivery of the project.

Project Risk Analysis

An agile project risk analysis refers to the process of identifying and assessing potential risks that could impact the successful completion of an agile project. It is an essential component of agile project management disciplines, which focus on adaptability and continuous improvement.

Risk analysis in the context of agile projects involves identifying both internal and external risks that may arise during the project's lifecycle. Internal risks can include factors such as resource constraints, skill gaps within the team, or changes in project scope. External risks may arise from factors such as market conditions, technology dependencies, or legal and regulatory changes.

The purpose of conducting a risk analysis is to proactively anticipate potential risks and develop strategies to mitigate or minimize their impact. This involves considering the likelihood of each risk occurring, as well as the potential impact it may have on project objectives. Agile project teams typically prioritize risks based on their severity and likelihood of occurrence, then allocate resources and develop contingency plans accordingly.

By integrating risk analysis into the agile project management process, teams can improve project outcomes by being prepared for potential roadblocks and obstacles. This approach allows for flexibility and adaptability, as risk analysis helps to identify areas where adjustments or changes may be necessary to keep the project on track.

Project Risk Assessment Matrix

A Project Risk Assessment Matrix is a tool used in the Agile Process and Project Management disciplines to help identify and evaluate project risks. It provides a systematic approach for assessing the likelihood and impact of potential risks on a project.

The matrix consists of a grid that categorizes risks based on their likelihood and impact. The likelihood represents the chances of a risk occurring, while the impact represents the potential consequences if the risk were to materialize. The grid is typically divided into different levels or ratings for both likelihood and impact, ranging from low to high.

The purpose of the matrix is to prioritize risks so that the most critical ones can be addressed first. Risks that have a high likelihood and high impact are deemed high-priority and require immediate attention, while those with a low likelihood and low impact may be considered low-priority and can be monitored or mitigated at a later stage.

By using the Project Risk Assessment Matrix, project teams can proactively identify and manage risks, enabling them to take appropriate actions to minimize their negative impact. It also facilitates communication and collaboration among team members and stakeholders, as it provides a clear visual representation of the risks associated with the project.

Project Sponsor

A project sponsor, in the context of Agile Process and Project Management disciplines, is an individual or a group that provides the necessary resources, support, and direction for a project. They have a vested interest in the success of the project and are responsible for ensuring that it aligns with organizational objectives and delivers the expected value.

The project sponsor plays a crucial role in Agile project management by setting the project vision, defining the business objectives, and prioritizing the project backlog. They have the authority to make key decisions, allocate resources, and remove any impediments that hinder the project's progress.

Project Sponsorship Agreement

A project sponsorship agreement in the context of Agile Process and Project Management disciplines is a formal document that outlines the responsibilities, expectations, and commitments between a project sponsor and the project team.

The agreement serves as a mutual understanding between the sponsor and the project team, ensuring alignment on the project's objectives, scope, timeline, budget, and success criteria. It facilitates effective communication, collaboration, and decision-making throughout the project's lifecycle.

Sponsorship in Agile processes is crucial as sponsors play a vital role in providing guidance, support, and resources to ensure project success. They are responsible for securing project buy-in from stakeholders, setting the strategic direction, and making critical decisions when needed. The project sponsor also takes on the role of meeting the project's needs and removing any roadblocks that may impede progress.

The project sponsorship agreement typically includes key elements such as the project's purpose and goals, the sponsor's responsibilities, the project team's composition, the project's budget and timeline, communication channels, and escalation procedures. It may also include specific metrics or indicators to measure project progress and success.

By formalizing the project sponsor's role and responsibilities, the agreement helps foster a collaborative and accountable environment, enhancing the chances of project success. It provides clarity and guidance to both the sponsor and the project team, enabling them to work together efficiently and achieve the project's desired outcomes.

Quality Assurance Audit Plan

A Quality Assurance Audit Plan is a formal document that outlines the procedures and criteria used to assess the quality of a product or process in the context of Agile Process and Project Management disciplines. It serves as a roadmap for conducting audits, ensuring that best practices are followed, and identifying areas for improvement.

In an Agile environment, where projects are executed incrementally with frequent iterations, it is crucial to have a well-defined Quality Assurance Audit Plan. This plan provides a systematic approach to assess the compliance of project deliverables with quality standards and ensures that all relevant aspects are thoroughly examined.

Quality Assurance Audits

Quality Assurance Audits in the context of Agile Process and Project Management disciplines refer to systematic evaluations and assessments conducted to ensure adherence to quality standards, best practices, and project requirements throughout the entire project lifecycle.

These audits play a crucial role in Agile projects as they help identify any deviations or non-compliance with established quality criteria. They are conducted at various stages, such as planning, execution, and delivery, to identify risks, issues, and areas for improvement.

During the planning phase, Quality Assurance Audits involve reviewing project documentation, such as requirements, user stories, and acceptance criteria. This ensures that the project team has a clear understanding of quality expectations, and that proper planning and risk mitigation strategies are in place.

During the execution phase, audits focus on progress monitoring, adherence to Agile principles, and adherence to project management techniques. They evaluate team collaboration, communication, and compliance with Agile ceremonies and tools, such as daily stand-ups, sprint planning, and sprint reviews. These audits provide an opportunity to identify potential bottlenecks, impediments, and process inefficiencies, enabling teams to take corrective actions promptly.

At the delivery stage, audits ensure that the final product meets all quality acceptance criteria and meets customer expectations. They involve detailed inspections and testing to verify that the implemented solution aligns with the defined scope and requirements.

Overall, Quality Assurance Audits in Agile Process and Project Management disciplines contribute to enhancing overall project quality, identifying potential risks, and fostering continuous improvement throughout the project lifecycle.

Quality Assurance

Quality Assurance (QA) in the context of Agile Process and Project Management disciplines refers to the systematic and planned activities implemented to ensure that the deliverables produced during a project meet the defined quality standards. QA is an integral part of the Agile methodology, where it focuses on preventing defects rather than detecting them at a later stage.

The primary goal of QA in Agile is to proactively identify and address quality-related issues throughout the entire project lifecycle. This involves continuously monitoring the development processes, identifying potential risks and defects, and implementing appropriate measures to mitigate them. QA activities are performed by dedicated QA teams or individuals who work closely with the development team to ensure that the quality of the software or product being developed is maintained at all times.

Quality Control Chart

A Quality Control Chart is a visual representation of data, used in the Agile Process and Project Management disciplines, to monitor and control the quality of a product or process throughout its development. It provides a graphical display of variation in the data over time, allowing the team to identify and address any potential quality issues or deviations from the desired standards. The chart typically consists of a horizontal axis representing time or the order of the items being inspected, and a vertical axis representing the measured values or characteristics of the product or process being monitored. Data points are plotted on the chart to show the actual values or measurements taken at specific intervals. The QC chart helps the team to determine if the product or process is within control limits, which are predefined statistical boundaries indicating acceptable variation. If data points fall within these limits, it indicates that the quality of the product or process is stable and meets the desired standards. However, if data points exceed the control limits, it suggests that there are causes of variation that need to be investigated and addressed to improve the quality. In Agile Process and Project Management, QC charts are used as a tool for continuous monitoring and improvement. They enable the team to identify trends, patterns, and abnormalities in the quality metrics, facilitating timely corrective actions and preventing potential defects or deviations from customer requirements. By visually representing the quality data, the QC chart helps in making informed decisions and maintaining a high level of quality throughout the project.

Quality Control Measurements Standards

Quality Control Measurements Standards refer to a set of predetermined criteria and guidelines used in Agile Process and Project Management disciplines to ensure that the deliverables and processes of a project comply with the established quality expectations. These standards are applied throughout the project lifecycle to identify and rectify any deviations or non-conformances that may affect the overall quality of the project.

In Agile Process, quality control measurements standards play a crucial role in facilitating incremental and iterative development. They help teams monitor and assess the quality of their work at regular intervals, allowing them to identify and address any issues or defects early on. These standards often include metrics and key performance indicators (KPIs) that are used to measure and evaluate the quality of deliverables, such as software code or documentation.

Quality Control Measurements

Quality Control Measurements in the context of Agile Process and Project Management disciplines refer to the systematic activities and processes undertaken to ensure that the deliverables produced meet the predefined quality standards and requirements. These measurements are implemented as part of the quality control process, which aims to identify defects, errors, or deviations from the defined standards and implement corrective actions to improve the overall quality of the project.

Agile methodologies, such as Scrum or Kanban, emphasize the importance of constantly monitoring and evaluating the quality of the project deliverables throughout the development lifecycle. This is achieved through various quality control measurements, which include:

1. Automated Testing: Agile teams rely heavily on automated testing tools and frameworks to continuously test the software codebase. This helps identify any functional or regression issues early on, enabling quick resolution and preventing the accumulation of defects.

2. Peer Reviews: Regular peer code reviews and inspections are conducted to ensure the codebase aligns with coding standards, design patterns, and best practices. This collaborative approach helps identify and rectify any potential issues during the development process.

3. Continuous Integration and Deployment: Agile teams frequently integrate the individual components and deploy them to a testing or staging environment. This enables early detection of integration issues and provides stakeholders with a working prototype to validate against the project requirements.

By implementing these quality control measurements, Agile teams can proactively identify and address any quality-related issues, thus ensuring the final product meets the desired quality standards.

Quality Control

Quality Control is a critical part of the Agile Process and Project Management disciplines. It encompasses the activities and processes that ensure deliverables meet defined quality standards.

Within the Agile Process, Quality Control involves continuous evaluation of work products, such as software code or documentation, throughout the iteration. This evaluation ensures that the deliverables are complete, accurate, and adhere to the defined requirements and standards. It also involves identifying any defects or issues present in the deliverables, allowing for prompt resolution.

In Project Management, Quality Control focuses on ensuring that the final product meets the specified quality requirements. This includes defining the quality standards and metrics to be used, as well as implementing procedures and processes to assess and monitor the quality of the project deliverables. Quality Control activities can involve inspection, testing, and verification against the predetermined quality criteria.

By implementing effective Quality Control processes, Agile teams and Project Managers can detect and address quality issues early on. This allows for timely corrections and helps prevent defects from being carried forward into subsequent iterations or project phases. Additionally, Quality Control helps improve overall product quality, customer satisfaction, and the success of the project.

Quality Function Deployment (QFD) Matrix

Quality Function Deployment (QFD) Matrix, in the context of Agile Process and Project Management disciplines, is a structured approach that helps teams identify and prioritize customer requirements and align them with the project's technical capabilities. It is a powerful tool that enables the translation of customer needs into specific project goals and tasks.

The QFD Matrix consists of a grid that organizes customer requirements, project features, and technical specifications. The rows represent the customer requirements, while the columns represent the project features or technical specifications. The intersection points in the matrix provide a visual representation of the relationships and priorities between customer requirements and project features.

With an Agile approach, the QFD Matrix can be used iteratively throughout the project lifecycle to capture and incorporate evolving customer needs. In Agile methodologies, such as Scrum, the QFD Matrix can be utilized during Sprint Planning sessions to prioritize backlog items based on customer value and align them with the project's technical capabilities.

By using the QFD Matrix in an Agile context, project teams can ensure that they are focusing on delivering value to the customer by continuously refining and adapting the project goals and tasks. It facilitates collaboration and communication among team members, stakeholders, and customers, allowing for a more customer-centric and iterative approach to project management.

Quality Function Deployment (QFD)

Quality Function Deployment (QFD) is a systematic method used in Agile Process and Project Management disciplines to ensure that customer requirements are accurately translated into product or service attributes. It is a highly structured approach that focuses on understanding the voice of the customer and aligning it with the development process.

In Agile Process and Project Management, QFD involves a series of steps that start with gathering customer needs and expectations. This is typically done through interviews, surveys, and market research. These requirements are then analyzed and converted into technical specifications that can be used by the development team.

Once the customer requirements are identified, they are translated into prioritized product or service attributes that can be quantified and measured. This helps in setting clear goals and objectives for the development team. The QFD process ensures that these attributes are aligned with the overall project goals and objectives.

QFD in Agile Process and Project Management also involves the creation of a matrix known as the House of Quality. This matrix helps in visually mapping the relationships between customer requirements, product or service attributes, and engineering characteristics. It provides a structured way to prioritize and address customer needs in the development process.

The use of QFD in Agile Process and Project Management disciplines ensures that customer requirements are not only captured accurately but also incorporated into the development process. It helps in reducing the risk of developing products or services that do not meet customer expectations. By aligning customer needs with development goals, QFD improves the overall quality and success of Agile projects.

Quality Management Plan

A Quality Management Plan is a document that outlines the processes, procedures, and activities that will be implemented throughout the Agile Process and Project Management disciplines to ensure high-quality deliverables and customer satisfaction. It serves as a roadmap for the project team, providing guidance on how quality will be planned, monitored, and controlled.

The Quality Management Plan is a fundamental component of the overall project management process. It defines the quality objectives and standards that will be used to evaluate project deliverables and ensures that the project team has a clear understanding of what is expected in terms of quality.

The plan begins with an assessment of the project's quality requirements, including the identification of key stakeholders and their quality expectations. It then outlines the quality assurance and control activities that will be performed throughout the project lifecycle, such as design reviews, code inspections, and testing methodologies.

In addition, the Quality Management Plan outlines the roles and responsibilities of the project team members, including the Project Manager, Product Owner, Scrum Master, and other stakeholders. It also defines the communication channels and reporting mechanisms that will be used to track and monitor quality throughout the project.

By following the guidelines and practices outlined in the Quality Management Plan, Agile Process and Project Management disciplines can effectively manage and control quality, ensuring that deliverables meet or exceed customer expectations. This, in turn, increases customer satisfaction, reduces rework, and enhances the overall success of the project.

Quality Management

Quality Management in the context of Agile Process and Project Management disciplines refers to the systematic approach of planning, controlling, and improving the quality of deliverables throughout the project lifecycle. It encompasses activities that ensure that the project meets the specified requirements and fulfills the customer's expectations while continuously enhancing the overall quality of the project.

Agile Quality Management emphasizes the principles of collaboration, flexibility, and continuous improvement. It focuses on delivering high-quality products and services by embracing change, adapting to evolving requirements, and involving stakeholders at every stage of the project. Agile methodologies, such as Scrum and Kanban, provide frameworks that enable teams to deliver value incrementally, gather feedback, and respond promptly to changes.

The Agile Quality Management process comprises several key components. It includes establishing clear quality objectives, conducting frequent inspections and reviews, implementing continuous integration and automated testing, and utilizing customer feedback to drive improvements. Agile teams utilize various techniques and practices like Test-Driven Development (TDD), Behavior-Driven Development (BDD), and Continuous Delivery to ensure the quality and reliability of the project deliverables.

By embracing Agile Quality Management, organizations can reduce the risk of project failures, improve customer satisfaction, and achieve faster time to market. It fosters a culture of collaboration, transparency, and accountability, where all team members take ownership of the quality of their work and actively contribute to the overall project success.

Quality Metrics Baseline Report

A Quality Metrics Baseline Report is a formal document that is used in the context of Agile Process and Project Management disciplines to establish a set of performance measurements and benchmarks for evaluating the quality of a project or process. It provides a comprehensive overview of the quality metrics that will be used to assess the success and effectiveness of a project or process, and serves as a baseline reference point for future evaluations and improvements.

The report typically includes a combination of both quantitative and qualitative metrics, which are used to measure various aspects of quality such as customer satisfaction, defect rates, code quality, and delivery timeliness. These metrics are selected based on the specific needs and objectives of the project or process, and may be derived from industry standards, best practices, or customized to suit the unique requirements of the organization.

The purpose of the Quality Metrics Baseline Report is to establish a common understanding and agreement among stakeholders regarding the key quality indicators that will be monitored throughout the duration of the project or process. It provides a standardized framework for measuring and reporting on quality, and enables the project team to proactively identify areas of improvement and take corrective actions as necessary.

By establishing a baseline measurement of quality at the start of the project or process, the report allows for ongoing monitoring and measurement of progress, and facilitates the identification of trends and patterns over time. This information can inform decision-making, drive continuous improvement, and help ensure that quality objectives are met or exceeded.

Quality Metrics Baseline

Quality Metrics Baseline refers to the established set of measurable criteria used to assess the quality of a product or project within Agile Process and Project Management disciplines. These metrics serve as a standardized benchmark against which the performance, progress, and success of a project can be evaluated.

In an Agile environment, where iterative development and continuous improvement are central, quality metrics play a crucial role in monitoring and managing project quality. These metrics are typically defined and agreed upon by the project team during the planning phase, and they help to guide the team's efforts towards delivering a high-quality product.

Quality Metrics

Quality metrics in the context of Agile Process and Project Management disciplines refer to the quantitative measures used to assess and evaluate the quality of deliverables, processes, and outcomes within an Agile project. These metrics provide objective data that can be used to track progress, identify areas for improvement, and make informed decisions to ensure high-quality outcomes.

One commonly used quality metric in Agile project management is the Defect Density, which measures the number of defects found per unit of the product or code. This metric helps the team assess the product's overall quality and identify areas of improvement in the development process. Another important metric is the Cycle Time, which measures the time taken to complete a user story from start to finish. This metric helps evaluate the efficiency and productivity of the development team.

Other quality metrics in Agile include Test Coverage, which measures the percentage of code covered by automated tests, and Velocity, which measures the amount of work completed in each iteration. These metrics provide valuable insights into the quality of the software being developed and the team's ability to deliver value consistently.

By tracking and analyzing quality metrics, Agile teams can identify patterns, trends, and potential risks related to the project's quality. This enables them to take proactive measures to improve quality throughout the project lifecycle. Quality metrics also promote transparency, facilitate effective communication, and help stakeholders make data-driven decisions.

Quality Review

The Agile Process in project management is a set of principles and practices used to manage a project in a flexible and iterative manner. It focuses on delivering value to the customer through continuous collaboration, adaptation, and improvement. In Agile, projects are divided into small increments called iterations or sprints, with each iteration delivering a potentially shippable product.

Agile project management emphasizes the importance of responding to change, rather than following a rigid plan. It promotes open communication and frequent feedback between the project team and stakeholders, to ensure the project is on track and delivering the desired outcomes. Agile relies on self-organizing and cross-functional teams, where members work collaboratively to achieve project goals.

Quality Standards Compliance Checklist

A quality standards compliance checklist in the context of Agile Process and Project Management disciplines refers to a comprehensive document that outlines the specific criteria and requirements that need to be met in order to ensure that a project adheres to the established quality standards. This checklist serves as a tool for project managers and teams to assess the level of compliance and identify any areas that need improvement.

With Agile methodologies, the focus is on delivering value to customers through iterative and incremental development. The quality standards compliance checklist helps teams ensure that the project remains aligned with these principles. It covers various aspects such as product functionality, performance, security, user experience, and regulatory compliance.

Quality Standards Compliance

Quality Standards Compliance refers to the process of ensuring that a project or product adheres to established quality standards. In the context of Agile Process and Project Management disciplines, it involves continuously assessing and verifying that the developed software or deliverables meet the defined quality criteria and standards.

Agile processes emphasize the importance of delivering high-quality products to customers in shorter iterations or sprints. Quality standards compliance plays a crucial role in achieving this by identifying and rectifying any quality issues early in the development lifecycle. This approach helps in reducing rework, improving customer satisfaction, and enhancing overall project success.

Quality Standards

A quality standard refers to a predefined set of criteria or requirements that are established to determine the level of excellence or superiority of a product, process, or service. It serves as a benchmark or reference point against which performance, effectiveness, and efficiency can be measured or evaluated.

In the context of Agile Process and Project Management disciplines, quality standards play a crucial role in ensuring that the deliverables meet the expected level of quality. Agile methodologies emphasize the importance of delivering working software that satisfies customer requirements and expectations. Quality standards help guide the development team in producing high-quality software by setting clear expectations and defining the criteria for acceptance.

RACI Matrix

In the context of Agile Process and Project Management, a RACI Matrix is a tool used to clarify and define the roles and responsibilities of team members involved in a project. RACI stands for Responsible, Accountable, Consulted, and Informed, which are the four key roles identified in the matrix.

The RACI Matrix helps project teams establish clarity and alignment by clearly outlining who is responsible for completing specific tasks, who is accountable for the overall success of the project, who needs to be consulted for input or expertise, and who needs to be kept informed of project progress and decisions. This ensures that everyone involved in the project understands their role and can effectively contribute to its success.

The matrix is typically represented in a tabular format, with tasks or project deliverables listed on the left-hand side and the four roles (Responsible, Accountable, Consulted, and Informed) listed on the top. Each cell in the matrix is then filled with the appropriate role(s) for each task or deliverable.

The use of a RACI Matrix in Agile Process and Project Management allows for improved project planning, better collaboration, and increased accountability. It helps prevent confusion, duplication of efforts, and gaps in responsibility, ultimately leading to more efficient and successful project outcomes.

RACI-VS Matrix Template

The RACI-VS matrix is a project management tool commonly used in Agile processes to clarify and communicate roles and responsibilities within a project team. It helps ensure that everyone understands who is accountable, responsible, consulted, and informed for each task or deliverable.

RACI-VS stands for Responsible, Accountable, Consulted, Informed, and Verifies and Signatures. Each role or individual involved in the project is assigned one or more of these labels for each task or deliverable, making it clear what their role is in relation to that specific item.

RACI-VS Matrix

The RACI-VS matrix is a tool used in Agile Process and Project Management disciplines to clarify and define roles and responsibilities within a project. It helps to clearly assign tasks, activities, and decisions to specific individuals or groups, ensuring transparency and accountability throughout the project lifecycle. The acronym RACI-VS stands for Responsible, Accountable, Consulted, Informed, Verifier, and Support. These roles are assigned to project team members, stakeholders, and other relevant parties to outline their involvement and level of authority in various project activities. - Responsible (R): This role signifies the individual or group responsible for completing a specific task or activity. They are responsible for action and execution. - Accountable (A): The accountable role represents the individual or group ultimately responsible for the outcome or completion of a task or activity. They have the overall ownership and decision-making authority. - Consulted (C): The consulted role involves individuals or groups who provide input, guidance, or expertise in the decision-making process. They are consulted before a decision or action is taken. - Informed (I): The informed role includes individuals or groups who need to be kept informed about the progress, decisions, and outcomes of a task or activity. They are not directly involved in its execution but are provided with updates. - Verifier (V): The verifier role is responsible for ensuring the quality and accuracy of the completed task or activity. They verify that all requirements and standards have been met. - Support (S): The support role provides assistance, resources, or expertise to the responsible individual or group. They assist in completing the task or activity. The RACI-VS matrix is often represented in a matrix format, where tasks or activities are listed on one axis, and roles are listed on the other. This visual representation helps project teams understand their respective roles and responsibilities, fostering collaboration and synergy.

Regression Testing Strategy

Regression testing is a strategy employed within the Agile Process and Project Management disciplines to ensure that modifications or enhancements to a software system do not unintentionally introduce defects or regressions in existing functionalities. It involves retesting previously validated features or areas of the system to verify their continued correctness and stability after changes have been made.

This iterative testing approach aims to identify any unexpected behavior or issues that may arise due to the integration of new elements or modifications. It helps to mitigate the risk of inadvertently introducing defects in the software system while ensuring that the existing functionalities remain intact and perform as intended.

Regression Testing

Regression testing is a crucial process in the Agile Process and Project Management disciplines. It refers to the repetition of test cases that have been previously executed to ensure that any changes or modifications made to the software did not introduce new defects or negatively impact existing functionalities. In the Agile framework, software development is done in short iterations or sprints. This means that changes and enhancements are continuously added to the software during each iteration. However, these changes can unintentionally introduce new bugs or interfere with previously working features. Regression testing is performed to detect and identify these defects before they impact the overall functionality of the software. It involves retesting the affected areas of the software and the interconnected components to ensure that they still function as expected. The goal is to ensure that the software maintains its functionality and stability despite the continuous changes introduced during the development process. This form of testing is especially important in Agile project management as it helps teams identify defects early on, enabling them to fix the issues promptly and maintain the integrity of the software. Additionally, regression testing helps in maintaining the confidence of stakeholders and clients in the quality and reliability of the software product. Regression testing includes both manual and automated testing methods. While manual testing involves executing test cases step-by-step, automated testing uses tools to automate the execution of test scenarios. The adoption of test automation helps Agile teams to perform regression testing more efficiently and effectively, allowing faster feedback and ensuring maximum test coverage. Overall, regression testing plays a vital role in the Agile Process and Project Management disciplines by ensuring the continuous reliability and quality of the software product, facilitating the timely identification and resolution of defects. It helps Agile teams maintain a high level of software functionality and stability throughout the development process.

Resource Allocation Matrix (RAM) Template

A Resource Allocation Matrix (RAM) is a tool used in Agile Process and Project Management disciplines to allocate resources efficiently and effectively for a project. It provides a visual representation of the resources needed for each task and helps in proper planning and utilization of resources.

The main purpose of the RAM is to ensure that the right resources are allocated to the right tasks at the right time. It helps in identifying any resource gaps or conflicts, allowing project managers to take immediate actions to resolve them. By having a clear overview of resource availability, the RAM enables better decision-making and ensures that the project progresses smoothly.

Resource Allocation Matrix (RAM)

A Resource Allocation Matrix (RAM) is a key tool used in the Agile Process and Project Management disciplines to effectively manage and allocate resources to specific tasks or activities within a project. The RAM provides a visual representation of how resources are assigned and utilized throughout the project lifecycle.

The RAM typically includes a list of resources, such as team members or departments, and a list of tasks or activities that need to be accomplished within the project. The matrix then indicates which resources are assigned to each task or activity, allowing project managers to see at a glance who is responsible for what.

Resource Allocation Matrix

A Resource Allocation Matrix is a tool used in Agile Process and Project Management disciplines to effectively allocate resources to tasks or activities within a project. It provides a visual representation of the resources available, such as team members, equipment, or other assets, and the tasks they are assigned to complete.

The matrix typically consists of a grid with resources listed along one axis and tasks listed along the other axis. Each intersection in the grid represents the assignment of a specific resource to a specific task. The matrix allows project managers to easily identify which resources are responsible for which tasks, and helps in ensuring that resources are effectively utilized and not overburdened.

The Resource Allocation Matrix can also be used to identify resource constraints and potential bottlenecks in the project. By examining the matrix, project managers can identify situations where resources are overloaded with tasks or where certain tasks are not assigned to any available resources. This allows for proactive resource management and allocation adjustments to be made to ensure project success.

Furthermore, the matrix can facilitate effective resource planning, as it provides visibility into the availability and capacity of resources. Project managers can use the matrix to make informed decisions about resource allocation, taking into consideration factors such as skills, expertise, and availability. This helps in optimizing resource utilization and avoiding resource conflicts or shortages.

In summary, the Resource Allocation Matrix is a valuable tool in Agile Process and Project Management disciplines that aids in effective resource allocation, identification of bottlenecks, and resource planning. By providing a clear visual representation of resource assignments, it helps project managers ensure that tasks are appropriately distributed and completed in a timely manner, contributing to the overall success of the project.

Resource Allocation

Resource allocation in the context of Agile Process and Project Management disciplines refers

111

to the process of assigning and utilizing various resources effectively and efficiently to accomplish project goals and objectives.

In Agile, resource allocation is a dynamic and iterative process that takes into account the ever-changing needs and priorities of the project. It involves identifying and assigning resources such as team members, equipment, tools, and facilities based on their skills, availability, and expertise. This allocation is done in a way that maximizes the utilization of resources while ensuring that project goals and deliverables are achieved within the given time frame.

Agile resource allocation follows the principle of self-organization and cross-functional teams. It empowers team members to collaborate and make decisions collectively, ensuring that resources are allocated appropriately for each task or iteration. This allows for flexibility and adaptability, as resources can be reallocated as needed to address emerging priorities or changing requirements.

Effective resource allocation in Agile requires continuous monitoring and assessment of resource utilization. It entails tracking resource availability, workload distribution, and overall project progress to identify any imbalances or bottlenecks. This information is then used to make informed decisions and adjustments to ensure optimized resource allocation throughout the project lifecycle.

Resource Contouring

Resource contouring is a practice in Agile project management that involves optimizing the allocation and utilization of resources to meet project goals and deliverables. It aims to ensure that resources are used efficiently and effectively throughout the duration of a project.

In the Agile process, resource contouring is based on the principle of prioritization and flexibility. It requires the project manager to continuously assess the availability and capacity of resources, such as human resources, materials, and equipment, and adjust their allocation based on the changing needs of the project. This may involve reassigning resources from one task or team to another, redistributing workloads, or bringing in additional resources when necessary.

The goal of resource contouring is to avoid bottlenecks and maximize productivity by ensuring that resources are neither underutilized nor overburdened. By balancing resource allocation with project requirements and constraints, Agile project managers can optimize project delivery times, reduce risks, and enhance overall project success.

Resource contouring also plays a crucial role in managing project dependencies and interdependencies. By aligning resource allocation with task dependencies, project managers can minimize delays and conflicts, thereby improving project efficiency and collaboration.

Resource Histogram

A resource histogram is a visual representation of resource allocation and availability in an Agile project. It provides a high-level overview of the resources required for the project tasks and their availability over the project timeline. The histogram can be created using a horizontal bar chart where the x-axis represents the time periods and the y-axis represents the resources.

In an Agile process, where teams work in iterations, the resource histogram helps in identifying potential resource overloads or underutilization. It allows project managers to plan and allocate resources efficiently, ensuring that the right resources are available when needed.

Resource Leveling

Resource leveling is a technique used in Agile Process and Project Management disciplines to ensure that the workload for each team member is balanced and optimized throughout the project. It involves analyzing and adjusting the project schedule to evenly distribute the workload, avoiding resource overutilization or underutilization.

The objective of resource leveling is to minimize any resource bottlenecks and make the most efficient use of available resources. This helps to prevent burnout, fatigue, and frustration among team members, ensuring that they can deliver high-quality work consistently over the project's duration.

Resource Loading Analysis

A resource loading analysis is a crucial aspect of project management in the Agile process. It involves assessing the availability and allocation of resources within a project to ensure efficient and effective execution. In the Agile methodology, projects are divided into iterations or sprints, with each iteration having its own set of tasks and objectives. During the planning phase, a resource loading analysis is conducted to determine the number and type of resources required for each task. This analysis takes into account factors such as the skillset, availability, and capacity of the resources. The goal of resource loading analysis is to avoid overloading or underutilizing resources, both of which can lead to delays, inefficiencies, and poor productivity. By accurately assessing the resource needs and availability, project managers can create a balanced workload and distribute resources effectively. The analysis starts by identifying all the resources that will be required for the project, including human resources, equipment, and materials. Once identified, the availability and capacity of each resource are determined. This information helps project managers make informed decisions concerning resource allocation and scheduling. Resource loading analysis also helps in identifying any resource constraints or bottlenecks that may impact the project schedule. By identifying these constraints early on, project managers can take proactive measures to address them, such as hiring additional resources, redistributing workload, or adjusting the project timeline. In summary, resource loading analysis plays a vital role in Agile project management by ensuring that resources are allocated optimally, maximizing productivity, and minimizing delays. It helps project managers make informed decisions regarding resource allocation, identify constraints, and maintain a balanced workload throughout the project.

Resource Loading

Resource loading refers to the process of assigning and allocating resources to tasks and activities in an Agile process and project management discipline. In this context, resources can include personnel, equipment, tools, and facilities that are necessary to complete the project or task. The goal of resource loading is to ensure that the right resources are allocated to the right tasks at the right time, in order to maximize efficiency and productivity. By properly loading resources, project managers can effectively manage workloads, avoid bottlenecks, and optimize resource utilization. In Agile project management, resource loading is typically done during the project planning phase. It involves identifying the tasks and activities required to complete the project, estimating their resource requirements, and determining the sequence and dependencies between tasks. Once the tasks and activities are identified, project managers allocate resources based on their availability, skills, and expertise. This involves scheduling resources to work on specific tasks within specific timeframes, considering any constraints or dependencies. The allocation of resources should be done in a way that ensures the project is completed within its specified timeline without compromising on quality. Resource loading is an ongoing process throughout the project lifecycle. As the project progresses, project managers may need to adjust resource allocations based on changes in project priorities, resource availability, or unforeseen events. Regular monitoring and analysis of resource usage is essential to identify any imbalances or gaps and make necessary adjustments to ensure the project stays on track. Effective resource loading requires collaboration and coordination among project stakeholders, including project managers, team members, and resource managers. Continuous communication and feedback are crucial for successfully managing resources and adapting to evolving project needs. In conclusion, resource loading plays a vital role in Agile project management by facilitating efficient allocation and utilization of resources. It helps to optimize productivity, minimize delays, and ensure successful project execution.

Resource Management

Resource management in the context of Agile Process and Project Management disciplines refers to the strategic allocation, utilization, and optimization of resources to effectively execute and deliver projects within an Agile environment.

Agile methodologies, such as Scrum or Kanban, emphasize the importance of cross-functional teams and collaboration. Resource management ensures that resources, including human capital, technology, equipment, and budget, are allocated appropriately to support project goals and objectives in an Agile project.

The process of resource management begins with the identification of required resources for the project, considering the unique needs of the Agile project and its iterations or sprints. This involves assessing the skills and expertise of team members, determining the availability of tools and technology, and considering any external resources that may be required.

Once the resources are identified, the next step is to allocate them based on project needs, priorities, and timelines. This includes assigning team members to specific tasks or user stories, ensuring that they have the necessary skills and training, and optimizing their utilization to prevent bottlenecks or overloading.

Resource management in Agile project management also involves monitoring resource usage and making necessary adjustments throughout the project lifecycle. Regular tracking and reporting of resource allocation and utilization help identify any imbalances or constraints, allowing for proactive resource management decisions to be made to mitigate risks and ensure optimal project performance.

Resource Optimization

Resource Optimization refers to the process of aligning and utilizing resources in an optimized and efficient manner to achieve project goals and deliverables. In the context of Agile Process and Project Management disciplines, resource optimization involves effectively managing the allocation of various resources such as human resources, equipment, and budget to maximize productivity and minimize waste.

Agile methodologies, such as Scrum or Kanban, emphasize resource optimization by promoting collaboration, flexibility, and adaptability. These methodologies emphasize the importance of self-organizing and cross-functional teams, where members collectively work towards achieving project objectives. By leveraging the skills, expertise, and knowledge of team members, Agile teams aim to maximize resource utilization and optimize efficiency.

Resource Smoothing

Resource smoothing is a technique used in Agile Process and Project Management disciplines to maximize the efficiency and utilization of resources. It involves adjusting and redistributing the workload of resources over a period of time to eliminate peaks and valleys in resource demand.

The primary goal of resource smoothing is to achieve a more balanced and even distribution of resources, thus avoiding underutilization and overutilization of resources. By carefully managing resource allocation, organizations can optimize productivity, reduce the risk of burnout, and maintain a consistent pace of work throughout the project.

Risk Analysis

Risk analysis in the context of Agile Process and Project Management disciplines refers to the systematic evaluation and assessment of potential risks that may impact the successful delivery of a project using the Agile methodology. It involves identifying, analyzing, and prioritizing risks to develop effective mitigation strategies and contingency plans.

The Agile approach emphasizes adaptability, collaboration, and iterative development. As such, risk analysis is an integral part of Agile project management as it enables teams to proactively address potential obstacles and uncertainties. By identifying risks early in the project lifecycle, Agile teams can minimize their impact and increase the chances of project success.

Risk Appetite Statement Template

Risk Appetite Statement is a formal definition that outlines the overall willingness of an organization or project team to accept and embrace risks during the Agile process and project management activities. It serves as a guiding document that establishes the boundaries and level of acceptable risk exposure for the organization or project.

The Risk Appetite Statement enables project stakeholders to collectively understand and agree upon the degree of risk tolerance within the Agile framework. It helps in setting clear expectations and defining the risk management strategy by specifying the acceptable level of risk exposure in terms of probability, impact, and time frame.

This statement is crucial in aligning the risk management approach with the organizational objectives and Agile principles. It provides a framework for decision-making by highlighting the level of acceptable risk that the organization or project team is willing to undertake. This allows for better risk assessment, mitigation, and contingency planning throughout the Agile process.

Moreover, the Risk Appetite Statement also acts as a foundation for risk communication and stakeholder engagement. It facilitates effective risk dialogue between the Agile team, project sponsors, and other stakeholders, enabling them to have a shared understanding of risk tolerance and its impact on decision-making.

Overall, the Risk Appetite Statement promotes a proactive and collaborative approach to risk management in Agile projects. It helps in balancing the need to embrace innovative practices and the responsibility to mitigate potential risks, thus contributing to the successful delivery of projects within the defined risk boundaries.

Risk Appetite Statement

A Risk Appetite Statement in the context of Agile Process and Project Management disciplines is a formal statement that outlines the organization's or project team's willingness to tolerate risks in order to achieve their objectives. It provides guidance on the level of risk that the organization or project team is willing to accept, and it helps in making informed decisions regarding risk management strategies.

The Risk Appetite Statement reflects the organization's or project team's risk appetite, which is influenced by various factors such as the industry, business goals, regulatory requirements, stakeholders' expectations, and the organization's risk culture. It sets the tone for risk management activities and helps in aligning risk tolerance with business objectives.

Risk Appetite

Risk appetite, in the context of Agile Process and Project Management disciplines, refers to the level of risk that an organization or project team is willing to accept in pursuit of their goals and objectives.

Agile methodologies emphasize adaptability and the ability to quickly respond to changes in requirements and market conditions. However, every project carries inherent risks, such as budget overruns, scope creep, technological challenges, and external factors that can impact the project's success.

Having a clearly defined risk appetite ensures that stakeholders have a shared understanding of the acceptable level of risk for the project. It helps project teams make informed decisions about the level of risk they are comfortable with and enables them to prioritize risks and allocate resources accordingly.

A risk appetite statement typically outlines the types and magnitudes of risks that the organization or project team is willing to accept. It may consider factors such as financial impacts, operational impacts, reputational impacts, and regulatory compliance. This statement serves as a guiding principle for risk management activities throughout the project lifecycle.

By understanding and aligning their risk appetite, project teams can avoid taking unnecessary risks or being overly cautious, finding the right balance between innovation and stability. It allows for more efficient decision-making, as they can confidently assess and respond to risks based on their predetermined risk tolerance.

Ultimately, a well-defined risk appetite ensures that project teams are proactive in identifying and mitigating risks, leading to more successful project outcomes within the Agile framework.

Risk Assessment

Risk assessment in the context of Agile Process and Project Management disciplines is the process of identifying, analyzing, and evaluating potential risks that could impact the success of a project. It involves assessing the likelihood and impact of risks and determining appropriate response strategies to minimize their negative effects. In Agile, risk assessment is an ongoing and iterative process that takes place throughout the project lifecycle. It is a collaborative effort involving all members of the Agile team, including the product owner, Scrum Master, and development team. The aim is to proactively identify and address risks early on to ensure timely and successful project delivery. During risk assessment, risks are categorized based on their potential impact on the project's objectives, such as scope, schedule, budget, and quality. Risks are then assigned a rating based on their likelihood and impact, which helps prioritize the team's response efforts. This rating can be represented using a risk matrix or a heat map. Once risks are identified and evaluated, the Agile team develops appropriate risk response strategies. These strategies can include risk avoidance, risk mitigation, risk transfer, or risk acceptance. The team collaboratively determines the most suitable response strategy for each identified risk, keeping in mind the Agile principles of flexibility and adaptability. Throughout the project, the Agile team monitors and reviews risks regularly, reassessing their likelihood and impact and updating response strategies as needed. This ensures that risks are actively managed and that the project remains on track. By integrating risk assessment into the Agile process, project managers and teams can proactively address potential risks and increase the chances of project success.

Risk Management Plan

A Risk Management Plan is a formal document that outlines the process and strategies to identify, assess, and mitigate risks in an Agile Process and Project Management disciplines. It is an essential tool for project teams to proactively identify potential risks, analyze their impact on project objectives, and develop effective strategies to prevent or mitigate these risks.

In the Agile process, risk management is an iterative and continuous process that is integrated into the overall project lifecycle. The Risk Management Plan focuses on identifying and addressing risks that may impact the project's scope, schedule, cost, quality, and overall success.

The Risk Management Plan typically includes:

- Risk Identification: This step involves identifying and documenting potential risks that may arise during the project. It includes conducting brainstorming sessions, analyzing historical data, and leveraging the expertise of the project team and stakeholders.

- Risk Assessment: Once the risks are identified, they are assessed and analyzed to understand their likelihood of occurrence and potential impact on the project. This step involves prioritizing risks based on their severity and developing risk response strategies.

- Risk Response Strategies: This step involves developing strategies and actions to avoid, transfer, mitigate, or accept risks. It includes defining contingency plans, establishing risk thresholds, and identifying responsible parties for managing specific risks.

- Risk Monitoring and Control: Throughout the project, risks are monitored and controlled to ensure that the identified strategies are effective and the project is not affected by unforeseen events. This step involves regular risk reviews, tracking risk status, and implementing necessary adjustments to the risk management approach.

A well-executed Risk Management Plan enables project teams to proactively address potential risks, minimize their impact on project objectives, and ensure successful project delivery in the Agile environment.

Risk Matrix Template

A risk matrix is a visual tool used in the Agile Process and Project Management disciplines to assess and prioritize potential risks within a project. It provides a systematic approach for identifying, analyzing, and categorizing risks based on their likelihood of occurring and the impact they would have on the project. The risk matrix typically consists of a grid or a matrix with two axes representing the likelihood and impact of each risk. The likelihood axis represents the probability of a risk occurring, while the impact axis represents the severity of the risk's consequences. These axes are divided into multiple levels or categories to allow for a more detailed assessment. Each identified risk is placed in the appropriate cell of the matrix based on its calculated likelihood and impact. The cells are usually color-coded or labeled to indicate the risk level, with different colors or labels representing different levels of severity. This visual representation helps project managers and teams to quickly identify and prioritize the risks that require immediate attention and mitigation. By utilizing a risk matrix, Agile teams can effectively identify and address potential risks early on in a project. It allows for a proactive approach to risk management, ensuring that appropriate strategies and actions are implemented to minimize the impact of risks on the project's success. Regularly reviewing and updating the risk matrix throughout the project lifecycle helps in tracking the progress of risk mitigation efforts and adapting the risk management strategy accordingly.

Risk Matrix

A risk matrix is a visual tool used in Agile Process and Project Management disciplines to identify and assess potential risks associated with a project or process. It provides a structured approach to evaluate the likelihood and impact of risks, allowing project teams to prioritize and address them accordingly.

The risk matrix typically consists of a grid with different levels of likelihood and impact, creating a matrix of possible risk scenarios. Likelihood refers to the probability of a risk occurring, while impact represents the magnitude of its potential effects on the project. Each risk is categorized within the matrix based on its assessed likelihood and impact, resulting in a graphical representation that enables stakeholders to easily understand and manage risks.

By using a risk matrix, Agile teams can proactively identify and prioritize risks, allowing them to develop appropriate mitigation strategies. The matrix helps to focus resources and attention on high-priority risks, ensuring that potential issues are addressed before they escalate and impact project objectives.

Moreover, the risk matrix fosters collective decision-making by providing a common language and framework for discussing risks. It enables project stakeholders to have a shared understanding of the potential risks, facilitating effective communication, and enabling timely risk response actions.

Risk Register

A Risk Register in the context of Agile Process and Project Management disciplines is a tool used to identify, assess, prioritize, and manage risks throughout the duration of a project. It serves as a central repository for all potential risks that could impact the project's success.

The Risk Register captures various types of risks, including but not limited to technical risks, resource risks, schedule risks, and external risks. It allows project teams to proactively anticipate and address potential issues before they occur, minimizing the negative impact on project outcomes.

When using Agile methodologies, the Risk Register is particularly important as it supports the iterative and incremental nature of Agile development. It helps the project team in continuously identifying and managing risks as the project evolves.

The Risk Register typically includes a detailed description of each identified risk, its potential impact on the project, the likelihood of occurrence, and the proposed mitigation or contingency plans. It also includes information on the owner or responsible party for each risk, allowing for clear accountability and tracking of risk management activities.

117

Regular review and updating of the Risk Register is essential to ensure that new risks are identified and existing risks are appropriately managed. The Agile team should revisit the Risk Register during project retrospectives or any time there are significant changes in project scope, timeline, or resources.

SWOT Analysis Workshop Agenda

SWOT Analysis is a strategic planning technique used to assess the strengths, weaknesses, opportunities, and threats of a project or organization in the context of Agile Process and Project Management disciplines. The SWOT Analysis Workshop Agenda serves as a structured guide for conducting a SWOT Analysis session within an Agile team or project management setting.

The agenda typically consists of the following key components:

1. Introduction and Overview: The workshop begins with an introduction to the purpose and objectives of conducting a SWOT Analysis. The facilitator provides an overview of the process and its relevance to the Agile process or project management discipline.

2. Explanation of SWOT Elements: The facilitator explains each element of the SWOT Analysis - strengths, weaknesses, opportunities, and threats. The team members are encouraged to brainstorm and share their understanding of these elements, ensuring a common understanding among all participants.

3. Identification of Strengths: The team members collectively identify and discuss the internal strengths of the project or organization. This may include resources, skills, technologies, or any other factors that contribute to its success within the Agile context.

4. Identification of Weaknesses: The team members identify and discuss the internal weaknesses of the project or organization. These could be areas that need improvement, bottlenecks, or constraints that might hinder progress in the Agile process or project management.

5. Identification of Opportunities: The team members identify and discuss the external opportunities that can be leveraged to benefit the project or organization within the Agile context. These could be market trends, partnerships, or any other factors that create additional advantages.

6. Identification of Threats: The team members identify and discuss the external threats that may pose risks or challenges to the project or organization within the Agile context. These could be competition, changing regulations, or any other factors that may impact the success of the project.

7. Action Planning: Based on the outcomes of the SWOT Analysis, the team discusses and plans specific actions or strategies to capitalize on strengths, address weaknesses, seize opportunities, and mitigate threats. These actions are aligned with the Agile process or project management practices to ensure effective implementation.

A SWOT Analysis Workshop Agenda in Agile Process and Project Management disciplines provides a structured framework for teams to collectively evaluate internal and external factors that can influence the success of their projects, leading to informed decision-making and action planning.

SWOT Analysis Workshop

A SWOT Analysis Workshop is a collaborative activity conducted in the Agile Process and Project Management disciplines to analyze and assess the strengths, weaknesses, opportunities, and threats associated with a project or a specific aspect of it. It is a structured approach that brings together cross-functional teams or stakeholders to identify and evaluate the internal and external factors that may impact project success.

During the workshop, participants engage in brainstorming sessions and open discussions to identify and document the project's strengths, which represent its unique capabilities or advantages. These strengths may include highly skilled team members, a supportive organizational culture, or access to specialized resources. Conversely, weaknesses are identified as internal factors inhibiting project progress, such as limited budget, resource constraints, or skill gaps within the team.

The workshop also aims to identify and evaluate opportunities, which are external factors that could potentially contribute to project success. These opportunities may arise from market trends, technological advancements, or strategic partnerships. On the other hand, threats are external factors that may pose risks to the project, such as competing projects, changing regulations, or unexpected market shifts.

The SWOT Analysis Workshop serves as a strategic assessment tool, allowing project teams to gain a comprehensive understanding of the project's current state and its environment. By identifying and exploring these factors, the workshop facilitates informed decision-making and enables the development of effective strategies to maximize strengths, minimize weaknesses, capitalize on opportunities, and mitigate threats. The outcome of the workshop is a SWOT matrix, which visually represents the findings and serves as a reference for project planning, risk management, and continuous improvement efforts.

SWOT Analysis

A SWOT analysis is a strategic planning tool used in Agile Process and Project Management disciplines to identify and evaluate the strengths, weaknesses, opportunities, and threats associated with a project or an organization. It allows teams to assess their current position and make informed decisions based on their internal capabilities and external factors.

The strengths component of the analysis focuses on the positive attributes of the project or organization. This includes the team's expertise, resources, and unique selling proposition that sets them apart from competitors. By understanding their strengths, agile teams can leverage them to gain a competitive edge and deliver high-quality products or services.

The weaknesses component highlights the areas where the project or organization may be lacking or vulnerable. It could be a skill gap within the team, limited resources, or poor infrastructure. Identifying weaknesses helps the team to devise strategies for improvement and address any potential obstacles that may arise during the project lifecycle.

Opportunities refer to the external factors that have the potential to benefit the project or organization. This could include emerging markets, new technologies, or changes in customer preferences. Agile teams can exploit these opportunities by aligning their project goals and strategies to take advantage of external circumstances, thereby gaining a competitive advantage.

Finally, threats encompass the external factors that can potentially harm the project or organization. These could include competitors, economic downturns, or regulatory changes. By identifying threats, agile teams can develop contingency plans and take proactive measures to mitigate any risks or obstacles.

Scenario Analysis

Scenario analysis is a technique used in Agile Process and Project Management disciplines to understand and evaluate the potential impact of various future scenarios on a project. It involves identifying and analyzing different possible futures and their associated risks and opportunities.

The purpose of scenario analysis is to help project teams anticipate and plan for different outcomes, allowing them to be more flexible and adaptable in their approach. By considering a range of potential scenarios, project managers can develop contingency plans, identify potential bottlenecks, and make informed decisions to mitigate risks and maximize opportunities.

Schedule Performance Index (SPI) Calculation

The Schedule Performance Index (SPI) is a metric used in Agile Process and Project Management disciplines to measure the efficiency of time management in a project. It is a ratio that compares the amount of work completed with the amount of work planned for a specific period of time.

To calculate the SPI, divide the Earned Value (EV) by the Planned Value (PV). The EV represents the budgeted cost of the work actually completed, which is determined by measuring completed tasks. The PV represents the budgeted cost of the work that was planned to be completed. By dividing EV by PV, the SPI reveals if the project is ahead or behind schedule.

If the SPI is greater than 1, it indicates that the project is ahead of schedule, meaning that more work has been completed than planned within the specified time. A SPI less than 1 indicates that the project is behind schedule, with less work completed than planned. An SPI of 1 suggests that the project is on schedule, as the amount of work completed aligns with the planned work for the given period.

The SPI is a valuable tool for Agile project management as it provides insight into the project's time performance. It helps project managers and stakeholders assess the progress of the project and make informed decisions to optimize time management and efficiency. By regularly calculating the SPI during the project's lifecycle, project teams can identify early warnings of schedule slippage and take necessary corrective actions to keep the project on track.

Schedule Performance Index (SPI)

The Schedule Performance Index (SPI) is a metric used in Agile process and project management disciplines to measure the efficiency and effectiveness of scheduling activities. It provides a quantitative measure of how well a project is adhering to its planned schedule.

In Agile, the SPI is calculated by dividing the Earned Value (EV), which represents the value of completed work, by the Planned Value (PV), which represents the value of scheduled work. The resulting ratio indicates how efficiently the project is utilizing its resources and time.

Scope Change Control Board (SCCB) Charter

The Scope Change Control Board (SCCB) Charter is a formal document that defines the purpose, responsibilities, and authority of the SCCB in an Agile Process and Project Management environment.

The SCCB is a governance body consisting of key stakeholders, such as project managers, product owners, and senior leadership, who are responsible for evaluating and approving changes to the project scope.

Scope Change Control Board (SCCB)

Scope Change Control Board (SCCB) is a governing body in Agile Process and Project Management disciplines that is responsible for evaluating and managing changes to the project scope. It is comprised of key stakeholders and subject matter experts who assess the impact of proposed scope changes and make decisions regarding their implementation.

The SCCB plays a crucial role in ensuring that scope changes are carefully evaluated and controlled to minimize disruption and maximize project success. Its primary objectives are to maintain project focus, manage scope creep, and prevent unnecessary rework.

Scope Change

Scope change, in the context of Agile Process and Project Management disciplines, refers to any modification or alteration to the defined scope or requirements of a project during its execution. It is a common occurrence in Agile methodologies, where change is embraced and accommodated throughout the project lifecycle.

Agile processes, such as Scrum or Kanban, recognize that requirements often evolve as a project progresses and stakeholders gain a better understanding of their needs. Therefore, they allow for scope changes to address these evolving requirements effectively.

When a scope change request arises, Agile teams follow a transparent and collaborative approach to evaluate and incorporate the proposed modifications. The Product Owner, along with the stakeholders, reviews the change request and identifies its impact on the project's overall objective, timeline, and budget.

The Agile team then analyzes the feasibility of the scope change and assesses its potential benefits against the project's goals. If approved, the team incorporates the change into the project backlog and updates it accordingly. This ensures that the change is prioritized alongside existing requirements.

Throughout the Agile project, scope changes are managed using various techniques such as backlog grooming, sprint planning, and continuous communication with stakeholders. These techniques allow the team to adjust the project's direction while maintaining transparency and minimizing disruption to ongoing work.

Scope Creep

Scope Decomposition Structure

A Scope Decomposition Structure in the context of Agile Process and Project Management disciplines refers to a methodical breakdown of the project scope into smaller, more manageable components. This process helps to clearly define the project's deliverables, tasks, and activities, allowing for better planning, estimation, and tracking of progress.

In Agile Project Management, the Scope Decomposition Structure is typically represented using a hierarchical structure, often called a Work Breakdown Structure (WBS) or a Product Breakdown Structure (PBS). The structure starts with the highest-level deliverables or project objectives and then breaks them down into smaller, more detailed components.

Scope Decomposition

Scope decomposition is a key technique used in Agile Process and Project Management disciplines to break down a project or product into smaller, more manageable components or work packages. It involves dividing the overall scope or requirements of the project into smaller, more specific deliverables or features, which can then be prioritized, estimated, and assigned to the team members.

This decomposition helps in understanding the complexity of the project and allows for a more effective planning and execution. By breaking down the scope into smaller pieces, it becomes easier to estimate the effort and duration required for each component, as well as assign them to different team members based on their skills and availability.

Scope Document

Scope Document, in the context of Agile Process and Project Management disciplines, refers to a formal document that outlines the objectives, deliverables, and boundaries of a project. It serves as a comprehensive reference for all project stakeholders, including the project team, stakeholders, and clients, to understand and agree upon the project's scope and its limitations.

The main purpose of a Scope Document is to provide clarity and define the boundaries of a project. It helps in avoiding scope creep, which is the tendency of a project to gradually expand beyond its original objectives and requirements. By clearly defining what is within and outside the project's scope, the Scope Document ensures that all stakeholders have a shared understanding of what the project will deliver and what it will not.

Typically, a Scope Document contains sections such as project objectives, project deliverables, project boundaries, project constraints, and project assumptions. It may also include a high-level timeline and budget estimates. The Scope Document is usually created at the beginning of the project during the project initiation phase. It is a living document that may evolve and be refined throughout the project lifecycle as new information becomes available or changes are requested.

Overall, the Scope Document plays a crucial role in effective project management. It helps prevent misunderstandings, manage expectations, and serves as a reference point for project scope decisions. By clearly defining the project's scope, the Scope Document enables the project team to focus on delivering the agreed-upon objectives and successfully meet project goals.

Scope Statement

A scope statement is a concise and formal document that outlines the project deliverables, objectives, and constraints. It provides a clear understanding of the project's goals and what is expected to be achieved. In the context of Agile Process and Project Management disciplines, a scope statement plays a crucial role in defining the project scope and boundaries.

The scope statement in Agile projects is typically created and refined throughout the project's lifespan due to the iterative and incremental nature of Agile methodologies. It helps the team prioritize and communicate the work that needs to be done, ensuring that everyone is aligned and focused on the same objectives.

Scope Validation

Scope validation is a process within the Agile methodology and Project Management disciplines that involves confirming and validating the project's scope. It ensures that the defined objectives, requirements, and deliverables align with the client's expectations and the project's overall goals.

During scope validation, the project team reviews and evaluates the project's scope statements, requirements documentation, and any other relevant artifacts. The primary objective is to verify that all key components of the project are included and that they accurately represent the client's needs and expectations. It also ensures that any changes or modifications to the scope are approved and documented properly.

Scope Verification

Scope Verification in the context of Agile Process refers to the formal process of reviewing and validating the project's deliverables with the stakeholders to ensure that they meet the requirements and are in line with the project objectives.

In Agile Project Management, the scope of work is divided into smaller chunks called user stories or features, which are prioritized and planned for delivery in iterative cycles called sprints. During each sprint, the project team develops and tests the features and then presents them to the stakeholders for review.

Scope

Scope refers to the boundaries and extent of a project or task. In the context of Agile Process and Project Management disciplines, scope defines the work that needs to be accomplished during a project. It outlines the goals, deliverables, tasks, and features that need to be included within the project's timeframe.

In Agile, the scope is dynamic and can change throughout the project as new information and requirements emerge. It is common for scope to be defined and refined during each iteration or sprint. Agile teams prioritize the most valuable features and adjust the scope accordingly to ensure the project stays on track and delivers the highest value to the stakeholders.

Sensitivity Analysis Report

Sensitivity Analysis in the context of Agile Process and Project Management disciplines refers to a technique that is used to evaluate the potential impact of variations in specific input variables on the outcomes or results of a project. It is a form of "what-if" analysis that allows project managers to understand the sensitivity of project outcomes to changes in different factors.

The process of sensitivity analysis involves identifying the key variables or factors that might affect the project outcomes, determining the range of values for each variable, and then systematically assessing the impact of varying these values on the project. This analysis helps project managers to understand the level of sensitivity of project outcomes to different factors and make informed decisions based on this understanding.

Sensitivity Analysis

Sensitivity analysis in the context of Agile Process and Project Management disciplines refers to a technique used to assess the impact of changes in project parameters or assumptions on project outcomes. It helps project managers and teams identify the factors that are most critical or sensitive to changes, allowing them to make informed decisions and adjustments to their project plan.

Agile projects are characterized by their flexibility and adaptability, as they emphasize iterative and incremental delivery. However, changes in project parameters or assumptions can have significant consequences on the success of the project. Sensitivity analysis allows project managers to evaluate the potential impact of such changes before implementing them.

Software Development Life Cycle (SDLC)

The Software Development Life Cycle (SDLC) is a conceptual framework that describes the various stages involved in the development of a software product. In the context of Agile Process and Project Management disciplines, SDLC refers to an iterative and incremental approach to software development.

Agile SDLC follows a series of short development cycles, known as sprints, where requirements and solutions evolve through the collaborative effort of self-organizing and cross-functional teams. The process is characterized by continuous feedback, flexibility, and adaptability, allowing for quick response to changes or improvements.

Sponsor

A sponsor, in the context of Agile Process and Project Management disciplines, refers to an individual or an organization that provides financial support, resources, and guidance to a project or initiative. The sponsor is typically a senior executive or a stakeholder who plays a crucial role in the success of the project.

The sponsor's primary responsibility is to champion the project and ensure its alignment with the organization's strategic goals. They establish the project's objectives, define its scope, and provide the necessary authority and resources for its execution. The sponsor also helps in securing the buy-in and support of other key stakeholders and facilitates effective communication across different levels of the organization.

Furthermore, the sponsor acts as the project's advocate and represents its interests at higher levels within the organization. They help remove any obstacles and provide guidance to the project manager, helping them navigate any challenges that may arise. The sponsor also ensures that the project remains on track, monitors progress, and evaluates its success against predetermined metrics.

Overall, the sponsor's involvement in Agile Process and Project Management is crucial for establishing a strong foundation for success. Their financial support and guidance not only ensure the project's viability but also provide the necessary resources and authority to execute it effectively. The sponsor's active engagement in the project allows for better decision-making, efficient resource allocation, and effective risk management. Their role extends beyond mere financial support, making them an integral part of the project's overall success.

Sponsorship

Sponsorship is a critical aspect of Agile Process and Project Management disciplines. It refers to the financial and strategic support provided by a sponsor to ensure the successful execution of a project or initiative.

The sponsor, typically a senior executive or a key stakeholder, plays a crucial role in championing the project, securing necessary resources, and removing any impediments that may hinder progress. They are responsible for aligning the project with the organization's strategic goals and ensuring that it delivers the expected value.

Stage Gate Process

A stage gate process refers to a structured approach used in Agile Process and Project Management disciplines to manage and evaluate projects at various stages or gates, in order to make informed decisions about whether to proceed or terminate the project. It provides a systematic framework for breaking down a project into distinct stages and reviewing its progress and viability at each stage, based on predefined criteria.

The process typically consists of several stages or gates, with each gate representing a milestone in the project. At each gate, the project undergoes a thorough evaluation, which includes comprehensive analysis, assessment, and review by relevant stakeholders and decision-makers. The evaluation is based on specific criteria and metrics, which are defined in advance and aligned with the project objectives and goals.

If a project meets the criteria set for a particular gate, it progresses to the next stage. Conversely, if a project fails to meet the criteria, it may require further refinement, reevaluation, or termination. The stage gate process helps ensure that resources are efficiently allocated, risks are properly managed, and the project remains aligned with the overall business objectives. It also enables stakeholders to have a clear understanding of the project status, risks, and potential outcomes at each gate, facilitating better decision-making and reducing the likelihood of unforeseen issues.

Stakeholder Analysis

Stakeholder Analysis is a critical process in Agile Project Management that involves identifying, categorizing, and prioritizing the individuals, groups, or organizations that have a vested interest in or will be affected by the project. It is an essential tool for understanding and managing the expectations, needs, concerns, and influence of stakeholders throughout the project's lifecycle.

The primary purpose of Stakeholder Analysis is to ensure the project team can effectively communicate, collaborate, and engage with stakeholders. By understanding their perspectives, the team can align project goals, manage risks, and make informed decisions. The analysis helps identify potential conflicts, address challenges, and build positive relationships with stakeholders.

The Agile approach emphasizes continuous engagement and collaboration with stakeholders, considering them as crucial contributors and a source of valuable input throughout the project. By involving stakeholders early and frequently, Agile teams can incorporate their feedback, adjust priorities, and deliver solutions that meet their needs effectively.

In stakeholder analysis, stakeholders are typically categorized based on their influence, interest, and impact on the project. The categories can include project sponsors, clients, end-users, product owners, developers, testers, managers, and other impacted individuals or groups. It is essential to identify their needs, expectations, roles, responsibilities, and any potential challenges or conflicts they may face during the project.

Conducting a stakeholder analysis helps project managers and Agile teams to proactively manage communication, collect relevant requirements, build consensus, and engage stakeholders effectively. By addressing stakeholder concerns and keeping them informed, the project is more likely to achieve success and deliver value to all involved parties.

Stakeholder Communication Plan Template

A Stakeholder Communication Plan is a formal document that outlines the strategies and methods for effectively communicating with stakeholders involved in an Agile process or project management discipline. It provides a structured approach for identifying, engaging, and managing diverse stakeholders throughout the project lifecycle.

The purpose of a Stakeholder Communication Plan is to establish clear guidelines on how to communicate project-related information, expectations, and updates to stakeholders in a timely and comprehensive manner. This includes defining stakeholder roles and responsibilities, determining communication channels, and specifying the frequency and format of communication.

By creating a Stakeholder Communication Plan, Agile teams and project managers can ensure that the right stakeholders receive the right information at the right time, enabling effective collaboration, decision-making, and alignment throughout the project. It helps to minimize miscommunication, confusion, and conflicts by providing a framework for proactive and transparent communication.

An effective Stakeholder Communication Plan includes elements such as stakeholder identification and analysis, communication goals and objectives, key messages, communication methods and frequency, escalation procedures, and evaluation and feedback mechanisms. It is a flexible document that may evolve and adapt based on the changing needs and requirements of the project.

Overall, a Stakeholder Communication Plan is an essential tool in Agile project management, fostering effective stakeholder engagement, promoting transparency, and enabling successful project delivery. It helps to build and maintain strong relationships with stakeholders, ensuring their support and participation throughout the project lifecycle.

Stakeholder Communication Plan

A stakeholder communication plan is a formal strategy that outlines how project stakeholders will be effectively and consistently informed and engaged throughout the Agile process and project management disciplines. It is a crucial component of project planning that ensures stakeholders are aware of project progress, key decisions, and potential impacts on their interests.

The stakeholder communication plan identifies the specific stakeholders, their roles, and their communication preferences. This information helps project managers determine the most appropriate channels and frequency of communication, ensuring that stakeholders receive relevant and timely updates. The plan also defines the purpose and objectives of the communication, whether it is to provide information, seek feedback, or gain support. By clearly stating the purpose, project managers can tailor their messaging to achieve desired outcomes.

In Agile project management, stakeholder communication plans are particularly valuable due to the iterative and collaborative nature of Agile processes. Agile teams frequently interact with stakeholders to gather requirements, provide progress updates, and obtain feedback on deliverables. The stakeholder communication plan ensures that these interactions are intentional, structured, and aligned with the Agile principles.

Overall, a stakeholder communication plan fosters transparency, trust, and collaboration between project teams and stakeholders. It helps prevent misunderstandings, manage expectations, and minimize potential conflicts. By keeping stakeholders informed and engaged, the plan contributes to the overall success of Agile projects by ensuring the right stakeholders are involved at the right time and that their perspectives are taken into consideration throughout the project lifecycle.

Stakeholder Communication

Stakeholder Communication in Agile Process and Project Management refers to the proactive and ongoing exchange of information, feedback, and updates with individuals or groups who have a vested interest or influence in a project's outcome. The Agile approach emphasizes collaboration, transparency, and regular communication among team members and stakeholders throughout the project's lifecycle.

This communication process involves identifying stakeholders, understanding their needs, expectations, and concerns, and effectively conveying relevant project information to them. It aims to build understanding, trust, and alignment among the project team and stakeholders, ensuring that everyone has a shared understanding of project goals, progress, and changes.

Stakeholder Engagement

Stakeholder engagement in the context of Agile Process and Project Management disciplines refers to the active involvement and collaboration of individuals or groups who have a vested interest or influence in the project. These stakeholders contribute their knowledge, insights, and perspectives throughout the project lifecycle to ensure its success.

In Agile, stakeholder engagement is crucial for several reasons. Firstly, it helps gather and incorporate diverse perspectives, allowing for a more comprehensive understanding of the project requirements, goals, and potential challenges. This can lead to better decision-making and problem-solving throughout the project. Secondly, stakeholder engagement ensures that the project remains aligned with the expectations and needs of various stakeholders, ultimately delivering a product or service that meets their requirements.

Stakeholder Register

A Stakeholder Register is a documented record that identifies and provides relevant information about individuals, groups, or organizations that have an interest in or can be affected by the Agile process or project being managed. This register serves as a central repository of stakeholder-related information, allowing Agile teams and project managers to effectively identify, analyze, and engage with stakeholders throughout the duration of the project.

The Stakeholder Register captures key details about each stakeholder, such as their roles, responsibilities, and level of influence. It also includes their specific interests, concerns, and expectations, which can help project managers anticipate and address potential challenges or conflicts. In an Agile context, the register may include additional information related to stakeholder engagement strategies, such as preferred communication channels or frequency of updates.

By maintaining a Stakeholder Register, Agile teams can ensure that stakeholders are actively involved in the decision-making process and that their needs and expectations are appropriately considered. This promotes transparency, collaboration, and alignment among all project participants, allowing for more efficient and effective delivery of value.

The Stakeholder Register is a dynamic document that should be regularly reviewed and updated as new stakeholders emerge or as existing stakeholders' information changes. It serves as a vital tool for Agile project management, enabling teams to prioritize and manage stakeholder relationships, mitigate risks, and ultimately deliver successful outcomes that meet stakeholder expectations.

Stakeholder

A stakeholder is an individual or group who has a vested interest or is affected by the outcome of a project in the context of Agile Process and Project Management disciplines. They have the potential to impact the project positively or negatively and can influence its success or failure.

In Agile, stakeholders play a crucial role in providing input, feedback, and guidance throughout the project. They include individuals or groups such as the project manager, product owners, developers, business owners, customers, users, and other key decision-makers.

Statistical Sampling

Statistical sampling is a crucial method used in Agile Process and Project Management disciplines to collect data and make informed decisions based on a representative subset of the population. It involves selecting a subset of items or individuals from a larger group, known as the population, in order to gather information about the characteristics and behaviors of the entire population.

The purpose of statistical sampling in the context of Agile Process and Project Management is to minimize the resources and time required to collect data while still obtaining reliable and meaningful results. By selecting a smaller sample from the population, it becomes feasible to gather relevant and accurate data within the constraints of an Agile project.

Strategic Alignment Matrix Tool

A Strategic Alignment Matrix Tool is a framework that helps organizations align their strategic objectives and initiatives with the Agile process and project management disciplines. It provides a structured approach for organizations to prioritize and track their projects based on their strategic goals and objectives.

The tool enables organizations to map their strategic objectives onto different Agile methodologies and project management practices, such as Scrum or Kanban. This allows organizations to ensure that their projects are in line with their strategic goals and objectives, and that they are delivering value to the stakeholders.

The Strategic Alignment Matrix Tool helps organizations to identify the most critical and high-priority projects that are aligned with their strategic objectives. It provides a visual representation of the projects in a matrix, where the X-axis represents the strategic goals and the Y-axis represents the Agile methodologies or project management practices.

By using the tool, organizations can evaluate and prioritize their projects based on their strategic importance. They can also track the progress of the projects and make adjustments as needed to ensure that the projects are delivering the desired outcomes.

Strategic Alignment Matrix

A Strategic Alignment Matrix, within the context of Agile Process and Project Management disciplines, is a framework that facilitates the integration of organizational objectives with project goals and the strategic decision-making process. It helps stakeholders, including project managers, product owners, and team members, to align their efforts and resources with the strategic direction of the organization.

The matrix consists of two key dimensions: strategic objectives and project initiatives. The strategic objectives represent the high-level goals and priorities of the organization, while the project initiatives represent the specific tasks and activities required to achieve those goals.

Strategic Alignment

Strategic alignment refers to the process of ensuring that all activities, projects, and initiatives within an organization are directly linked to its overall strategic goals and objectives. It involves aligning the resources, capabilities, and efforts of the organization in a way that supports the strategic direction and maximizes the chances of success.

In the context of Agile Process and Project Management disciplines, strategic alignment plays a crucial role in ensuring that the projects undertaken by the organization are in line with its strategic objectives. It involves continuously assessing and prioritizing project opportunities based on their alignment with the organization's strategic goals, and making informed decisions on which projects should be pursued.

Strategic Planning

Strategic planning, within the context of Agile Process and Project Management disciplines, refers to the proactive and iterative process that organizations undertake to determine and align their long-term goals, objectives, and initiatives with their overall vision and mission. It involves analyzing the internal and external environment, identifying opportunities and challenges, and formulating strategies and action plans that enable the organization to effectively respond to changing market dynamics and achieve sustainable success.

In an Agile context, strategic planning takes into account the principles and practices of Agile methodologies, such as Scrum or Kanban, which emphasize flexibility, collaboration, and adaptability. Instead of relying on rigid, pre-determined plans and fixed timelines, Agile strategic planning involves continuous evaluation and adjustment based on feedback and learning obtained through the iterative cycles of development and delivery.

Agile strategic planning incorporates the concept of the product backlog, which serves as a prioritized list of features, enhancements, and tasks that need to be accomplished to achieve the strategic goals. It involves the active involvement of cross-functional teams, stakeholders, and customers in the planning process, driving alignment and ensuring that the strategies formulated are realistic, feasible, and customer-centric.

The primary goal of strategic planning in Agile Process and Project Management disciplines is to enable organizations to navigate dynamic and unpredictable business landscapes and to make informed decisions that maximize value and minimize risk. By fostering a culture of learning, collaboration, and continuous improvement, Agile strategic planning helps organizations stay responsive to market changes and customer needs, delivering products and services that meet or exceed expectations.

Success Criteria

Success Criteria in the context of Agile Process and Project Management disciplines refer to specific measurable objectives or goals that define what project success looks like. These criteria are used to determine whether a project or process has achieved its desired outcomes or not.

In Agile Project Management, success criteria are crucial for tracking and evaluating the progress of the project. They are often defined during the project planning phase and are used as a baseline for measuring the project's success throughout its lifecycle. These criteria help the project team and stakeholders to clarify what is expected from the project and provide a common understanding of success.

Succession Planning Process Framework

A succession planning process framework in the context of Agile Process and Project Management disciplines refers to a structured approach for identifying and developing potential future leaders within an organization. This framework focuses on ensuring a smooth transition of leadership roles by strategically preparing and grooming individuals who possess the necessary skills and competencies to take on key positions.

The succession planning process framework typically involves several key steps. Firstly, there is an assessment of the organization's current and future needs, as well as an identification of critical roles that require succession planning. This step is essential for understanding the specific leadership requirements and potential gaps that need to be addressed.

Next, individuals within the organization are assessed to identify those with high potential for leadership roles. This assessment considers both their current performance and their potential for growth and development. Those identified as high-potential candidates are then provided with opportunities for skill development and experience, such as through targeted training programs or leadership assignments.

Throughout the succession planning process, regular assessments and evaluations are conducted to track the progress of potential leaders and provide them with feedback and guidance. Additionally, mentorship and coaching from current leaders and executives can be implemented to further support their development.

By establishing a succession planning process framework, organizations can ensure a continuous pipeline of qualified individuals who are ready to step into key roles when vacancies arise. This approach not only mitigates the risks associated with leadership gaps but also fosters a culture of continuous learning, development, and growth within the organization.

Succession Planning Process

Succession planning is a systematic process in Agile Process and Project Management disciplines that ensures the continuous flow of skilled individuals to take on key leadership positions within an organization. It is a strategic approach that identifies and develops potential future leaders, equipping them with the necessary competencies and knowledge to successfully fulfill critical roles.

The succession planning process involves a series of steps that effectively fills talent gaps and mitigates the risk of losing critical knowledge and expertise within the organization. Firstly, potential successors are identified through a comprehensive assessment of their performance, skills, and potential for growth. This step is vital in order to determine the suitability of individuals for future leadership positions.

Once potential successors are identified, the next step is to provide them with the necessary training, mentoring, and development opportunities to enhance their leadership capabilities. This development phase may involve formal training programs, rotational assignments, coaching, and mentorship from experienced leaders. By investing in their development, organizations can ensure a steady pipeline of talented individuals capable of leading Agile projects and teams effectively.

In addition to talent development, succession planning also involves monitoring and regularly reviewing the progress of potential successors. This allows organizations to assess their growth, address any performance gaps, and make necessary adjustments to the succession plans if needed. It is important to regularly evaluate the effectiveness of the succession planning process and make any necessary improvements to ensure its continued success.

Succession Planning

Succession planning in the context of Agile Process and Project Management disciplines refers to the proactive identification and development of individuals within the organization who can take on key roles and responsibilities in the event of turnover or critical resource gaps. It involves creating a talent pipeline that ensures continuity and minimizes disruption in project delivery.

Succession planning in Agile Process and Project Management disciplines involves several key steps. Firstly, it requires identifying critical roles and positions within the organization that are essential for project success. This includes project managers, Scrum masters, product owners, and other key team members.

Once these roles have been identified, organizations need to assess the skills, knowledge, and competencies required for each position. This involves analyzing the specific Agile frameworks and methodologies used in the organization and determining the core capabilities needed to effectively execute projects.

Next, organizations need to identify high-potential individuals who have the potential to fill these critical roles in the future. This can be done through performance evaluations, feedback from peers and managers, and individual development plans.

Finally, organizations need to invest in the development and coaching of these high-potential individuals to prepare them for future leadership roles. This can include training in Agile methodologies, providing opportunities for hands-on experience, and mentoring by experienced Agile practitioners.

In conclusion, succession planning in the context of Agile Process and Project Management disciplines is a strategic approach to ensure the continued success of projects by identifying and developing the next generation of leaders. It involves identifying critical roles, assessing the required skills, identifying high-potential individuals, and investing in their development.

Sustainability

Sustainability in the context of Agile Process and Project Management refers to the ability of a project or process to maintain its effectiveness and efficiency over the long term while minimizing negative impacts on the environment and society.

Agile Process and Project Management emphasize iterative and adaptive approaches that promote collaboration and flexibility. Sustainability principles align with these approaches by

129

encouraging continuous improvement, environmental responsibility, and social impact considerations.

Task Dependency

Task dependency in the context of Agile Process and Project Management refers to the relationship between different tasks in a project, where the completion or progression of one task is dependent on the completion or progression of another task.

In Agile, task dependency is managed through the use of a task board or a Kanban board, where tasks are visualized and categorized in different stages (such as "To Do", "In Progress", and "Done"). The board helps the team understand the flow of work and identify the dependencies between tasks. For example, if Task A cannot start until Task B is completed, there is a dependency between these two tasks.

Understanding and properly managing task dependencies is crucial for successful project execution. By identifying dependencies, project managers can allocate resources and plan schedules more effectively. They can identify critical paths and potential bottlenecks, ensuring that tasks are executed in the correct order and that the project progresses smoothly.

In Agile, task dependencies are often managed using techniques such as Backlog Refinement or Sprint Planning, where the team collaboratively identifies and prioritizes tasks based on their dependencies and the available capacity. By breaking down complex projects into smaller, manageable tasks and mapping out their dependencies, teams can optimize their workflow and ensure that tasks are completed in the right sequence.

Task Duration

Task duration refers to the amount of time required to complete a specific task or activity within a project. In the context of Agile Process and Project Management disciplines, task duration is a crucial element in planning and monitoring progress.

Agile methodologies, such as Scrum, emphasize the iterative and incremental approach in project execution. Tasks are broken down into smaller units, often called user stories or backlog items, and assigned a duration estimate based on team consensus. The duration estimate represents the team's best guess of how much effort or time it will take to complete the task.

Task

Agile Process is a project management approach that focuses on flexibility and adaptability. It emphasizes iterative and incremental development, allowing teams to respond quickly to changes in requirements and deliver working software at regular intervals.

The Agile Process is guided by the Agile Manifesto, which promotes collaboration, customer satisfaction, and continuous improvement. It encourages cross-functional teams to work together closely and prioritize customer needs. Agile Process relies on regular feedback from customers and stakeholders to ensure the project is on track.

Team Building

Team building in the context of Agile Process and Project Management disciplines refers to the process of bringing together a group of individuals with diverse skills, knowledge, and experience to work collaboratively towards a common goal. It involves fostering mutual trust, respect, and open communication among team members to enhance their collective performance and productivity.

The Agile approach emphasizes the importance of cross-functional teams working closely together in an iterative and incremental manner. Team building plays a crucial role in creating an environment that promotes collaboration, creativity, and continuous improvement. It involves various activities and strategies aimed at enhancing team dynamics and fostering a sense of shared purpose and ownership.

Team Charter Template

A team charter is a formal document that outlines the purpose, goals, roles, and responsibilities of a team in the context of Agile Process and Project Management disciplines. It serves as a blueprint or guide that establishes a shared understanding among team members and stakeholders about the objectives and expectations of the team.

In Agile Process, the team charter plays a vital role in fostering collaboration, alignment, and transparency. It outlines the project's vision, scope, and deliverables, ensuring that all team members are on the same page and working towards the same goal. Additionally, the team charter helps in defining the roles and responsibilities of each team member, promoting accountability and enabling efficient task allocation.

Moreover, the team charter supports the Agile principles of self-organization and continuous improvement. It empowers the team by providing them with the autonomy to make decisions and adapt their processes as necessary. The charter also serves as a reference point for resolving conflicts and making project-related decisions.

Overall, the team charter is an essential document in Agile Process and Project Management disciplines. It aligns the team members, stakeholders, and project objectives, facilitating effective communication and collaboration. By establishing a clear framework and shared understanding, the team charter lays the foundation for successful project execution and delivery.

Team Charter

A team charter in the context of Agile Process and Project Management disciplines is a formal document that outlines the purpose, goals, roles, and responsibilities of a project team. It serves as a reference point for team members, stakeholders, and leadership, providing clarity on the overall objectives and expectations of the project.

The team charter typically includes key information such as the project's mission statement, scope, deliverables, timelines, and any constraints or assumptions. It also outlines the team's composition, identifying individual roles, skills, and level of authority. This helps to establish clear lines of communication and decision-making within the team.

Furthermore, the team charter promotes a shared understanding of project goals and objectives. By explicitly stating the team's purpose and intended outcomes, it helps align all members towards a common vision. This shared understanding enhances collaboration, coordination, and ultimately, the team's ability to achieve project success.

In an Agile context, the team charter is particularly crucial as it sets the foundation for the iterative and flexible nature of Agile methodologies. It establishes the team's autonomy and empowerment to make decisions and adapt to changing requirements throughout the project lifecycle.

Overall, the team charter serves as a vital tool in Agile Process and Project Management disciplines, providing a concise yet comprehensive guide to the project team. By clarifying goals, roles, and expectations, it fosters effective communication, collaboration, and success within the team.

Team

The Agile Process is a project management approach that emphasizes flexibility, collaboration, and delivering value to the customer in incremental iterations. It is an iterative and incremental method that focuses on adaptability and responsiveness to change. Agile teams work collaboratively to break down large projects into smaller, more manageable tasks called user stories. These user stories are prioritized and assigned to team members for implementation in short development cycles, usually referred to as sprints.

Agile project management disciplines promote frequent communication, transparency, and continuous improvement. The team conducts daily meetings, known as daily stand-ups or stand-ups, to discuss progress, address challenges, and align goals. These meetings enable the team to identify and resolve any potential roadblocks as early as possible. Additionally, Agile emphasizes self-organization, empowering teams to make decisions and adapt their processes to optimize productivity and achieve project goals.

Technical Specification

A technical specification in the context of Agile Process and Project Management disciplines refers to a document that outlines the detailed requirements for a software product or system. It serves as a blueprint for developers, designers, and other stakeholders involved in the project, providing them with a clear understanding of what needs to be built and how it should work.

The technical specification document typically includes various sections such as:

- Functional requirements: Describes the specific features and functionalities that the software should have, including user interactions, data handling, and system capabilities.

- Non-functional requirements: Specifies the quality attributes and performance expectations of the software, such as scalability, security, and reliability.

- Architecture and design: Outlines the overall structure and design principles of the system, including the choice of technologies, frameworks, and programming languages.

- Data models and diagrams: Presents the data structures and relationships required by the software, often accompanied by Entity-Relationship diagrams or UML diagrams.

- Test and acceptance criteria: Provides a set of conditions that must be met for the software to be considered complete and ready for deployment, including both functional and non-functional aspects.

The technical specification document is an essential component of Agile project management, as it helps facilitate effective communication and collaboration among team members. It enables developers to create accurate estimates, supports the identification and management of project risks, and serves as a reference during the iterative development cycles characteristic of Agile methodologies.

Test Case Specification Format

A test case specification is a formal document that outlines the steps to be taken, conditions to be met, and expected results for testing a specific aspect or feature of a software application. In the context of Agile Process and Project Management disciplines, test case specifications are an essential tool for ensuring the quality and functionality of the software being developed.

In Agile, test case specifications play a crucial role in the iterative and incremental development process. They provide clear instructions for testers to validate that a particular user story or requirement has been successfully implemented. By defining the expected results and conditions, test case specifications help ensure that the system meets the desired functionality and that any defects or issues are identified and resolved promptly.

Test Case Specification

A test case specification is a formal document that outlines a set of conditions or actions to be performed on a system under test (SUT) to verify its adherence to specified requirements. In the context of Agile Process and Project Management disciplines, test case specifications play a crucial role in ensuring the quality and functionality of software deliverables.

Agile Process emphasizes frequent feedback and collaboration among cross-functional teams. Test case specifications within this context are typically characterized by their concise nature, focusing on the essential requirements and user stories to be tested. They are often written in a BDD (Behavior-Driven Development) format, using the Given-When-Then structure to describe the preconditions, actions, and expected outcomes.

Test case specifications aid Agile Project Management practices by allowing teams to clearly define and prioritize test scenarios during Sprint Planning or Backlog Grooming sessions. These documents facilitate effective communication and alignment among stakeholders, developers, testers, and product owners. Additionally, they serve as a reference for test planning, execution, and automation, enabling teams to efficiently track progress and evaluate the system's behavior against expected results.

In conclusion, test case specifications in Agile Process and Project Management disciplines act as a foundation for ensuring quality and consistency in software development. They provide a common understanding of system behavior, support effective collaboration, and aid in validating compliance with specified requirements.

Time Management

Time management in the context of Agile process and project management disciplines refers to the practice of effectively allocating and prioritizing time to optimize productivity and meet project objectives within the given timeline.

Agile methodology emphasizes the value of time management to ensure a steady and efficient flow of work. It emphasizes the iterative and incremental approach to project delivery, with regular intervals of planning, executing, and reviewing. Time management techniques, such as timeboxing, help Agile teams stay focused and deliver incremental value.

Time And Materials (T&M) Contract

Time and Materials (T&M) contract is a type of contract commonly used in Agile project management where the client agrees to pay the contractor based on the actual time and materials used for a specific project or task. This type of contract is flexible and allows for adjustments as the project progresses and requirements change.

In an Agile project management context, T&M contracts are often preferred when the scope and requirements of the project are not fully defined or may evolve during the course of the project. The Agile approach emphasizes adaptability and collaboration, and T&M contracts provide the necessary flexibility to accommodate changes and uncertainties that may arise.

Time-Phased Budget Tracking

Time-Phased Budget Tracking is a crucial aspect of the Agile Process and Project Management disciplines, which enables accurate monitoring and control of project expenses over time. It involves the systematic allocation and tracking of budgeted funds across various stages or phases of a project.

In Agile Project Management, the budget is divided into specific time intervals or increments, typically iterations or sprints. These time increments are defined based on the project's duration and the Agile framework being followed. The process starts with the creation of an initial time-phased budget, which outlines the estimated costs for each iteration or sprint.

As the project progresses, the actual expenditures are regularly tracked and compared to the initial estimates. This allows project managers to identify any deviations or discrepancies and take appropriate actions to address them. By closely monitoring the budget on a time-phased basis, project teams can proactively manage and adjust their spending to ensure the project stays within its financial boundaries.

Time-phased budget tracking offers several benefits in the Agile context. It provides transparency and visibility into the project's financial status, allowing stakeholders to make informed decisions. It also facilitates effective resource allocation and helps to identify any areas of over or under-spending, enabling timely course corrections.

In summary, Time-Phased Budget Tracking in Agile Process and Project Management disciplines involves the systematic allocation and monitoring of budgeted funds in specific time increments. By closely tracking expenditures against initial estimates, this approach enables effective financial management and control throughout the project's lifecycle.

Time-Phased Budget

A time-phased budget is a planning and control tool used in both Agile Process and Project Management disciplines to establish and track the financial resources needed at each stage of a project. It provides a comprehensive breakdown of financial estimates and allocations over a specified time period, typically divided into smaller intervals such as months or quarters.

In the Agile Process, a time-phased budget plays a crucial role in facilitating iterative planning and prioritization. It enables the project team to determine the financial implications of various features or user stories and make informed decisions on resource allocation. By breaking down the budget into smaller intervals, it becomes easier to adjust and adapt based on changing requirements and priorities during each sprint or iteration.

In Project Management, a time-phased budget serves as a roadmap for project financials. It outlines the estimated costs and expenses at different milestones or time periods, helping to monitor and control the project's financial health. It enables stakeholders to identify and address budget variances and take corrective actions if necessary. Additionally, it aids in forecasting and determining the overall project cost, contributing to better project planning and decision-making.

Overall, a time-phased budget is a valuable tool that aligns financial planning with the project's scope, milestones, and timeline. It allows project teams to gain visibility into the financial aspects of the project, make data-driven decisions, and ensure efficient utilization of resources.

Timebox

Timeboxing is a time management technique used in Agile Process and Project Management disciplines. It involves allocating a fixed duration, known as a timebox, to a specific activity or task. The purpose of timeboxing is to create a sense of urgency and focus, ensuring that work is completed within the designated time frame.

Timeboxing allows teams to prioritize and schedule their work effectively. By setting strict time limits, it encourages the team to make decisions quickly and avoid excessive analysis or unnecessary delays. This helps to improve productivity and efficiency, as well as promote accountability and transparency.

During a timebox, the team commits to delivering a valuable and potentially shippable increment of work. This incremental approach allows for frequent feedback loops and enables the team to make adjustments and improvements along the way. It also promotes early and continuous delivery, allowing stakeholders to see progress and provide input throughout the project.

The duration of a timebox may vary depending on the nature of the task or activity. It could range from a few hours to a few weeks, but it is important to define a specific and realistic time limit that allows for meaningful progress and completion.

Overall, timeboxing is a powerful technique that helps Agile teams manage their time effectively, prioritize work, and maintain a steady pace of delivery. By setting clear boundaries and focusing on incremental progress, it drives efficiency and ultimately leads to successful project outcomes.

Timeline

The timeline in the context of Agile Process and Project Management disciplines refers to a visual representation of the evolution of a project or the progress of tasks over time. It depicts the planned and actual duration of activities, milestones, and deliverables. The timeline provides a clear overview of the project's schedule, allowing team members and stakeholders to track progress and ensure that deadlines are met.

In the Agile approach, the timeline is often represented in the form of a sprint backlog or a Kanban board. These visual tools display the tasks or user stories to be completed within a specific time frame, usually a sprint or iteration. Each task is assigned a duration or effort estimate, which helps the team prioritize and plan their work accordingly.

The timeline is a crucial component of Agile project management as it enables teams to monitor their progress and adapt their plans as needed. It facilitates transparency and collaboration, allowing team members to have a shared understanding of the project's status and upcoming activities. By regularly reviewing and updating the timeline, the team can identify any bottlenecks or delays and take corrective actions to stay on track.

In addition to tracking the progress of tasks, the timeline also helps to manage dependencies and allocate resources effectively. By visualizing the sequence and duration of activities, the team can identify any interdependencies or risks that may impact the project's timeline. This allows for timely adjustments or prioritization to ensure that critical tasks are completed on schedule.

Tolerance

Tolerance, in the context of Agile Process and Project Management disciplines, refers to the acceptable amount of deviation or variation from the planned or expected outcomes or deliverables of a project. It recognizes that in complex and unpredictable environments, it is not always possible to accurately plan and estimate every aspect of a project from the outset. Therefore, tolerance allows for flexibility and adaptability in managing the project, acknowledging that things may change and adjustments may need to be made along the way.

In Agile methodologies, such as Scrum, tolerance is integrated into the planning and execution processes. It is recognized that requirements may evolve, priorities may shift, and new information may emerge that could impact the project's trajectory. Rather than trying to control and eliminate all uncertainty, Agile embraces it and ensures that the project is resilient enough to handle changes effectively.

Tolerance is typically defined and agreed upon during the project's inception or during the early stages of planning. It may be expressed in terms of time, cost, scope, or quality. For example, a project may have a tolerance of up to 10% for cost overrun or a tolerance of a three-day delay in the delivery date. These tolerance limits help project teams understand the boundaries within which they can make adjustments and decisions without requiring explicit approval or formal change requests.

By embracing tolerance, Agile teams can foster a culture of openness, collaboration, and continuous improvement. They can respond swiftly to changes, adapt their plans, and make informed decisions based on the current context. Tolerance ensures that the project remains on track and delivers value even in the face of uncertainty and emerging complexities.

Total Cost Of Ownership (TCO)

Total Cost of Ownership (TCO) is a metric that measures the financial impact of owning and operating a system or software over its entire lifecycle. In the context of Agile Process and Project Management disciplines, TCO provides an estimation of the overall expenses associated with developing, deploying, and maintaining a product or project.

TCO encompasses various cost components, including initial investment, operational costs, and potential costs of upgrading or replacing the system. It considers both direct and indirect expenses, such as hardware and software costs, training, maintenance, support, and any associated infrastructure costs. By considering all these factors, TCO provides a holistic view of the financial impact of a project or product.

Training Needs Analysis

A Training Needs Analysis is a systematic process used in Agile Process and Project Management disciplines to identify the training needs and requirements of individuals or teams within an organization. It involves assessing the current skill levels, knowledge gaps, and performance deficiencies of team members in order to determine the specific areas where training and development are required.

This analysis is typically conducted at the beginning of a project or initiative to ensure that the right resources are allocated to the right tasks and that the team has the necessary skills and knowledge to successfully execute the project. By identifying the training needs, organizations can provide targeted training programs that address the specific areas of improvement.

User Acceptance Criteria (UAC)

User Acceptance Criteria (UAC) in the context of Agile Process and Project Management disciplines refer to specific conditions or requirements that a product or system must meet in order to be accepted by the end user or customer. UAC is a vital aspect of the Agile methodology as it helps ensure that the developed product meets the customer's expectations and requirements.

Unlike traditional software development approaches, Agile emphasizes frequent collaboration and feedback loops with the customer throughout the development process. User Acceptance Criteria serve as a bridge between the customer's needs and the development team's implementation, helping to align both parties' understanding of the delivered product's functionality and quality.

UAC must be specific, measurable, and testable, and they are typically written in user-focused language to ensure clarity and understanding. They aid in defining the boundaries and scope of the development effort while also serving as a benchmark for validating the completion of user stories or features.

During Agile project planning and development, User Acceptance Criteria are determined collaboratively with the customer or product owner. They are typically created by breaking down user stories or requirements into actionable criteria that can be tested and verified. These criteria help guide the development process, enable prioritization, and aid in avoiding scope creep.

Overall, User Acceptance Criteria play a crucial role in Agile project management by enabling effective communication, clarifying expectations, and ensuring customer satisfaction. They help foster transparency, collaboration, and high-quality product delivery by aligning the development team's efforts with the customer's needs.

User Acceptance Testing (UAT)

User Acceptance Testing (UAT) is a critical phase in the Agile process and Project Management disciplines. It involves testing the software or system from an end-user's perspective to ensure its readiness for production. UAT is typically performed by a group of end-users or business stakeholders who simulate real-world scenarios and validate whether the application meets their business requirements.

During UAT, the focus is on verifying the functionality, usability, and compatibility of the software or system. It aims to identify any defects or issues that may impact the end-users' experience or hinder their productivity. UAT helps uncover any gaps between what was intended during the project's requirements phase and the actual implementation.

The Agile approach to UAT involves collaboration between the development team, product owner, and end-users throughout the project lifecycle. This ensures that the software or system meets the users' needs and aligns with their expectations. UAT is an iterative process, allowing for feedback from end-users to be incorporated into subsequent development cycles.

UAT is an essential step in mitigating risks before the application is released into the production environment. It helps validate the system's stability and reliability and reduces the likelihood of costly issues emerging when the users start using the software or system.

In summary, UAT is a crucial part of the Agile process and Project Management disciplines. It involves testing the software or system from the end-users' perspective to ensure its functionality, usability, and compatibility. Through collaborative efforts and iterative cycles, UAT helps to mitigate risks and ensure the success of the final product.

User Documentation

User Documentation is a formal definition that refers to a comprehensive set of documents created for Agile Process and Project Management disciplines. It encompasses a wide range of informational material designed to assist users in understanding and effectively using a software product or system. In the context of the Agile Process, User Documentation acts as a vital communication tool between the development team and end-users. It provides essential instructions, guidelines, and reference materials that enable users to navigate and utilize the software effectively. While the Agile Methodology focuses on continuous iteration and rapid delivery, User Documentation ensures that users are equipped with the necessary information to make the most of the software's features and functionality. In the realm of Project Management, User Documentation plays a critical role in facilitating project planning, execution, and control. This documentation serves as an essential resource for project teams, enabling them to conceptualize, document, and communicate project requirements, design specifications, and implementation details. It aids in aligning the project team's objectives, clarifying expectations, and ensuring that all stakeholders have a common understanding of the project's scope and deliverables. User Documentation typically includes various types of documentation, such as user manuals, installation guides, troubleshooting guides, FAQs, and release notes. These documents are often created iteratively throughout the Agile development process, ensuring that they are up-to-date and relevant to the software's current features and functionalities. Overall, User Documentation in the context of Agile Process and Project Management disciplines serves as a comprehensive resource that empowers users and project teams with the necessary information to effectively utilize and manage software products or systems.

User Interface (UI) Design Prototyping

User Interface (UI) Design Prototyping is a crucial aspect of the Agile Process and Project Management disciplines. It involves creating visual representations of the proposed user interface design for a software application or website. These prototypes serve as a blueprint to communicate and validate design ideas and requirements among stakeholders, developers, and designers. The purpose of UI design prototyping is to ensure that the final product meets the users' needs and expectations, enhancing usability and user satisfaction.

UI design prototyping significantly contributes to the success of Agile projects by facilitating a collaborative and iterative approach. It allows for early feedback and detection of design flaws or usability issues, reducing the risk of rework or revisions later in the development process. The prototypes serve as a design reference and foundation for discussions, enabling the whole team to align their understanding and vision of the final product.

User Interface (UI) Design

User Interface (UI) Design, in the context of Agile Process and Project Management disciplines, refers to the process of creating visually appealing and user-friendly interfaces for software applications or websites. It involves the design and arrangement of visual elements, such as buttons, menus, icons, and layouts, to enhance user experience and usability. In an Agile process, UI Design plays a crucial role as it helps in aligning the design elements with the project objectives and user needs. It focuses on iterative development and collaboration, ensuring continuous improvement and adaptation based on user feedback and changing requirements. The UI design process within Agile typically begins with understanding user requirements and conducting user research to gather insights about user preferences, behaviors, and goals. This information is used to create user personas, which are fictional representations of target users that help guide the design decisions. Once the user requirements are established, UI Designers collaborate closely with the development team to create wireframes or prototypes that illustrate the structure and functionality of the interface. These wireframes are refined and iterated upon based on feedback from stakeholders and user testing. During the development phase, UI Designers work closely with developers to implement the visual design specifications and ensure that the interface is consistent with the project's brand guidelines. They also conduct usability testing to identify any usability issues and make necessary adjustments. Overall, UI Design in Agile Project Management focuses on creating intuitive and visually appealing interfaces that enhance user satisfaction and drive business outcomes. It involves continuous collaboration, iteration, and adaptation to ensure that the final product aligns with user needs and business objectives.

User Story

137

A user story is a concise, written description of a feature or functionality from an end-user's perspective. It typically follows a specific format: "As a [role/persona], I want [goal/desire] so that [benefit/value]." User stories are used in Agile Process and Project Management disciplines as a way to capture and communicate requirements in an iterative and collaborative manner.

Unlike traditional requirements documents, user stories focus on the end-user's needs and desired outcomes rather than detailed technical specifications. They are often written on index cards or digital tools and are kept visible to the project team as a constant reminder of the desired functionality. User stories are a key element of Agile methodologies such as Scrum and Kanban, where they are used as the primary unit of work or "backlog items."

Value Engineering

Value engineering is a systematic and organized approach used in Agile Process and Project Management disciplines to identify, analyze, and improve the value of a product, service, or process. It involves a collaborative effort by cross-functional teams to optimize the overall value delivered to the customer while reducing costs and maximizing resource utilization.

The primary goal of value engineering is to enhance the value proposition of a project by ensuring that all functionalities, features, and requirements are necessary and contribute directly to the customer's needs. This is achieved by examining each component of the project and evaluating its cost-effectiveness, performance, and alignment with the project goals and objectives.

Value engineering follows a structured methodology that includes various stages such as information gathering, functional analysis, creativity, evaluation, development, and implementation of alternative solutions. It encourages out-of-the-box thinking and innovation to explore potential improvements and efficiencies.

Through value engineering, Agile teams can identify and eliminate non-value adding activities, redundancies, bottlenecks, and unnecessary complexities in the project. It helps in streamlining processes, reducing waste, enhancing productivity, and facilitating continuous improvement.

Furthermore, value engineering in Agile Process and Project Management disciplines emphasizes the need for continuous communication, collaboration, and feedback between team members to ensure that the changes and improvements align with the Agile principles and methodologies being followed. It promotes a data-driven decision-making approach, taking into account the trade-offs between cost, quality, time, and scope.

In conclusion, value engineering is an essential practice in Agile Process and Project Management disciplines that aims to enhance the overall value delivered to the customer while optimizing resources, reducing costs, and driving continuous improvement.

Value Stream Analysis Report

A Value Stream Analysis is a systematic approach used in Agile Process and Project Management disciplines to identify and analyze the flow of value within a process or project. It involves mapping out the steps and activities involved in delivering a product or service and highlighting areas of waste, delays, and inefficiencies. The main goal of a Value Stream Analysis is to optimize the value stream by eliminating non-value-added activities and streamlining the overall flow of value.

During a Value Stream Analysis, the entire value stream is examined from start to finish, including both the steps that directly contribute to the creation of value and the steps that do not add any value but are necessary for the process to function. This analysis helps identify areas where value is being added efficiently as well as areas where there are bottlenecks, wait times, or excessive handoffs, which can lead to delays and waste.

Value Stream Analysis

Value Stream Mapping (VSM)

Value Stream Mapping (VSM) is a visual representation technique used in Agile Process and Project Management disciplines to identify and analyze the flow of value in a given process or project. It provides a high-level overview of the entire value stream, from the initial concept or customer request to the delivery of the final product or service.

The main objective of VSM is to identify and eliminate inefficiencies, delays, and waste in the value stream, ultimately improving the overall value and customer satisfaction. It helps to highlight areas of improvement, identify bottlenecks, and streamline the process to reduce lead time and increase productivity. Additionally, VSM also facilitates communication and collaboration among team members, promoting a shared understanding of the process and alignment towards common goals.

Vendor Evaluation

Vendor Evaluation is a crucial process in Agile Project Management that involves assessing and selecting external suppliers or vendors for a particular project. It is a formal assessment of potential vendors based on predetermined criteria, such as their expertise, resources, track record, and ability to meet project requirements and timelines.

The evaluation process typically begins by identifying the project's specific needs and requirements. These may include technical capabilities, financial stability, geographic reach, and industry experience. Once the criteria are established, the project team solicits proposals from various vendors who may be capable of meeting these requirements.

During the evaluation, each vendor's proposal is carefully reviewed and scored against the predetermined criteria. The project team may conduct interviews, request references, and review past work samples or case studies to gain a better understanding of the vendor's capabilities and approach. This evaluation process helps determine the suitability of each vendor and their compatibility with the project goals.

After completing the evaluation, the project team selects the most suitable vendor(s) based on the assessment results. The selected vendor(s) enter into contractual negotiations, during which the terms and conditions are finalized. Once the contract is in place, the project team collaborates with the vendor(s) to ensure effective communication, alignment of expectations, and successful project delivery.

Vendor Evaluation plays a vital role in Agile Project Management, as it helps ensure that the project team engages with reliable and competent vendors who can contribute to project success. By conducting a thorough evaluation, organizations can minimize the risks associated with outsourcing and enhance their chances of achieving project objectives.

Vendor Management Office (VMO)

The Vendor Management Office (VMO) is a critical component in the Agile Process and Project Management disciplines. It serves as a centralized function within an organization responsible for managing vendor relationships and ensuring that vendors are meeting the organization's objectives and requirements. The VMO is tasked with facilitating effective communication and collaboration between the organization and its vendors, ultimately ensuring that the organization receives the maximum value from its vendor relationships.

In the context of Agile Process and Project Management, the VMO plays a key role in the selection and onboarding of vendors. It is responsible for conducting vendor assessments, evaluating vendor capabilities, and coordinating the procurement process. The VMO also establishes and maintains the necessary contracts and agreements with vendors, ensuring that they align with the organization's Agile practices and project management methodologies.

Once vendors are engaged, the VMO provides ongoing oversight and management of vendor performance. This includes monitoring vendor delivery, tracking key performance indicators, and addressing any issues or concerns that may arise during the course of the project. The VMO acts as a point of escalation for vendor-related issues, working closely with both the organization and the vendor to resolve any issues in a timely manner.

In addition to managing vendor relationships, the VMO also plays a crucial role in driving continuous improvement in vendor management practices. It conducts regular vendor evaluations and assessments to identify areas for improvement and drives the implementation of best practices. The VMO also fosters knowledge sharing and collaboration among stakeholders, ensuring that lessons learned from vendor engagements are captured and shared across the organization.

Vendor Selection Criteria Evaluation

Vendor Selection Criteria Evaluation is a systematic process carried out in the Agile Process and Project Management disciplines to assess and choose the most suitable vendor for a project or initiative. It involves evaluating potential vendors based on predefined criteria to determine their ability to meet project requirements and deliver value.

The evaluation process typically starts with identifying the specific criteria that are essential for the success of the project. These criteria may include factors such as experience, expertise, track record, financial stability, technical capabilities, cultural fit, and cost-effectiveness. Once the criteria are determined, a thorough assessment is conducted to evaluate each vendor against these criteria.

During the evaluation process, project managers and stakeholders may utilize various techniques such as requests for proposal (RFP), interviews, reference checks, product demonstrations, and pilot projects to collect relevant information and gather insights about the vendors. They analyze the gathered data to assess the vendor's strengths, weaknesses, and overall suitability for the project.

The evaluation and selection of a vendor play a crucial role in ensuring project success and mitigating risks. By thoroughly evaluating potential vendors based on predefined criteria, project managers can minimize the possibility of poor vendor selection decisions that can lead to project failures or cost overruns. It helps in selecting a vendor who possesses the necessary expertise, resources, and capabilities to deliver high-quality products or services within the allocated budget and timeline.

Vendor Selection Criteria

Vendor selection criteria are the specific qualifications and characteristics that an organization evaluates when choosing a vendor to work with in the context of Agile Process and Project Management disciplines. These criteria help ensure that the selected vendor is capable of meeting the organization's project requirements and aligns with their Agile values and principles.

In the Agile Process, it is crucial to select vendors who can effectively collaborate with the organization's internal teams. The ability to communicate transparently and openly, as well as the willingness to actively participate in Agile ceremonies, such as daily stand-ups and sprint planning meetings, are important criteria to consider. Vendors should also demonstrate their understanding of Agile methodologies, including their knowledge of Scrum, Kanban, or other frameworks commonly used in Agile environments.

From a Project Management perspective, the vendor's experience and expertise in delivering similar projects using Agile methodologies should be assessed. This includes evaluating their track record in managing projects within budget and on schedule, as well as their ability to adapt to changing project requirements and deliver high-quality work.

Other critical selection criteria include the vendor's ability to offer flexible pricing models and negotiate contracts that fit the organization's needs. Their financial stability and reputation within the industry should also be considered, as these factors can impact the ongoing support and maintenance of the delivered solutions.

Finally, organizations should assess the vendor's compatibility with their corporate culture and values. This includes evaluating their commitment to continuous improvement, their ability to foster collaborative relationships, and their willingness to embrace change and adapt their processes to fit the organization's Agile practices.

140

Virtual Team Management Guidelines

Virtual Team Management is the process of effectively coordinating and overseeing a team of remote individuals in order to achieve project goals within an Agile framework. It involves implementing strategies and practices that promote collaboration, communication, and accountability among team members, while also addressing the unique challenges of working in a virtual environment.

Within the Agile process, Virtual Team Management is crucial for ensuring the successful execution of Agile principles, such as frequent iterations, customer collaboration, and adaptive planning. It involves defining clear goals and roles, establishing communication channels, and fostering a culture of trust and autonomy that empowers team members to work independently while staying aligned with the project objectives.

Virtual Team Management

Virtual Team Management, within the context of Agile Process and Project Management disciplines, refers to the practice of effectively leading and coordinating teams composed of individuals who are geographically dispersed or work remotely. It involves the utilization of technology and communication tools to ensure efficient collaboration, cooperation, and productivity among team members.

In an Agile environment, where iterative development and continuous improvement are key, virtual team management is crucial to the success of a project. Agile teams are often cross-functional and self-organizing, and they require effective communication and coordination to achieve project goals. Virtual team management provides the necessary guidance and support to ensure that team members can work together seamlessly, regardless of their physical location.

Virtual team management involves establishing clear goals and expectations, assigning appropriate roles and responsibilities, and providing timely feedback and support. It emphasizes open and transparent communication channels, fostering a culture of trust and collaboration. Team members are encouraged to actively participate, share ideas, and collectively solve problems. The use of tools such as video conferencing, instant messaging, and project management software facilitates real-time communication, file sharing, and task tracking.

Effective virtual team management helps overcome the challenges and potential disadvantages of working in a dispersed environment. It promotes inclusivity, ensures that everyone is aligned and aware of project progress, and encourages a sense of accountability and commitment. By effectively managing virtual teams, Agile project managers can leverage the diverse skills and perspectives of team members, adapt quickly to changing requirements, and deliver high-quality results consistently.

Virtual Teams

Virtual teams are teams composed of members who are located in different geographical locations, and communicate and collaborate primarily through electronic means. In the context of Agile Process and Project Management disciplines, virtual teams play a crucial role in ensuring the successful implementation of projects.

The Agile Process emphasizes close collaboration and communication among team members, and virtual teams enable this by using various technology tools such as video conferencing, instant messaging, and shared project management systems. Virtual teams allow individuals with diverse skills and expertise to work together towards a common goal, without being restricted by physical distance.

Waste

Waste, in the context of Agile Process and Project Management disciplines, refers to any activity or resource that does not add value to the final product or result. It is a concept derived from Lean thinking, which aims to eliminate waste in order to increase efficiency and deliver maximum value to the customer.

In Agile methodologies, waste is typically classified into seven categories:

1. Partially Done Work: This refers to work that has been started but not completed, leading to delays and increased effort to finish the task later on. Agile teams strive to complete work within a single iteration to minimize partially done work.

2. Extra Features: These are features or functionalities that are not required by the customer or end user. Including such features in the product adds unnecessary complexity and can result in wasted time and effort.

3. Relearning: When team members have to relearn or redo work that has already been done due to lack of documentation or communication, it leads to waste. Agile teams focus on clear communication and documentation to avoid relearning.

4. Handoffs: Handoffs occur when work is passed from one team member or department to another. Each handoff introduces the risk of miscommunication and delays, making it a potential source of waste. Agile teams aim to minimize handoffs by promoting collaborative and cross-functional work.

5. Task Switching: When team members are frequently disrupted or forced to switch between different tasks, it can lead to loss of focus and productivity. Agile methodologies advocate for minimizing interruptions and allowing team members to concentrate on completing one task at a time.

6. Delays: Delays in any part of the project or process can lead to wasted time and resources. Agile practices emphasize the importance of identifying and addressing delays as early as possible to prevent further waste.

7. Defects: Defects or bugs in the product can result in rework, delays, and customer dissatisfaction. Agile teams aim to address defects as they are identified to prevent waste caused by additional work or customer complaints.

Work Authorization System Workflow

A work authorization system workflow is a defined set of processes and procedures that govern how work authorizations are requested, reviewed, approved, and monitored within a project or organization. It serves as a key component in Agile process and project management disciplines, providing structure and control for managing the allocation of resources and ensuring that work is completed in a timely and efficient manner.

In Agile, work authorization systems are typically used to manage the flow of work within a project, enabling teams to prioritize and schedule tasks based on their importance and dependencies. The workflow begins with the submission of a work authorization request, which includes details about the work to be performed, such as scope, objectives, and resources required. The request is then reviewed by the project management team to assess its feasibility, alignment with project goals, and resource availability.

If the request is approved, the work authorization is granted and assigned to a team or individual responsible for completing the work. Throughout the execution of the work, progress is regularly monitored and reported to ensure that it remains on track and within budget. If any issues or obstacles arise, they are addressed promptly to minimize delays and mitigate risks. Once the work is completed, a review is conducted to evaluate its quality and alignment with project objectives.

The work authorization system workflow is designed to promote collaboration, transparency, and accountability in Agile project management. By providing a structured process for requesting, approving, and monitoring work authorizations, it enables teams to effectively manage their workloads, streamline decision-making, and ensure that resources are effectively allocated to achieve project goals.

Work Authorization System

A work authorization system, in the context of Agile Process and Project Management disciplines, refers to a structured approach and set of procedures for granting permission to perform specific tasks or activities within a project. This system is typically used to control and manage the allocation of resources, ensure proper authorization for project work, and maintain accountability and transparency throughout the project lifecycle.

In Agile project management, where iterative and incremental development methodologies are followed, the work authorization system plays a crucial role in maintaining project control and facilitating collaboration within cross-functional teams. It enables the project manager to define and prioritize work packages, establish clear ownership and responsibilities, and allocate resources based on project requirements and priorities.

The work authorization system operates by documenting and communicating the scope of work required for a specific task or activity. It defines the project objectives, deliverables, milestones, and dependencies, ensuring that all team members are aware of their roles and the expected outcomes. The system also establishes criteria for initiating, reviewing, approving, and monitoring work packages to ensure they align with the project goals and objectives.

Through the work authorization system, the project team can track the progress of individual tasks, identify and resolve any bottlenecks or barriers to progress, and make informed decisions based on the project's evolving needs. It provides a framework for effective communication and coordination, enabling the team to adapt and respond to changes in a streamlined manner, while ensuring that work is authorized, controlled, and executed in a disciplined and efficient manner.

Work Authorization

Work authorization, in the context of Agile Process and Project Management disciplines, refers to the process of granting approval or permission to begin a specific task or project within an Agile team. It is a fundamental aspect of Agile project management that ensures efficient collaboration and progress within the team.

During the planning phase of an Agile project, the team identifies various tasks or user stories that need to be completed in order to achieve the project's objectives. These tasks are then assigned to team members based on their skills and availability. Before a team member can start working on a task, they need to obtain work authorization.

Work authorization is typically obtained through communication and agreement among the team members and stakeholders. It involves assessing the readiness of the task, ensuring that all necessary resources and dependencies are available, and obtaining the necessary approvals. The authorizing party, which could be a product owner or a project manager, reviews the task and provides the go-ahead to the team member.

This process allows for better coordination and prioritization of tasks within the Agile team. By obtaining work authorization, team members can be confident that they are working on the right tasks at the right time, avoiding unnecessary delays or conflicts. It also provides visibility and transparency, as everyone within the team is aware of the tasks that have been authorized and the ones that are still pending approval.

Overall, work authorization plays a crucial role in Agile project management by ensuring that tasks are properly authorized, facilitating collaboration and progress within the team, and ultimately contributing to the successful delivery of the project.

Work Breakdown Structure (WBS) Dictionary Template

A Work Breakdown Structure (WBS) Dictionary is a document that provides detailed descriptions of the tasks, deliverables, activities, and components within a project's work breakdown structure. It serves as a reference guide for all project stakeholders, ensuring a common understanding of the project scope, objectives, and key elements.

In the Agile process, the WBS Dictionary plays a crucial role in project management by facilitating effective communication and collaboration within the Agile team. It provides a comprehensive overview of all project-related activities, enabling team members to stay aligned and focused on shared goals throughout each iteration. By capturing relevant information such as task names, descriptions, dependencies, responsible parties, and estimated effort, the WBS Dictionary supports Agile practices like Sprint Planning, Daily Standups, and Retrospectives, enhancing transparency and accountability.

Work Breakdown Structure (WBS) Dictionary

A Work Breakdown Structure (WBS) Dictionary is a document that provides detailed information about the components and deliverables included in a Work Breakdown Structure (WBS). It serves as a reference guide for project teams and stakeholders to understand the scope, definition, and attributes of each work package or task within the project.

In the context of Agile Process and Project Management disciplines, the WBS Dictionary becomes an essential tool for organizing, planning, and managing projects using the Agile methodology. It breaks down the project into smaller, manageable components called work packages or tasks, which are then further detailed in the WBS Dictionary.

The WBS Dictionary typically includes information such as the unique identifier or code for each work package, a description of the work to be performed, the responsible individuals or teams, the estimated effort or duration, dependencies, resources required, associated risks, and any other relevant information. It provides a comprehensive overview of the project's scope, objectives, and deliverables, supporting effective communication and coordination among project stakeholders.

By having a well-defined and documented WBS Dictionary, Agile project teams can easily track progress, allocate resources, identify potential risks, and ensure that all project requirements are met. This allows for greater transparency, collaboration, and adaptability throughout the project lifecycle.

Work Breakdown Structure (WBS) Template

A Work Breakdown Structure (WBS) is a hierarchical decomposition of a project into smaller, more manageable components. It is a technique used in both Agile Process and Project Management disciplines to organize and define the scope of work.

In an Agile Process, the WBS is typically developed during the project planning phase, but it is also a tool that is continuously updated and refined throughout the project's lifecycle. It serves as a visual representation of the project's deliverables, allowing the team to identify and track progress, assign responsibilities, and estimate the time and resources required for each component.

Work Breakdown Structure (WBS)

A Work Breakdown Structure (WBS) is a hierarchical decomposition of the work needed to be completed for a project. It provides a visual representation of the project scope and delivers a systematic approach to divide the work into smaller, more manageable tasks.

In the context of Agile Process and Project Management disciplines, the WBS acts as a tool to organize and prioritize the project's deliverables. It helps teams to identify and understand the different work components, facilitating the planning and estimation processes. By breaking down the project into smaller tasks, the team can better manage their time and resources, ensuring the successful and timely completion of the project.

Work Package Closure Procedure

A work package closure procedure is a formal process within the Agile project management discipline that signifies the completion of a specific work package within a project. It involves several steps to ensure that all deliverables and objectives of the work package have been met and all necessary documentation is completed.

Firstly, the project team reviews the work package to ensure that all the agreed-upon deliverables have been accomplished. Any incomplete or outstanding tasks are identified, and necessary actions are taken to address them. This is to ensure that the work package is completed in its entirety.

Work Package Closure

The work package closure is a crucial process in the Agile Project Management discipline, where the completion of a work package is formally recognized and documented. It is a comprehensive step that ensures all the necessary deliverables, tasks, and activities within the work package are successfully accomplished, reviewed, and accepted by the stakeholders.

Within Agile, a work package refers to a specific unit of work that is manageable, measurable, and has a predefined boundary. It is an essential component of project planning and execution, enabling teams to effectively track progress, allocate resources, and monitor timelines.

The process of work package closure involves various steps, including:

1. Verification: The completion of all the planned work within the package, ensuring that all the deliverables are met and all the stakeholders are satisfied.

2. Documentation: The creation of comprehensive documentation comprising all the essential information about the work package, such as objectives, scope, outcomes, and lessons learned. This documentation serves as a valuable reference for future projects or audits.

3. Final Review: Conducting a final review to assess the overall performance, quality, and adherence to established project standards. This review involves the collaboration of key stakeholders, project team, and other relevant individuals to ensure the work package aligns with the project's objectives and requirements.

4. Formal Acceptance: Obtaining formal acceptance from the relevant stakeholders, signifying their approval and satisfaction with the completed work package. This acceptance is crucial for proper project closure and transitioning to subsequent project phases or packages.

In conclusion, work package closure in Agile is a critical process that confirms the successful completion of a specific unit of work, ensuring all the objectives are met, stakeholders are satisfied, and documentation is in place for future reference.

Work Package Description

A work package is a defined set of tasks and activities within a project that can be assigned to a team or individual for execution. It is a key component in Agile Process and Project Management disciplines as it provides a structured approach to completing work and helps in the effective management and tracking of project progress.

In Agile Process, work packages are often created during the sprint planning phase. They are derived from the product backlog and represent the granular units of work that need to be completed within a specified timeframe, typically a sprint. Each work package is defined based on the user stories or requirements that need to be addressed. It includes the tasks, deliverables, and acceptance criteria that need to be met to consider the work package as completed. The size of a work package can vary depending on the complexity and estimated effort required.

Within the context of Project Management disciplines, work packages play a crucial role in project planning, scheduling, and resource allocation. They help in breaking down the overall project into manageable chunks, allowing for better estimation and allocation of resources. Work packages also facilitate the assignment of tasks to different teams or individuals, enabling parallel execution and maximizing efficiency.

In summary, work packages are a fundamental element in Agile Process and Project Management disciplines. They provide a structured approach to tackling work, help in tracking progress, and enable effective resource allocation. By breaking down the project into smaller units, work packages contribute to the successful completion of the overall project objectives.

Work Package

A work package is a distinct and manageable unit of work that is part of a larger project. It is a well-defined set of activities or tasks that contribute to the overall completion of the project. In the context of Agile Process and Project Management disciplines, work packages are used to break down the project into smaller, more manageable chunks of work that can be easily assigned, tracked, and completed.

Each work package typically has its own deliverable(s), timeline, and assigned resources. It represents a specific objective or goal that needs to be achieved within a given timeframe. Work packages are often created based on the project's scope and requirements, ensuring that they align with the project's objectives and contribute to its successful completion.

www.ingramcontent.com/pod-product-compliance
Lightning Source LLC
Chambersburg PA
CBHW020519290526
45786CB00002B/681